THEY FOUGHT FOR EACH OTHER

THEY FOUGHT FOR EACH OTHER

THE TRIUMPH AND TRAGEDY OF THE HARDEST HIT UNIT IN IRAQ

KELLY KENNEDY

ST. MARTIN'S PRESS ☙ NEW YORK

THEY FOUGHT FOR EACH OTHER. Copyright © 2010 by Kelly Kennedy. All rights reserved. Printed in the United States of America. For information, address St. Martin's
Press, 175 Fifth Avenue, New York, N.Y. 10010.

www.stmartins.com

Library of Congress Cataloging-in-Publication Data

Kennedy, Kelly, 1970–
    They fought for each other : the triumph and tragedy of the hardest hit unit in
    Iraq / Kelly Kennedy.—1st ed.
        p. cm.
    ISBN 978-0-312-57076-7
    1. Iraq War, 2003—Campaigns—Iraq—A'zamiyah.   2. United States. Army.
    Infantry Regiment, 26th. Company C.   I. Title.
    DS79.766.A93K46 2010
    956.7044'342—dc22

                                                                    2009040088

First Edition: March 2010

10 9 8 7 6 5 4 3 2 1

To my grandfathers, Archie Kennedy and Arley Walton,

who both earned the title "Doc" during World War II

CONTENTS

Let him bear the palm who has won it.

ACKNOWLEDGMENTS

I first must thank the men of Charlie Company for watching out for photographer Rick Kozak and me on one of their worst days, June 21, 2007. Jared Purcell brought us continuous reports and made sure we had what we needed—and then helped us to meet up with the men when they came home to Germany; Gerry DeNardi brought a quick bit of comfort when he let me know Doc Timothy Ray, whom we had been following, was OK; Erik Osterman made sure I had water and brought me to tears with his kind words; the medics dragged me out of the sun and into the aid station, where Doc Tyler Holladay made me feel like a part of the group instead of a reporter just looking for a scoop; and Major Eric Tangeman drove us back through the treacherous streets of Adhamiya to relative safety just after losing one of his soldiers. And thank you Rick for being willing to talk about what we had witnessed while we were in Adhamiya. Your work there was amazing.

Almost as soon as my first accounts of that day appeared in *Army Times*, the soldiers and their families have been there for me when writing their tales made me cry. Thank you, Charles and Rhonda McKinney, for checking in on me and making me love your son. Thank you, Elizabeth DeNardi, for that very first note while I was still in Iraq telling me to keep telling their stories. Thank you, Cathy Baka, for welcoming us into your home and for the funny e-mails and photos. There have been so many notes and gestures that left me weeping, and I wish I could offer more than a glimpse of a son's last moments.

I don't think I could have written this without the jokes from De-Nardi, the beers and visit to Arlington with Derrick Jorcke, the phone conversations with Chad Smith, and certainly not without the timeline Jeremy Rausch provided. And I'll never forget salsa dancing with Ely Chagoya, Carlos Perez, Ernesto Martin, Ruben Chavez, and Armando Cardenas. You all went through so much, yet you understood how hard it was for an outsider, too. There were so many of you who told your stories and wanted people to understand what you experienced, and I'm honored to be able to write it. I owe any sense of relief I have in trying to get the facts straight to Kenny Hendrix and Mike Baka for telling their stories in such great detail, as well as for reading a draft of the book even though I know it hurt like hell to go back to their days in Adhamiya. Though I was only with Charlie Company for a few days, all of the quotes in this book come directly from interviews with the men, beyond a couple of jokes and exclamations.

Thank you also to *Army Times*—to Tobias Naegele, Elaine Howard, Alex Neill, Robert Hodierne, and especially Chuck Vinch for pushing for and appreciating the original Blood Brothers series, and for putting up with my nonsense while I tried to finish the book and meet daily newspaper deadlines. I'm sure I owe many people many drinks for that. Thank you to Sean Naylor for explaining the process and leading me to his agent, writing kind notes of encouragement, and being willing to listen as I muddled through this.

Kristin Henderson—you're my hero. This project would have been a mess without your suggestions and edits. And you are one of many friends and family members whom I owe much to for letting me talk when I got back without shutting me down. You let me heal.

Thank you Donald J. Davidson for copy-editing the book, and even making me laugh a bit. Many thanks go to my agent, Scott Miller, for treating me like someone capable of writing a book, and for being willing to answer any of my many questions. And finally, thanks to Marc Resnick at St. Martin's Press for taking a chance on me, and for being so encouraging and helpful and understanding as I made my way back through Adhamiya.

THEY FOUGHT
FOR EACH
OTHER

CHAPTER 1
Second Platoon Meets Adhamiya

At their tiny combat outpost in the Adhamiya neighborhood of Baghdad, the soldiers of second platoon acted like kids going to an amusement park: jumping around, grabbing gear, punching shoulders. They hugged the other members of the company like long-lost brothers, joyful to be part of a whole. Nothing could be worse than the two months they had spent separated from the rest of Charlie Company—they had not even lived on the same post. The men of second platoon had been attached to another unit, as often happens in war zones, and their company commander, Captain Mike Baka, had fought hard to get them back.

Baka, grinning at their antics and their proximity, gathered his boys in October 25, 2006, for their first formation back together in months. Now that he had them back, he had to prepare them to do battle in Baghdad's worst neighborhood.

"Second platoon!" he shouted, and the men stopped kicking up dust and stood still to listen. "Welcome to Adhamiya!"

Baka paused as a barrage of deep-voiced "Hooah!'s" erupted from the platoon and bounced off the khaki-colored buildings.

"If there's no violence in your sector, something's amiss," Baka continued. "If 1 percent of the 400,000 people who live in Adhamiya are shitheads, that's 4,000 shitheads. We're up against some bad odds."

"Roger that, sir!" yelled Private First Class Daniel Agami, and everybody laughed, eager to see their new sector.

"The enemy does not have a uniform," Baka said. "You won't know who you're up against, but they'll know who you are. There is no front line. There is no moving forward. You will have to get to know the people. You will have to assume they want to hurt you while you treat them like neighbors."

The guys grew quiet, having already met fear and pain two months into their deployment, but still not quite clear about the exact nature of the new mission—or, for that matter, the mission in Iraq. They knew they were part of the "surge," and they had heard the term "counterinsurgency," but many of the guys believed the two words were interchangeable without understanding the philosophy behind the new counterinsurgency manual written by General David Petraeus and his aides. In fact, they did not know the manual existed. According to the manual, they were supposed to spend just as much time sitting in living rooms drinking sweet, strong tea and trying to make connections with Iraqi citizens as they did rolling down the narrow streets shooting insurgents. But they would learn quickly.

Second platoon arrived at Combat Outpost Apache on a brilliantly sunny day and Baka decided to welcome them by taking them on a three-hour tour of the two-kilometer-by-three-kilometer neighborhood in northeastern Baghdad. Baka's other platoons—first, third, and the scouts—had been patrolling Adhamiya since late summer.

"The hardest part will be holding yourselves back," Baka told second platoon. "For every shithead, there are 99,999 people who just want to get on with their days. They don't want violence. They've been caught in the middle and are doing everything they can to help their families survive." He explained that the soldiers would gather intelligence by asking for it. They would spend much of their time offering up help in the form of water, electricity, soccer balls, and school supplies. But they would also have to memorize minute details, like how the street litter had changed from the previous patrol and how traffic should move at certain times of the day and what time the kids should be walking to school. Changes in the details signaled danger.

"Second platoon!" Baka said. "Let's go see the neighborhood."

They climbed into several up-armored Humvees, loaded with the usual amount of ammunition and water and bravado, and then rolled past a mural of the Grim Reaper a soldier from a previous unit had painted on a wall. Rumor was that the artist had died in Adhamiya.

Second platoon rolled out of the front gate onto one of Adhamiya's main roads. Baka, riding in the platoon leader's vehicle, decided to take them to a suburban area of town first, where things might be calmer but would still give them a sense of the place.

"Watch for IEDs," Baka warned First Lieutenant Ryan Maravilla, second platoon leader, and Maravilla's driver, Private First Class Jose Quinones, who rode in the lead vehicle. "IED" stands for improvised-explosive device—or roadside bomb. Baka spoke over an intercom system that allowed the whole platoon to hear him, including Sergeant First Class Tim Ybay, second platoon's platoon sergeant, and all of his noncommissioned officers: Staff Sergeant John Gregory, Sergeant Jose Villa, Sergeant Ryan Wood, Staff Sergeant Robert Morris, Staff Sergeant Raja Richardson, Sergeant Billy Fielder, Sergeant Alphonso Montenegro, and Sergeant Michael French. Ybay, thirty-eight and from the Philippines, served as platoon daddy for second platoon. A former drill sergeant, he came from a military family— grandfather, dad, aunts, cousins, brothers, and sister had all served. He'd gone to college for three years, studying criminal justice, but in his third year, he decided he just didn't want to be in school anymore. By infantry standards, he was an old man, but he needed the experience. He'd served in Bosnia and Kosovo, but Adhamiya was his first combat tour.

Ybay, pronounced "Ee-buy," liked to tease his men, making them drop for push-ups and telling jokes over the intercom system. But this day, he was quiet. "The insurgents hide bombs in the garbage," Baka continued. Maravilla's eyes instantly began sweeping the road for signs of the bombs, which could be placed in sewage drains, or hidden in a bag of trash, or even buried beneath the street. The "suburban" area of Ad-hamiya also boasted snipers and men tossing grenades.

"Watch that group over there," Baka said, nodding toward a few young men gathered on a corner. "Most of the insurgents are young males, so be on the lookout for any suspicious activity."

The platoon tried to take it all in, but in the middle of a city neighborhood, it was hard to focus on anything. In Iraq, traffic doesn't stay in lanes. Everyone crowds together and merges and turns with a haphazard hope that everyone else is paying attention. Horns blared constantly. With no electricity, the streetlights could offer no clue as to who had the right of way. People on bikes and pedestrians appeared from between cars parked—or abandoned—on the side of the road.

On the residential streets, children and chickens walked through sewage and filth. Generators roared to provide some homes with electricity. Occasionally, second platoon heard AK-47 fire in the distance, but that could have been caused by anything. Someone might have had a birthday or won a soccer match. Or killed a member of a rival group. Or started a firefight with the Iraqi army or police. Or killed a soldier.

"Focus," Baka admonished his men. "Pay attention to your sector."

Watching the sides of the road, Baka noticed something that seemed odd to him. "Hold up, hold up!" he said. Baka had taken a year of Arabic—the only class in which he had received an A+ at West Point—and the license plate on a car indicated it was from Dubai. "Foreign fighters?" Baka said, more to himself than to the others. Recent intelligence showed many of the insurgents were coming in from Iran, as was their weaponry. "Let's check it out."

He got out of the Humvee and started walking toward a house near where the car was parked, and then he noticed his guys were hanging back a little, trying to process their new neighborhood. But Baka didn't have time for them to think about it. "Hey!" he yelled. "I need some people on the ground with me!"

Instantly, Agami was by Baka's side, followed by Fielder and Montenegro, ready to watch the captain's back. As Baka approached the house, his soldiers turned away from him, M-4s up and ready. In the front yard, a man in a long white robe explained through Baka's interpreter that the Dubai tag was similar to a temporary plate in the United States, and all new cars came in through Dubai. The explanation seemed legitimate, so Baka loaded everybody back up to head into the city areas for their first encounter with Antar Square and the Abu Hanifa Mosque.

Baka led them through narrow streets, picking his way past burned-out cars that created an impromptu obstacle course, piles of garbage that had cluttered the roads for months, and streams of sewage that drizzled down the gutters. The fumes of sulfur and rot caused the soldiers' eyes to water. "Oh my God," Agami said, riding with his squad in a Humvee behind Baka. "How can people live here?"

"Hey!" Maravilla yelled. "Is that a person?"

One of the piles in the sidewalk looked human-shaped, but it couldn't be a body—people were walking past it, almost over it, as if there were nothing at all on the ground. Baka had the vehicles pull near for security, dismounted from his Humvee, and pulled back a scrap of cardboard covering the man's face. The man was young, shot between the eyes, and it looked as if he had been beaten. "Jesus," Maravilla muttered. "You'll see this often," Baka said. He called the location of the body back to the company command post so they could contact the Iraqi army to come pick the man up. With the help of an Iraqi interpreter, the soldiers interviewed some Iraqis on the scene, and received answers Baka had heard before: "He's not from here." "We don't know how this happened." "What a terrible accident."

Shaking his head, Baka turned to his soldiers and saw their mouths gaping in disbelief. He tried to explain that the Iraqis were trying to protect themselves, but he could see from his soldiers' faces that they weren't impressed by the explanation. Baka had them get back in the vehicles.

"OK! Load up!" he said.

"Watch the rooftops," Baka said again, as they entered an area with shopping centers, hotels, and four- and five-story apartment buildings, each fronted with arched balconies and latticed barriers that allowed women—or snipers—to look down at the street without being seen. Private First Class Ron Brown watched, but also tried to keep track of traffic and pedestrians. "Hey, Captain Baka," he said. "That dude's following us with a camera."

"Where?" Baka yelled.

Baka ordered the driver, Quinones, to turn the Humvee around as Baka let the others know over the radio that they were on the chase. The man was taking pictures of second platoon's patrol from the back of a car. Baka had already learned the insurgents liked to record everything—the grislier the better. But those videos and pictures could contain important intelligence for the Americans, if they could get their hands on them. They raced after the car and stopped it on a busy street. The soldiers surrounded it, pulled the driver out with his camera, and began to question him. But as they did, another car rushed through the intersection and slammed into a concrete post. "What the hell?" Maravilla said, looking over at Baka from the passenger seat.

"VBIED!" Quinones yelled, instantly assuming the car contained a vehicle-borne improvised explosive device—a suicide bomber in a car.

"Wait," Maravilla said, as they prepared to flee the scene. "That dude looks dead." The "suicide bomber" was slumped over his steering wheel.

"Let's check it out," Baka said, and sent a message over the radio for the guys in the trucks behind him to back him up. Baka had assumed the car belonged to another one of Adhamiya's bad drivers and had simply crashed into a concrete pole because the driver wasn't paying attention. But Baka's men were not yet familiar with Adhamiya's traffic.

"You gotta be kidding me," Montenegro said. "What if it blows up?" But he jumped out with the rest of the platoon, figuring the company commander must know what he was doing. Baka walked toward the car, followed by his men looking toward the rooftops for snipers and pointing their weapons out.

"Shit," Baka said as he got near the car. Blood poured from the side of the driver's forehead. "Gunshot wound to the head."

A sniper, apparently aiming for the soldiers and Baka, had hit the civilian driver instead as he chanced through the intersection.

"Where is he? Where is he?" Agami shouted as the guys realized they were in immediate danger and began looking for the sniper. They scanned the tops of buildings, but they did not see anybody. The platoon medic quickly bandaged the man's head. He had survived the gunshot wound, and was conscious and confused. "Load him up," Baka yelled. "We gotta get this guy to a hospital."

As they moved the Iraqi man into a Humvee, the patrol started taking fire. "Just go!" Baka yelled, and had Quinones lead the way, tires bumping over the curbs and soldiers bouncing hard in their seats.

"Sir, sir!" Maravilla shouted. "Don't you think we're going a little fast?"

Baka laughed.

"It's always a little fast," Baka said.

He told Quinones to hurry, and they hit a dip in the road, sending soldiers flying up out of their seats.

"Whoa," Maravilla said, eyes wide as he grabbed the dash. "So this is Adhamiya."

CHAPTER 2
Adhamiya Moves from Acceptance to Hatred

Second platoon's new neighborhood once bustled with shoppers and worshippers and visitors, Sunni and Shiite alike. Date palms provided spiky relief against the stuccoed, flat-roofed homes that seem as if they wouldn't be out of place in balmier areas of the United States. Sandal-clad men in white robes, or dishdashas, gathered on corners to drink chai, play chess, and chat about business.

Parts of the neighborhood in northeast Baghdad consisted of urban shopping areas, complete with five-story malls, hotels, and factories. On other streets, low-slung houses lined up side by side, shielded by high plastered walls.

Once, not long before, neighbors walked across the Bridge of the Imams, or al-Aima Bridge, to visit family and friends in Kadhamiya, the Shiite neighborhood on the other side of the Tigris River. The name of the bridge commemorates imams from both cities and both branches of Islam. For generations, at least socially, sect didn't matter. In fact, mannered people considered it impolite to ask. Marriages between the Sunni in Adhamiya and the Shiite in Kadhamiya didn't bring visions of Romeo and Juliet, as long as the accompanying wedding feast included good music and good food.

But even in Adhamiya, Saddam Hussein's favorite town, a river of fear ran deeper than the Tigris that bordered it. Neighbors didn't complain to neighbors about the government. They didn't talk about family members who disappeared in the night. When Saddam Hussein called for an annual celebration of his defeat of the Americans in 1991, no one denied his victory—they just wordlessly joined the party. And when Saddam Hussein killed an estimated 300,000 Kurds in the north and Shiite in the south after they rose up against him while the Americans were still in Iraq after Desert Storm, nobody said a word. If they had, they might have been spirited away in the dark of night themselves, leaving their families to wonder what had happened: Had they been murdered by the side of the road? Taken to one of Saddam Hussein's infamous prisons for years of torture and then, inevitably, death?

For those who played by the rules, Adhamiya represented a retirement community by the river. The neighborhood jutted out into the Tigris like a peninsula, creating waterfront property along three of its borders. Hussein's Ba'ath Party generals built their mansions along those edges, where the palm trees graced well-watered lawns, and sleeping porches provided pleasant breezes during hot summer nights. Farther from the river, sand defined the landscape, with scrappy shrubs popping up along perfectly straight, dusty streets. People filled the coffee shops and markets, students attended university classes, and children—boys and girls—with shiny black hair and red sweaters walked to their required school classes to learn together.

On the way, they passed the gold-domed shrine of the Abu Hanifa Mosque. Abu Hanifa was a Sunni scholar of Islam and religious law who, because he refused a position as a judge, or, according to other versions, because he said the wrong thing to the wrong person, was imprisoned and tortured until he died in 767. Sunnis built the mosque over his tomb in the eleventh century.

Though Hussein's government was sectarian, Hussein was a Sunni, and he used that to his advantage. Historically, Sunnis held the government jobs and filled the military. For that reason, it would take a generation of education for the Shia to fill those roles, even after the caste system loosened in the middle part of the twentieth century. But the same year Saddam Hussein became president—1979—Iran experienced an uprising that resulted in the Ayatollah Khomeini bringing Shiite reign to a formerly Persian country. Like Iraq, Iran was majority Shiite. Hussein immediately banned an ancient Shiite ceremony that could bring thousands of potential enemies to the streets in mourning for a martyr dead for centuries.

That's when the real rift between the Sunnis and the Shia began—with the bygone battle that caused that martyr's death. When the founding prophet of Islam, Muhammad, died in 632, he didn't say who should succeed him as the spiritual and political leader of the Muslim world. Muhammad had created a new system of law administered by tribal leaders. In many cases, he sought to make rights equitable for everyone—including those of other faiths—with respect to property rights, judicial equality, and even women's rights. Islam allowed women to own property and restricted men to marrying only as many women as they could afford to clothe, feed, and house. However, men could still "discipline" women—as long as they did it with kindness. Many of the punishments are extreme by today's standards, but at the time they were considered progressive because everyone could expect the same treatment for deeds deemed against Allah. But Muhammad lacked a successor. Who then would determine how those new laws should be carried out or what new laws should be created according to Muhammad's intent? And who would say what the proper interpretation of the Koran should be? Muhammad believed in the same God as the Jews of the Old Testament, but he thought mankind had lost the path along the way. He believed Jesus was a prophet—like Muhammad, Moses, and Abraham—sent by God to help lead people back to the correct path. Muhammad did not believe Jesus was the son of God.

When Muhammad died, some thought his rule should be passed through the bloodline. Others thought it should go to his dear friend, the man Muhammad shared his thoughts with about religion and society almost daily. That man, Abu Bakr, became the first caliph basically because the majority of Muslims believed he should. But Ali ibn Ali Talib, Muhammad's son-in-law, who the minority thought should replace Muhammad, became the fourth caliph. In 661, Ali ibn Ali Talib was murdered in Iraq.

Again, people argued over who should replace the caliph—Ali ibn Ali Talib's son Hussein or Muhammad's former companion, Muawiyah of Syria. The two groups met on a battlefield near Karbala in Iraq, and Muawiyah's followers killed Hussein and decapitated the body. That didn't settle things. Instead, Hussein became a martyr for the Shia. And the Shia continued to believe Ali's descendents were the true caliphs. The last one disappeared in 931, but the Shia believe he's in hiding and will appear again one day.

The Shiite holiday Saddam Hussein banned, Ashura, commemorates Hussein's death, and every year, until the ban, mourners marched through the streets beating their chests, crying, even flagellating themselves.

Muawiyah's followers became the Sunnis and quickly grew to a large majority, encompassing as much as 90 percent of the world's Muslims today. In Iraq, however, Shiites make up the majority. Still, the Sunni ruled.

The Abu Hanifa Mosque stood as the most important Sunni shrine in Baghdad. It is here that Saddam Hussein last appeared after the United States attacked Iraq in March 2003 and preached tales of martyrs and bloody battles—and victory. The same day, the Americans bombed Adhamiya and hit the cemetery behind the mosque. But Saddam Hussein had scurried away to hide in a hole from which he emerged ten months later dirty and unshaven.

Adhamiya withstood the Americans for longer than any other part of Baghdad, finally falling on April 10, 2003, after a big battle. Immediately, the neighborhood formed an armed "watch group" to prevent looting. Soon after, members of the Ba'ath Party rose up to avenge the deaths of their relatives, or because they'd lost their important positions in society, or because they didn't believe the United States should have attacked Iraq. In December 2003, the brigade command sergeant major for 1st Brigade, 1st Armor Division, Eric Cooke, was killed by a roadside bomb on Omar Street by Iraqis angered by the Americans' presence. But the definition of "insurgent" shifted and swayed as the war wore on. As in other Middle Eastern countries, many younger people moved away from the parties of their parents and toward a more militant belief system—namely, that jihad and a strict Islamic legal system would be the way to Allah.

By February 2005, only 2 percent of Sunnis would be willing to vote in the elections to determine who would be Iraq's first government, so the parliament quickly filled with Shiite Iraqis. The Sunnis said the elections were not legitimate because they hadn't voted in them. The Shiites said they should have control of the government, because they won. A December election brought more Sunni voters, but the balance of power continued to lie with the Shiites.

Still, many Adhamiyans basically decided to wait and see what would happen—or to duke it out politically—never imagining that being Sunni or Shiite would soon determine whether they stayed in the city where their families had lived for centuries, or even whether they would live.

One event represented how much things could change in the space of one season. In August 2005, the Shiites celebrated Ashura in Kadhamiya for the first time since Saddam Hussein had taken—and lost—control. The celebration hit television stations in Iraq and the United States as a demonstration of the freedoms Iraqis would have as the American government urged them toward democracy. The celebration in Kadhamiya started that way. Even as people mourned the loss of their ancient martyr, they cried with joy at being allowed to march. But during a stampede on the Bridge of the Imams, people began jumping off the bridge and into the Tigris. Sunnis from Adhamiya jumped into the river to help those who were drowning, and one Sunni man died as he tried to rescue a Shiite woman. At first, newspaper accounts mourned the loss of the Shiites and praised the heroism of the Sunnis who helped them. But within months, the Shiites denied that anyone had helped them, and the Sunnis also denied that they helped them.

The Americans closed the bridge for security reasons, but that didn't stop the rabid hatred from crossing the river. In February 2006, the Sunni insurgents bombed the Golden Mosque of Samarra, sparking an all-out civil war between the two sects. Soon, a soccer field in Adhamiya filled with the graves of people killed in mortar attacks launched by the Shiite Mahdi army, an insurgent group from Kadhamiya—which the Adhami- yans met in kind. Shops closed as militants attacked anyone selling music or wearing makeup or believed to be working for the government. The mutilated bodies of young men appeared on the streets near the Abu Hanifa Mosque—apparently the work of Shiite death squads looking for anything that might identify someone as Sunni. The name "Omar" im- mediately identifies a person as Sunni, so people obtained fake identifica- tions with new names. Other Adhamiyans were kidnapped and held for ransom. But as food, water, and electricity became scarce, so did jobs and money to pay that ransom. Many of the kidnapped were tortured and murdered when they couldn't bring the asking price.

Early in the war, the Americans had turned over the Adhamiya area to the Iraqi army and police units, but because the government was Shi- ite, so were the troops and police. Rumors flew that not only did Iraqi soldiers and police officers turn a blind eye to theft and violence toward the Sunni, they participated. American military transition teams, or MiT teams, as well as some U.S. Army military police, patrolled with the Iraqi army, but there were not enough of them to disperse the corruption. The MiT teams trained the Iraqi soldiers and police officers so that they would eventually be able to take over when the Americans left Iraq.

Many Adhamiyans fled—especially the professional class needed to rebuild and staff the hospitals, government, and learning institutions— leaving behind a neighborhood filled with outsiders and insurgents, as well as some who still hoped to see the progress the Americans promised.

By the summer of 2006, the neighborhood simmered, requiring

only one more ingredient to boil over. Bodies filled the streets, opposing sects shot at each other across the river, and intelligence officials believed Adhamiyans were hiding—and making—weapons. A political excuse, an enemy force, or a power grab could lead the area into even more violence, erupting as it had before in roadside bombings, random shootings, and attacks on American troops.

In August 2006, the U.S. military command added Charlie Company, 1st Battalion, 26th Infantry Regiment, 1st Infantry Division, to the pot.

CHAPTER 3

Charlie Company Learns to Fight the Insurgents

First Sergeant Kenneth Hendrix didn't actually have a nicotine habit. He just liked to check in on his men. The best way to do that was out on the stoop, smoke-'em-if-you-got-'em, chasing off boredom and sleep. The smoke mixed with the dust that covered everything, even in the built-up parts of Baghdad. The city couldn't keep the sand contained, and it clung to the soldiers' eyelashes and dug into their scalps and added grit to their food. They looked out over a field of gravel and sand toward sand-colored buildings and sand-colored sky.

"Twelve months, man," Agami said, cigarette emphasizing the former disc jockey's high cheekbones. "That's a long time to be looking at you girls."

"Honey, you know I'm hotter than anything you got going in Miami," said Sergeant Ryan Wood, a wiry bundle of "ornery" under a blond crew cut. For all his playfulness, Wood thought deeply and often served as the conscience of second platoon.

On the stoop, they were just boys telling jokes about women, talking about music, wishing for their futures. Hendrix encouraged it all. He served as the mother of this family, making sure everybody ate properly and kept his underpants clean. That's what the men called him—First Sergeant Mama—but they said it to his face with a certain amount of respect because he was bigger than they were.

Sitting on the stoop of their makeshift, rocket-damaged "barracks," he smoked cigarettes with men as much as twenty years younger than he—and Hendrix was only thirty-eight. Beyond the need to mother his men, he seemed the definition of male, from his high, square cheekbones to the square stance that came from the confidence of two previous deployments to Iraq and one to Panama, earning three Bronze Stars along the way. In a company nicknamed "Charlie Rock," Hendrix seemed like granite. A tall man—a good six feet—with dark scruffy eyebrows, he could get physical with a soldier who didn't follow an order. But ask him about that same man five minutes later? He wouldn't have anything bad to say about him, at least out loud. He'd move on, and that admonished private would know everything was cool—until he screwed up again, which, being a private, he inevitably would do. Just like a family.

Hendrix had not always been with the 26th Infantry Regiment. He had moved to the 1st Battalion, 18th Infantry Regiment, 2nd Brigade Combat Team, just in time to deploy as a platoon sergeant to Samarra. In October 2004, the battalion had been the first unit to move into the city during Operation Baton Rouge, in which Charlie 1-26th had also been involved. Baka had been a battle captain at the brigade tactical command post during that battle. Samarra had been controlled by former Ba'athists, members of Saddam Hussein's political party, under Abu Musab al-Zarqawi, who hoped to bring the country back under Sunni rule. The battle marked pure inner-city warfare as the Blue Spaders essentially went door-to-door rounding up insurgents while they tried to figure out which civilians wouldn't harm them. They were called the "Blue Spaders" because their unit patch featured a blue Indian arrowhead that looks like a spade one might use for digging. Though the initial attack went well, they faced insurgent uprisings in the following months, and they had several casualties. They witnessed events that would haunt their dreams for years.

Hendrix moved to Charlie Company of the 26th in May 2006 and found himself relieved that so many of his men had combat experience.

But there was something about Adhamiya that made Hendrix feel hypervigilant about his men. On his first deployment—before Samarra—war had made sense: They knew whom they were fighting. They understood the objective. They felt some love from Saddam Hussein's victims. Victory seemed clear. Sitting on the stoop, he tried to explain the difference. "There were no insurgents," Hendrix told his men, many of whom had been out of basic training only a few months. "You could walk down the street with no body armor taking pictures." He had the snapshots to prove it: Hendrix and his troops grinning in front of Saddam's victory gate of crossed swords, held in house-sized replicas of Saddam's fists. Hendrix with no body armor talking to Iraqi citizens. Hendrix surrounded by grinning children.

Many of his soldiers had served in Samarra with Charlie Company. But even with the violence they saw there, the company knew its mission and accomplished its goals. In the soldiers' minds, they had lost friends for the just cause of creating a democracy in Iraq.

But Adhamiya started with random, pointless violence, and Hendrix quickly realized the rules would be different than on previous deployments. He would have to find a way to help his men redefine success.

Hendrix hadn't joined the army for any altruistic reasons, such as serving mankind or a deep-seated patriotism: His dad had told him he needed either to join or go to college. Hendrix had a lot of fun not being in college, so he was in no hurry to go there. He tried the army. After three years, he reenlisted. He loved it—loved the people from all the different backgrounds, skin colors, orientations, looks, religions. In the army, none of those mattered.

But even for a man who created a career based on camaraderie, Charlie Company surprised him. No unit was this close-knit. All the noncommissioned officers had combat experience, and the soldiers respected them. A couple of platoon sergeants, including Ybay, hadn't deployed before, but they'd just come off drill-sergeant duty, so they knew how to take care of soldiers. Better, they knew how to listen to squad leaders who had deployed. Hendrix trusted his noncommissioned officers completely, which hadn't always been the case.

During his third deployment, Hendrix also took care of his captain, Mike Baka. Dark-haired and pale-skinned with a solemn gaze, Baka sorted out his world methodically, like an engineer. The guys always knew exactly what he wanted and usually why, and they loved comparing him to Dick Winters from *Band of Brothers*. The comparison made sense: Baka had been an Eagle Scout and grew up in a small town in rural New York. As a boy, he had spent his free time hunting, trapping, and fishing, before heading to West Point for a degree in aeronautical engineering. Baka had been with Charlie Company for twelve months before they deployed for Iraq, and he wrote a letter to every soldier's family before he left. He didn't want his first contact with the families to be bad news. Baka's West Point training helped his men trust his judgment. He looked like the epitome of an officer with his athletic stance, always a little bouncy on the toes, the knees slightly bent, as if he were going to spring up at any moment. Baka was a first-generation American, his mother coming over from Poland and his father from Romania. Growing up, his parents made sure he understood the importance of living in a free country. As an officer, those lessons served him with patience, ethics, and an extreme love of country that his soldiers intuitively followed. Baka seemed unaware of his effect on the men, probably because he so obviously loved them back.

For that reason, Baka did his best to give them time with their families before they left. As Hendrix made sure their training included all the infantry skills they would need to bring down the bad guys, Baka tried to get a handle on what a "hearts and minds" campaign meant. During the Vietnam War, that hadn't worked out so well. Military leaders had buried the old counterinsurgency manuals from that era that had explained how to work with the civilian populations to break the enemy. Instead, they dug out plans for the things that had worked in the past:

tanks and planes and Desert Storm. There they'd seen victory. After serving a tour in Iraq, General David Petraeus had gone back to those old Vietnam field manuals, updated them, and issued orders to "drink chai" with the locals. But the new counterinsurgency manual—a thousand-page behemoth filled with everything from why a private can cause a national uprising to how to build relationships with sheikhs—filtered down the chain slowly, with top officers being the first to know and privates being the last to learn.

Charlie Company did train for two weeks at the Joint Multi-National Readiness Center at Hohenfels, Germany. Rather than Iraqi or Arabic-speaking people, they trained with German linguists.

The linguists tried to show the soldiers that they might only understand a few words of the people they'd be working with, but expressions and hand signals could go a long way—as could condescension and uncalled-for roughness. But one part of the training surprised Baka. As he stood next to a German "mayor," an improvised explosive device went off, producing chaos and busting down the relations he'd just built with the mayor. That would turn out to be the most realistic part of his training.

Neither Baka nor Hendrix saw the counterinsurgency manual before they left for Iraq, and the deployment arrived unexpectedly quick. They went to the field for training in July 2006 thinking they had at least two months. And there had been rumors that the 1st Battalion, 26th Infantry Regiment, wouldn't deploy at all. But while they were still in the field, they learned they had two weeks until deployment, and much of that was spent packing and preparing. Charlie would be the first company in the battalion to deploy when they got on the airplanes on August 4, a month before the rest of the brigade. They spent the next ten days in Kuwait.

The U.S. military uses bases in Kuwait to acclimatize the troops before they head into battle, making them wear their body armor and getting them used to drinking bottles and bottles of water each day. In some ways, the base in Kuwait is worse than anywhere in Iraq. Boots sink ankle-deep into loose sand, almost like walking in sand dunes. A hot wind also blows, causing the soldiers to compare Kuwait to living inside a hair dryer. The hot blast seems to suck any moisture from the lungs, making it difficult to breathe, and everyone walks with his head down to avoid stinging bits of sand whipped by that hair-dryer wind. When Charlie Company arrived, the medics got some practice sticking people with IV needles as they became dehydrated.

On August 12, Charlie Rock flew to Baghdad.

Normally, the leadership would have spent time training in counter-insurgency methods after reaching Iraq, but Baka's battalion did not have time because the military was in such a hurry to get troops in place for the surge.

The guys thought they were going to Sadr City, and they knew its reputation of violence. When they found out they were going to Adhamiya, it relieved them of some of their anxiety. At first, the men lived at Forward Operating Base Loyalty, just south of the Sadr City neighborhood in Eastern Baghdad.

Loyalty itself proved rough. For a forward operating base, it was tiny. Charlie Company's building had been hit by a JDAM—a guided bomb—before they arrived. The top floors of the five-story building had collapsed and been condemned, but the Corps of Engineers said the first and second floors were structurally sound, so that's where Charlie Company lived. The scout platoon set up cots in a hallway because there weren't enough rooms for everybody. Loyalty got hit with incoming fire between twenty and twenty-five times a day, and some of the mortars landed on Charlie Company's already crumbling home. Before they ever went out on patrol, their vehicles had been damaged by mortars in the motor pool.

Nothing had been reinforced, so when the guys weren't on patrol, Hendrix had them filling sandbags to fortify windows, especially after a couple of guys were injured by shrapnel in their sleep. The company command post, or CP, was in an old Iraqi jail where the government had tortured people. The chain of command lived in jail cells, complete with metal hooks in the ceiling from which chains had hung.

Baka had hoped he would have good news from home before he left for Adhamiya, where he might not have access to a phone or the Internet for a while. His wife, Cathy, was due with their second daughter any day. The other soldiers with babies due in August remained in Schweinfurt; they would deploy to Iraq after their children were born. But Baka was the company commander and had to go.

On August 25, Hannah entered the world a few days early, and Baka got to hear her little baby noises and Cathy's voice over the phone. A couple of hours later, Charlie Company began its daily commute to Combat Outpost Apache, which sat within one mile of Abu Hanifa Mosque.

As they moved into their new area, the previous unit did not show Charlie Company their new sector; they hadn't patrolled it because it was too dangerous. They did tell the Blue Spaders to stay away from the mosque.

American units had not properly patrolled Adhamiya since January 2006, a month before the civil war broke out in Iraq. Instead, an MiT team from the 4th Brigade, 101st Airborne, went out with Iraqi army troops, and a Special Forces team performed special missions. During Charlie Company's first two weeks at Apache, a Stryker Brigade from Alaska cleared the area by checking for bombs and searching houses in the neighborhood so Charlie Company could move in.

"We've got zones 18 and 19," one of the MiT team soldiers told Headquarters Platoon as they did their left-seat, right-seat patrols. Soldiers call those initial patrols "left-seat, right-seat" because the troops moving out show the new guys how things work, and then they switch so the new guys can prove they learned it. But there wasn't much showing on those patrols.

"This area's been cleared, but you can have it," a soldier told Private First Class Gerry DeNardi, who served as the company smart-ass. When

DeNardi walked, his head tended to move ahead of his body, as if his brain moved too quickly for the rest of him to keep up.

"Uh, what do you mean exactly by 'cleared'?" DeNardi asked, as they rolled quickly through a neighborhood, not even bothering to stop to check things out or try to get information. "What is this, like drive-by patrols? Do you guys ever get out of the trucks?"

"Dude, there are places you just don't go," the soldier said, without even pretending at machismo.

"Then what's the point?" DeNardi said, not necessarily wanting to know the answer.

"Hey, kid, you wanna make it home or not?" the soldier asked. "This is my last day. You can patrol or not patrol. It won't make a bit of difference, except one way will get you out of here alive."

Out on the stoop at Loyalty, DeNardi dealt with that gnawing bit of fear in typical fashion.

"This is a Humvee," he said, sitting in a make-believe seat as if he were the day's tour guide. "This is how it works. If you want to go faster—and you always want to go faster—hit this pedal over here."

The guys laughed, but there was a nervousness about it that Hendrix captured.

"I'd be scared, too," he said, holding a lit cigarette that he didn't actually smoke. "That's too much for one platoon."

From November 2005 until November 2006, the 1st Battalion, 2nd Brigade, 6th Iraqi Army Division, ran the show while an eighteen-man team of Americans under the 4th Brigade Combat Team, 101st Airborne Division, acted as advisers. That MiT team ended up being the most decorated in the 506th Regiment.

But they weren't stupid. After a while, they avoided being hit.

By September, Baka's 190 men ended up patrolling all of Adhamiya, including the roads everybody else avoided.

Except for second platoon. Second platoon, upon landing in Iraq, had been sent to work with Bravo Company, 9th Engineer Battalion, and

Bravo Company's second platoon had been sent to work with Charlie Company.

At Charlie Company's home base in Schweinfurt, Germany, four platoons—first, second, third, and Headquarters—made up the company. Each platoon had about forty men. Charlie Company, along with Alpha, Bravo, and Headquarters companies, made up 1st Battalion of the 26th Infantry Regiment, nicknamed the Blue Spaders. Several battalions from different regiments, including the Blue Spaders, made up the 1st Division, known as "the Big Red One" from its shoulder patch. Baka served as commander—the top officer position—of Charlie Company, and Hendrix served as first sergeant—the top enlisted position within the company. Each platoon had a platoon leader, who was an officer, and a platoon sergeant, who was an enlisted man. Officers give the orders—sort of like management—and enlisted soldiers carry them out. Each platoon was broken down further into squads, all of which were headed by a sergeant.

In the war zone, companies usually switch out a platoon so they have different resources available in an area of operations. In Charlie Company's case, the engineers they had swapped for second platoon could help with building roads or setting up protective barriers, while second platoon could help the engineer company with security, capturing insurgents or searching buildings.

Second platoon covered the periphery of Adhamiya in zone 17, one of the areas the previous platoon had patrolled frequently because it was safer. They concentrated on the Shiite neighborhoods of Sha'ab and Waziriyah.

But even though second platoon ended up in a less-volatile zone, they still had to commute thirty to forty minutes into Adhamiya from Loyalty, like the rest of the company, and that commute would prove as dangerous as the bad areas of Adhamiya.

"That drive out there makes me sick at my stomach," Agami said, after DeNardi's performance on the stoop. Though Agami's physique expressed enough manliness to qualify for an army recruitment poster—which he had just modeled for—the guys loved to imitate the way he talked: He sounded like somebody's Jewish mother, and for good reason. Agami hung an Israeli flag over his cot and went by the moniker "G.I. Jew." "I just know somebody's gonna get hurt."

Quickly, Baka decided he needed to do something to try to keep his men safe during their commute. He worked best in pictures, so he jotted down plans and ideas, intense eyes staring at the sheets of paper in front of him in his jail-cell office. Baka decided that he would stay at Apache to keep an eye on his men, and First Sergeant Hendrix would handle logistics and the rear command post at Loyalty. The platoons would rotate in to Apache one at a time. The day shift would pull three four-hour patrols and stay at Apache, and the night shift two four- to six-hour-long patrols and would stay at Loyalty, traveling in darkness to avoid traffic. No Iraqis traveled at night because of the curfew. There were also fewer improvised explosive device attacks at night.

Charlie Company's accommodations at Apache made Loyalty seem luxurious. Early in the war, soldiers had moved into the palace there, known as Uday Hussein's "love palace." Overflowing with tackiness, it included a round bed and a multitude of nude paintings. Uday was Saddam Hussein's son. After giggling their way through, those soldiers had taken over the swimming pool, located offices underneath gilded chandeliers, and even created a putting green.

The Blue Spaders did not live in the palace. That's where the Iraqi army lived. Charlie Company occupied a basement of an outbuilding on the palace grounds, twenty-five men to a room. They had no running water or heat. Tiles from the ceiling left dust on their faces that they brushed away when they woke up in the morning in a haze of funk from the other men lined head-to-foot in the rooms.

Funk's much better dry, as it turns out.

At about 2:00 A.M. one night, trying to catch some sleep before waking up for a 6:00 A.M. patrol, Sergeant Shawn Ladue of third platoon woke up and saw something floating past his cot.

"What the hell?" he said, loudly. Loudly enough to wake up some of the other guys who were already half listening for mortars out of habit. And then, "What is that funky-ass smell?"

The sewage from the palace was pumping straight into the basement.

"Holy crap!" Private First Class Carlos Perez yelled, almost causing the guys to laugh. Almost. "Oh, you gotta be kidding me."

They spent the rest of the night dragging their cots and gear outside, trying to get clean uniforms and helmets to safety before they were infected by sewage.

Things weren't much better outside the building. Apache had some port-a-potties, which they used when they had to, but otherwise tried to avoid. On Fridays—the Muslim holiday—the Iraqi waste-sucker guy didn't come, and the guys had to face the "shit pyramid." It got so high they couldn't actually sit down, so they'd just hold it until Saturday.

Forget using the port-a-potties for urinating. No one would subject himself to being encased by plastic in that heat just to piss. They urinated into tubes that wove through a wall straight into the Tigris River, the splashdown an undeniably satisfying sound.

When the waste-sucker dude did show up on Saturday, eradicating the fear that the port-a-potties might explode from toxic gas buildup, the smell of what was being sucked spread throughout the outpost.

"Stagnant-ass bullshit," Ladue muttered, sitting on the Apache stoop for a cigarette. "Lazy-ass contractors."

At Apache, the soldiers had T-rations for breakfast and dinner, most of the time, and meals ready to eat, or MREs, the rest of the time. Apache had no Baskin-Robbins and no KBR (contractors who prepare meals). When they arrived, garbage filled the tiny outpost, which made sense, since the neighborhood hadn't had any garbage service for months.

An MiT team occupied several rooms in the building Charlie Company stayed in, but refused to give up space for the new guys, even when they had only two men to a room. And their cooks would make meals, but if there wasn't enough for Charlie Company, that was Charlie's tough luck. There were plenty of MREs to go around. But even as they treated Charlie Company as if they were invading the MiT team's space, the MiT team stopped going out on patrol. A Special Forces unit also set up camp at Apache, but no one was allowed near their part of the base.

"We're not welcome here," Hendrix told Baka, as they stood in the command post trying to figure out how to make things better for their men. "We're forced to commute those treacherous-ass roads because these assholes won't make room for us."

"They're moving out soon," Baka said, explaining that they would be replaced by a new MiT team. "When that happens, we'll just take what we need."

But even with the problems, Apache served as the only bit of safety they had in a dangerous neighborhood.

As soon as they took over Adhamiya, Charlie Company drove everywhere, including Route Absolut, which previous units had avoided because they knew there were roadside bombs there. Command Sergeant Major Cooke had been killed on Absolut. Most of Adhamiya's streets were too narrow for the Bradleys or Humvees to drive through, and just as they'd encountered on the commute from Loyalty, burning heaps of garbage and debris from bombed buildings blocked some of the major roads. The guys would go as far as they could in their vehicles and then patrol on foot. Charlie Company patrolled zones 18 and 19, bordered by the Tigris and divided by Omar Street. Alpha Company had zone 17. Each zone had idiosyncrasies. In the Tigris River, the soldiers found bodies. At the north end of Omar Street, home of the Abu Hanifa Mosque, the soldiers found bombs. In zone 18, there were taller, more-industrial buildings—malls and hotels that provided the perfect hiding spots for snipers and kids dropping grenades. The roads in zone 18 surrounding the mosque were especially tight and littered with improvised explosive devices. Zone 19, just north of zone 20, was more residential, but it had more dead bodies and more kidnapping cases. Zone 17 was generally calmer.

All of the streets had American code names—christened ironically for favorite brands of liquor and beer. The troops were not allowed to have alcohol in Iraq because it was prohibited by Islam, and the American government didn't want to offend the locals, so the street names literally offered up a taste of home: A soldier on Route Fat Tire knew that someone from Fort Collins, Colorado, had probably been there because that's where the tiny New Belgium brewery that makes Fat Tire is based. Other streets, such as routes Remy and Absolut, ultimately only offered up fear.

On patrol, Hendrix tried to intuit what Baka needed before Baka knew himself. They'd trained together for months, but now Hendrix worked to make sure both his men and his captain were able to do their jobs well. Sometimes it was obvious when he needed to interfere.

Shortly after they had finished their left-seat, right-seat "training," Charlie Company conducted a large-scale, companywide operation. One of the platoons busted through the door of a five-story building that looked as if it had been a hotel in a previous life—before the windows were shot out, before a wall crumpled from a mortar, and before squatters took up residence with AK-47s. A shopping area had filled the first floor, with a lobby for the hotel; rooms occupied the upper floors.

As the guys descended into the basement, they found about two dozen people, including a man covered with bruises. The soldiers began to zip-tie—or "handcuff," basically using plastic fasteners normally used for garbage bags—the men in the basement as another squad prepared to go upstairs. The first sergeant and company commander controlled the operation from the first floor. A squad leader asked a young soldier to watch the door leading into the building, but the soldier itched to go upstairs and see some action.

"Ah, man," he said, staring up the stairs after them and not at the door he was supposed to be watching. "Can't you find somebody else?"

But the squad went up without him, and he continued to look after them, checking the door, and then spinning back toward the stairs when he could hear the sound of someone getting tackled.

Hendrix looked over at Baka and could see he was fuming, hands clenched at his sides and staring down the private. The private was oblivious. By not watching the door, the soldier put everybody else inside the building at risk. But Baka held back. He liked to let his NCOs handle their enlisted men.

Hendrix stormed over to the door, grabbed the kid by his harness and slammed him against the wall.

"You better get your ass on security!" he yelled.

Watching the door suddenly seemed like the best option, and the private stood quietly in the doorway, blocking the sunshine, weapon pointed up and out.

Baka walked over to Hendrix. "I'm glad you did that," Baka said, "because I was about to."

Ten minutes later, Hendrix had the kid helping photograph detainees in the basement—no hard feelings.

Ultimately, Charlie Company detained twenty-five guys that day, tried to identify them, and then took their pictures. Only six were on the blacklist, the list of guys who needed to be arrested and turned in. But half of them, by the end of Charlie Company's deployment, would end up being high-value targets. If they hadn't raided the hotel, they would never have identified them in the first place. And because no one had been properly patrolling the area, Charlie had no way of knowing just how bad these men were.

So they let them go.

Even as they tried to determine who in their neighborhood was good and who was bad, both leaders—company commander and first sergeant—defined different roles for themselves. Baka went out with all his platoons, and Hendrix went out on company missions with members of headquarters platoon. Hendrix didn't go out with the other platoons because he didn't want the platoon sergeants to feel that he was checking up on them, but he did want to know what they faced every day.

Every day, they faced a battle. On September 16, as Sergeant First Class Stuart Walker, platoon sergeant for the engineer platoon attached to Charlie Company, patrolled with his men, a sniper shot him in the forearm. The wound took him out of Adhamiya for a month.

The next week, acting on a hunch, Baka had the engineer platoon raid a building near where Walker had been shot. Inside, they found an old man and his two sons—and grenades, AK-47s, shotguns, and pistols. It was the company's first large weapons cache discovery, and it helped the engineers recover their pride after the shooting of their platoon sergeant.

On October 2, Staff Sergeant Raja Richardson was also shot through the forearm by a sniper, which meant a trip home to Germany. As men were injured or killed, soldiers from headquarters platoon would move over to take their places.

As Charlie Company patrolled, they'd find as many as ten bodies a day, but the soldiers didn't usually see the action that led to the death.

The people Charlie Company found on the streets always died from gunshot wounds to the head. But for the soldiers, it almost felt as if the insurgents were trying to test them. Out on patrol, they'd hear a gunshot from two streets away, and they'd drive over to investigate. Inevitably, they'd discover another body with a fresh gunshot wound to the head, some still gasping for a last chance at life. The shooter had to know the Americans were nearby. Bradleys aren't subtle, and all the insurgents had cell phones they could use to report the soldiers' movement through Adhamiya, so the soldiers were sure it was a kind of tease: We know you're nearby. We're not afraid of you.

In early October, Captain Baka went out with First Sergeant Hendrix and headquarters platoon on patrol. They saw one dead guy lying on the street and another on the sidewalk. But again the Iraqi people had covered the guy on the sidewalk with cardboard.

"Wow," Hendrix said, letting out a low whistle as Baka had his driver pull to the side of the road so they could investigate.

"Must be easier to deal with if they can't see it," Baka said, scorn in his voice. He couldn't imagine the same thing happening in, say, Chicago. Who were these people? What would happen to them if they acknowledged the body and took care of it? The bodies were usually Shia, but still. They were people.

Hendrix and Baka walked over with some of their soldiers, and as they did, the cardboard moved and the man beneath jerked up. He was still alive.

"Hey, Doc!" Baka yelled. "Let's see what we've got."

Sergeant Kevin Guenther, Baka's medic, immediately pulled the man to a safe area, while Baka and Hendrix questioned the people on the street. Nobody saw anything.

"Hey, sir, he's not going to make it," Guenther said, his voice shaking from concern as he knelt down, hand on the man's shoulder to try to reassure him.

"What does he need?" Baka asked.

"Tracheotomy, but I don't think it's going to matter," Guenther said.

"Do what you can," Baka said, trying to reassure his soldier that he wouldn't be able to save everyone. "Go ahead and get some practice. You're going to need it."

Guenther performed his first tracheotomy, shaking a bit as he cut a slit in the man's throat. He slipped in a tube to try to help the man breathe, but he knew the man would die. He had a gunshot wound right between the eyes. As Guenther worked, people gathered to watch, but nobody called an ambulance, and they seemed more concerned about the young teenage men Baka and Hendrix had backed against a wall as they questioned them.

"What kind of country is this?" Baka asked Hendrix, not expecting an answer. Hendrix, numbed by the callousness, could only shake his head.

"I can't—I don't understand," he finally said. "That's a human being there on the ground, and nobody cares."

"Every household in this country has an AK-47, yet they don't take care of their own," Baka said. "And where are the ambulances? Why are we the only ones providing medical assistance?"

The scene infuriated the company's favorite interpreter, an Iraqi man they called Santana because they didn't know any of the 'terps' real names and because the Iraqi man looked like the musician Carlos Santana of the band Santana.

"Why are you letting this happen?" he screamed at the people in the street, almost in tears. "Why won't you help this man?"

The man on the sidewalk lived for an hour without anyone calling an ambulance. He carried a Shiite prayer card—at that time, a death sentence in a Sunni neighborhood. He was eighteen years old.

When the insurgents did aim at the soldiers, it seemed random—potshots for practice. But the snipers generally aimed well. Out on patrol in early October with Lieutenant Colonel Eric Schacht, the 1-26 battalion commander, Hendrix and Baka heard over the radio that a civil affairs team was out in their sector. And then they heard that someone got shot.

Charlie Company still fell under the command of 4th Brigade Combat Team, 101st Airborne Division, and the brigade commander from that unit—Colonel Thomas Vail—sent out a Stryker unit to help after hearing about the gunshot.

"Damn it," Baka said, kicking the toe of his boot into the dust. He hadn't asked for backup, and the Stryker soldiers wouldn't be friendly when they came through. They'd kick in doors and piss people off. "I don't need another unit shitting in my backyard."

But Colonel Vail rode up in his Humvee to let Baka know the decision had already been made and that he had plenty of time and resources with which to help out.

Baka stopped arguing when he realized he had cowboys coming in, guys who wanted to see action. They would "help" whether Baka needed it or not. "Micromanagement at its finest," Baka muttered as the colonel drove away.

The civil affairs soldier had been shot in a triangle-shaped neighborhood near Antar Square, which was really a circle. Roads came out like spokes from the square, creating each triangle. Apartments made up the area. Vail said he was going to use his Stryker unit to clear the neighborhood—Baka's neighborhood—and asked Baka if he would set up the cordon around the Stryker's operation. Colonel Schacht volunteered to take one leg of the triangle with his men, and then Baka had two of his platoons take the other legs.

The Stryker soldiers came in and started kicking in doors. Baka fumed.

"Hey, we didn't find anything" came in over the radio.

"No kidding," Baka said. In the meantime, Baka had his driver running the Humvee in laps around the neighborhood so Baka could check in on his guys. After doing so, Baka joined up with Schacht.

Boom!

A large explosion shook the ground and seemingly even the air.

"I'll bet it's a VBIED," Baka said to Schacht. "Sounds like it's north of us."

"I'll check it out," Schacht said, and walked toward his Humvee.

As he walked, a bullet caught the edge of his e-sapi body armor plate by his armpit, spinning the colonel in a complete circle. The insurgent had been aiming for the edge, hoping to hit flesh and not armor. The insurgents had learned that if they shot through the unit patch a soldier wore on his shoulder, the bullet would go straight through his heart.

This time the shooter was off by a centimeter.

But nobody heard the shot crack through the air. With all the sounds of a city—traffic and generators and music—they saw the battalion commander spin but didn't understand why. Schacht stumbled toward his truck and started pulling off his body armor and grabbing at his chest. Sergeant Major Steve McClaflin, usually standing nearby with a dour expression and a slug of chew in his lip, grabbed Schacht and laid him in the back of the Humvee. He got out his knife and cut open Schacht's shirt.

The bullet had not reached Schacht's skin, but the force of it had left a dark purple bruise that stretched the width of his chest.

"Don't call it in," Baka yelled at his driver. "The last thing we need is Headquarters in a frenzy."

Baka had his men clear a nearby building, searching for the sniper. Early in their deployment, they thought the insurgents were shooting from the top floors of the buildings. Later they would realize the bullets came from ground-floor levels or from people who were shooting from cars and that there was always someone with a video camera nearby recording it.

Schacht stayed in his truck as the soldiers worked, refusing to go back to Apache until the mission was over. Baka had his medic check the commander out.

"We can take you back in, sir," Baka said. "It's not a big deal."

"I'm fine," Schacht said. "I don't even need a Band-Aid. Let's just finish this up."

"OK," Baka said. "You're the boss."

Baka first met Schacht at a brigade ceremony in March 2005. At first, Baka felt a little intimidated by the gruff commander, and it took him a while to get used to Schacht's leadership style, which left subordinate commanders free to make decisions on their own. Then Baka realized this style allowed his own skills to flourish, and that all he had to do was walk in Schacht's door and ask for help—respectfully—when he needed it. Very quickly, the respect became mutual, and top leaders within the battalion began referring to Baka as "Schacht's boy," a mark of respect showing that Schacht counted on Baka to perform the hard jobs.

As Schacht remained in his up-armored vehicle, McClaflin remained nearby and vigilant. Baka's men didn't find the shooter, so three hours after Schacht had been shot, they headed back to Apache where Captain Joseph Whelchel, the physician assistant in charge of the medics, checked out the battalion commander further.

By that time, news of Schacht's near-death experience had gone up the chain. Schacht drove to Loyalty for a brigade meeting that afternoon, and as he stood in the back of the room, people discussed the shocking news of his injury and wondered if he was OK, not realizing he was there. After hearing he had been shot, everyone assumed Schacht was in bad shape in an aid station or hospital somewhere. Vail immediately began bad-mouthing Charlie Company.

"This company is out of control with negligent discharges," Vail said. "The soldiers don't know how to evade snipers and they can't handle their battle space."

Vail went on and on in front of all of his battalion commanders and executive officers, apparently trying to make it seem that the 101st's MiT team had had the situation under control in Adhamiya before Charlie got there. In Schacht's mind, the MiT team made it seem much easier to evade snipers and control battle space simply by never leaving the safety of Combat Outpost Apache.

But Schacht allowed Vail to finish.

Then, his voice tight with anger, Schacht said, "I'm here."

Vail did a double take at the front of the room, as if he'd just heard the voice of God. He looked for Schacht to verify that the man had actually shown up for a brigade meeting just after being shot, and then backtracked.

"I'm just saying the situation seems out of control out there," he said. He quickly changed the subject, but the story of Schacht's appearance at the meeting quickly spread through the brigade.

From then on, soldiers who didn't need immediate assistance after being checked out by a medic waited for the platoon to finish its mission before heading back to Apache.

Out on the stoop at Loyalty, the guys talked about having their battalion commander shot, and about how badass he was for staying out on patrol. But the randomness of the snipers didn't make sense to them.

"I don't get it," DeNardi said, drawing circles in the dusty ground with his finger. "It's like they occasionally take potshots at us, but aren't really after us."

"You know, they can see it's just one platoon out there," said Staff Sergeant Robin Johnson, cutting off his *r*'s with his South Boston accent. "Maybe we just don't scare them?"

Johnson, an NCO in the scout platoon, could have been DeNardi's big brother. Both had the high cheekbones and clear faces indicative of extreme youth, though Johnson was twenty-nine to DeNardi's twenty. Johnson acted like DeNardi's brother, pulling him in for a head rub or advising him about just how much smart-assedness DeNardi could get away with. DeNardi didn't always stick with the lesson plan, but he still followed Johnson around and took his word as gospel.

Adhamiya was Johnson's fourth deployment. It was DeNardi's first.

"Maybe they're afraid if they mess with us too much, it'll bring the heat down," reasoned Private First Class Armando Cardenas, one of DeNardi's best buddies. "Like if they only kill civilians we won't come after them. They treat us like target practice if we happen to be in the way."

Cardenas, twenty-one, enlisted when he was a senior—and an honor student—in high school. A stout kid with black hair and glasses that made him somehow more handsome in a smart-kid way, Cardenas joined the army because he was afraid he'd get bored in college. He'd grown up with stories of Vietnam from his uncle and thought that the infantry might be more interesting than algebra.

"They don't seem to have any problem with shooting at us when we're driving out to Apache, though," Johnson said, staring up into the dusty sky. "That's enough insurgents for me."

In Adhamiya that fall, Charlie Company did deal with some skirmishes, but again it seemed as if it were only when the soldiers got in the way. Some soldiers made a habit of getting in the way.

Staff Sergeant Ian Newland had laughed when he found out they would be at "COP Apache." The skinny, dark-haired NCO had come from the Apache tribe. "Apache are pretty fierce," he told his men, shrugging. "It's a pretty appropriate name if you're going Native American."

As he drove through Adhamiya one day with his men, they got a call that a military police unit was getting hammered. Newland was manning the Mark-19, an automatic grenade launcher that can shoot off sixty rounds a minute. A round will kill anyone within five meters of the target. As Newland's crew arrived at the scene, Newland saw someone lob a hand grenade at the end of an alleyway, as well as a group of young men with AK-47s. He aimed the Mark-19 in their direction and fired. Then he aimed again and hit an insurgent he saw shooting at the MPs.

But there were people everywhere. He saw an MP get hit, so Newland traversed in his turret and aimed for the second insurgent. As he was shooting, he felt an armor-piercing round hit the bracket of the Mark-19, then clatter down into the turret. A fragment slammed into Newland's side, but just as with Colonel Schacht, there was no blood. Newland had just slipped new side plates into his body-armor vest a couple of days before, and one of those plates kept the fragment from piercing his skin. Still, the force of the blow knocked Newland down, but he rose back up.

Newland kept going with the Mark, but the insurgents blew out his headlights and tires, concentrating on Newland's truck as if he were the one to beat. Finally, the Mark-19 died, too.

As the soldiers had been firing, a crowd of spectators gathered to watch, as if at a soccer game.

"Sir, we have to move this truck," Newland shouted to his platoon leader, Second Lieutenant Travis Atwood, over the radio. Helicopters flew in to provide cover while the rest of first platoon hauled Newland and his team back to Apache.

The guys thought of that as a good day: They knew who they were fighting. Other days, they didn't participate so much as just witness the violence. At dinner that night, the soldiers sat on cots eating ravioli and chili and beef stew out of khaki-colored plastic bags with khaki-colored plastic spoons.

"Samarra was rough, but I felt a lot safer last time," Newland said, dumping Tabasco on his cold ravioli.

"Why?" asked Private Ross McGinnis, big brown eyes always questioning everything. "Weren't they shooting at you in Samarra?"

"It's the senseless violence," Newland tried to explain. "This deployment, every patrol, you're finding dead people—one to twelve a patrol. I didn't see this shit last time—these people with their eyes gouged out and their arms broken and their bodies bruised. I didn't see any torture crap last time."

"I guess I just thought that was how it was supposed to look," said McGinnis. He was nineteen years old and on his first deployment.

On a recent patrol, they had found a prepubescent boy who had been shot ten to fifteen times. The boy's cousin had been shot in the head. The boy's father had been shot through both hands and both shoulders, and then laid out on the floor like Jesus.

"Remember that?" Newland said. "Just blood everywhere. That sticks with you."

The family had been Shiite living in Sunni Adhamiya.

As they felt their way through the first month of their mission, Baka had his guys run fourteen hours of patrol: four nights on, eight days on, and then four days off. Baka would go to bed at 3:00 A.M.—or later—every day. The guys would ride back to Loyalty every night after night patrols. They'd spend eight nights sleeping at Apache if they were on day patrols. Then they'd have three or four days at Loyalty doing maintenance or acting as the quick reaction force. They had an hour break between patrols. Baka upped it to an hour-and-a half as the patrols grew worse.

The men hated the night patrols. They viewed the world through night-vision goggles, which offered an eerie green picture with no peripheral vision. Objects that looked like rocks or a curb could easily be molded fiberglass designed to conceal an explosive device. A bush could easily be a human. A human that looked like the enemy could be a friend. Once they found a body outside a Christian church in zone 19. In the darkness, it took them a while to realize what the shape was. Charlie Company knocked on doors to try to find out what had happened, but the neighbors were terrified and said they hadn't seen anything. Neighbors who talked to the troops ended up bodies on the streets.

Days weren't much better. Talking to locals on patrol inevitably brought in sniper fire or ambushes, which always failed. So the troops questioned people during cordon-and-knock missions. "Cordon and knock" meant they set up a security ring around an area to keep the troops safe, and then they knocked on doors. Charlie Company also spent much of its time looking for dead bodies, marking down the coordinates, and alerting the Iraqi army to come pick up the corpses.

The troops knew exactly what jobs they needed to perform as infantrymen, but some things fell outside the realm of anything they had done in training. In those cases, a few soldiers came up with their own solutions, often excluding everyone else to try to protect their friends.

Sergeant Erik Osterman walked through Apache with impossibly perfect posture. It's the first thing a person notices, just before the intense, straightforward gaze. He doesn't stare—that implies that he didn't see what he was looking at. Osterman saw everything. A former bouncer and concealed-permit trainer, he instinctively watched to see what would happen next. In Iraq, it meant he knew what his guys were thinking before they did.

The reason for his perfect posture was more complicated, but helps explain why he was a good noncommissioned officer. When he was eight, he went from being a kid who insisted on being involved in everything from Boy Scouts to Bible study—even if he had to get there on his own—to a kid with knees so bad he couldn't move. During a tae kwon do class, Osterman kicked his foot out in front of him. Normally, knees only hinge backward, so his kick should have ended as his leg straightened. But it didn't. His knee bent ninety degrees forward. His kneecaps had moved from the fronts of his knees to the sides, which meant there was nothing to keep his legs stable.

From ages eight until eleven, Osterman had to use crutches. Without them, his knees would buckle and he would collapse.

His knees were so bad that a doctor at Children's Memorial Hospital in Chicago used Osterman as an example of the worst knees a child could have in a book the doctor wrote. The doctor performed two surgeries, putting Osterman out of action—and in bed—for another year.

After the surgery, Osterman's knees were well enough that he spent all his time skateboarding. But his experience—not being able to play, as well as knowing that the other kids didn't want to play with "the cripple"— brought a level of compassion, as well as an expectation of other people, that would play out well in Adhamiya. In Charlie Company, he served as the commo guy and set up every bit of communications from Apache back to Loyalty, but he quietly took on much tougher duties.

The first time Osterman saw a Humvee come in with his friends' blood sprayed across the inside, he took over.

On October 2, Staff Sergeant Joe Narvaez of Headquarters Company's mortar platoon was out on patrol with Bravo Company, 1st Battalion, 77th Armor Regiment. Bravo Company had been attached to the Blue Spaders for the deployment to Iraq. They were heading to Apache for a battalion meeting, but on the way the soldiers saw two bodies on the ground. It was a setup. As Narvaez talked to his company commander, Captain Will Wade, near one of the bodies, a sniper shot Narvaez in the head.

His medic, Specialist Ahmed Uddin, worked long past the point when Narvaez had already died to try to save him, finally having to be pulled back. But Uddin wasn't finished yet.

The mortar platoon loaded Narvaez up and drove into Apache, where Osterman waited with First Sergeant Hendrix.

"I gotta do something for him," Uddin told Osterman. "I couldn't save him."

Uddin kept reaching out to Narvaez, trying to figure out what he could do, touching his chest, checking for a pulse.

"Hey, man," Osterman said, his hand on Uddin's shoulder. "You've done all you could. It wasn't your fault."

But Uddin wanted to help clean out the vehicle that had been doused in his friend's blood. Narvaez's teammates stood outside the Humvee staring at the blood.

"Go get some bleach," Osterman said, trying to give the medic a mission that would take him away from the scene.

Osterman grabbed a couple of people to help—Sergeant Jeremy Bracken and Sergeant Billy Fielder. As the other men came back with sponges and scouring pads and bleach, Osterman accepted the supplies and sent the Headquarters Company men back inside. He made it an order.

"There's no way in hell they're going to help clean up," Osterman said to Bracken and Fielder as they sprayed and scrubbed, pools of red forming in the dust. "And they're not going to roll back out in the vehicle like that. They wouldn't see anything else."

A switch had flipped for Osterman. This would be his job from now on. Quietly. He didn't talk about it. Even as he sprayed out the inside of Narvaez's helmet, his stomach roiling, he decided that no one else would see that part of Adhamiya.

When they had finished, Osterman went to Hendrix.

"Every time it happens, come and get me," Osterman said. "It's not like I need to be the den mother, but I have to do it."

Osterman's request didn't surprise Hendrix. He knew Osterman well enough to know he'd be the best person for the job, but Hendrix also understood the size of the request.

"You're right," Hendrix said, watching Osterman's face for any signs that he was making the offer in the moment rather than as a permanent gift to his men. "I don't want the platoons doing this. I don't want it to be any harder than it already is. But I need for you to be OK."

"Top, it would hurt them forever," Osterman said. "It hurts me."

From then on, every time someone was hurt or killed, Osterman washed away the remains of their fear and pain.

CHAPTER 4

Charlie Company Faces Its First Losses

The guys who had deployed together to Samarra became inseparable at Loyalty. Closer in rank and age, Staff Sergeant Robin Johnson, Sergeant Ryan Wood, Sergeant Alphonso Montenegro, and Sergeant Willsun Mock spent every spare moment working out. Specialist. Daniel Agami, beefing up bigger than any of them, soon joined the group. At Loyalty, there was nothing else to do—not even a PX, or post exchange, where they could buy new video games or music. A couple of them, including Johnson, were into extreme fighting back home, so they made a pact: They'd gain fifteen pounds of muscle by March.

At the gym, where they'd spend hours each day, Johnson and Mock had a running argument: Who was better, the Spartans or the Romans?

"The Spartans," Johnson said, grinning as he brought a bar of weight toward his chest for bench presses, Mock spotting, Johnson's "Spartans" came out without an *r*. His Boston accent added an odd modernity to the ancient argument. "The whole society was military. They didn't do anything but war."

"Romans," Mock calmly replied, pushing Johnson for one more set. "Back then, the rich people were the soldiers, instead of sending in the kids who couldn't afford college."

"That doesn't even make sense," Johnson said, sweat pouring in the un-air-conditioned gym. "Why would you send in the rich guys?"

"They could afford the best weapons," Mock said, switching spots with Johnson. "And then the rich people—the best educated—decided who would do what, so you end up with the best-organized army in the world—in history."

"No chance," Johnson argued. "The Spartans sent everybody in. Dude, they didn't even stand for weak babies. They tossed them in a chasm. You didn't go to Boy Scout camp, you got sent off in the wild by yourself to prove you could survive."

"It doesn't matter how tough they are if they don't know what to do with it," Mock said, grunting as he paused the conversation to push up the bar. "Tossing babies into chasms ain't strategy."

"I don't know, man," Johnson said, realizing the argument would never be resolved. "I don't want a bunch of nerds heading up my army."

They based a lot of their argument on movies, but then ramped it up with research they did online when they weren't on patrol. Every day, they had to have a new point for their argument. But they loved to hear the hero stories, too, Roman or Spartan, and they would regale each other with the ancient tales. Eventually, Mock one-upped Johnson: He had "Strength" and "Honor" tattooed down his arms, a reference to the movie *Gladiator*. When he greeted Johnson—or anyone else, including Baka—he would grip him high on his wrists and repeat those two words. Johnson would respond in the same way. Those images of courage and pure animal instinct became increasingly important as they talked about what could happen this tour. "I've seen friends get shot in the head, legs torn off," Johnson told his friends in a moment of quiet at Loyalty. Even though he set up house in the hallway with the rest of the scout platoon, he spent more time with his friends than on his own cot. "So much terrible stuff."

They all expected it to be worse in Adhamiya, more from gut feeling than anything else.

They'd take out their stress on the weight sets, spending two or three hours a day trying to bulk up. In Iraq, soldiers don't have a lot of control over what they will do from day to day or even whether they will live, but the gym was a different matter.

"I'm gonna cut down and shred up," Agami said again as he slammed down another protein shake. The army chose him as a model troop for a recruitment campaign, and the new job made perfect sense. Every time the media showed up at Apache, there'd be a shot of Agami, neck like a tree stump but well proportioned to his muscular body and handsome face: pure soldier. Bill O'Reilly even featured him for a "Hanukkah in the Green Zone" special on Fox News.

One afternoon, bored as usual, the guys decided to do their own photo shoot. Sitting on top of a Bradley with a leg on either side of the five-foot-long gun, it quickly became obvious what Agami was thinking. "This is my weapon and this is my gun," he said, pointing to the Bradley gun both times. "This is for shooting and this is for fun." Cardenas crawled up next to him and sat the same way with a much-smaller metal rod sticking out. "I'll be picking up all the chicks when we get back," he said, grinning so hard it pushed his glasses up on his nose.

"Hey, check this out," said Specialist Ernesto Martin as he pretended he was being chased by the Bradley, one knee high in the air as if he were running, mouth opened as he called for help.

Agami jumped down into a similar pose, and Cardenas went to one knee, shoving his foot under the Bradley track so it looked like he was about to be smashed, even as a cigarette hung from his lip. Agami clenched his jaw like a superhero in an action movie, arms pumping.

Before joining the army, Agami had worked as a DJ in Miami. He pulled party shifts on private yachts, seemingly constantly surrounded by gorgeous women—at least based on the pictures he liked to show the guys—and worked a constant tan. After he joined the army, he settled on one girl, relaxed into the role of a patriot, and only brought out bits of his old self when it was time to go out. "You're not wearing that," he told Johnson before a night out in Schweinfurt. Johnson had offended by daring to wear a T-shirt and sneakers, rather than, say, a button-down ox-ford and leather shoes. "I'm not going out with you looking like that."

He headed into Johnson's closet with him to help him pick some-thing out.

Johnson's upbringing had been completely different. He tried to explain it to Agami as they sat on his cot one night playing spades over an MRE box.

"I was in a really bad place when I joined the army," he said. "I was mixed up with drugs, violence—living in the projects. I thought, 'If I don't find a way out from here, I'm going to be dead or in prison by the time I'm thirty.'" He needed someone to tell him what to do. He'd grown up in South Boston in a traditional working-class Irish-Catholic neigh-borhood. His grandparents raised him, and he grew up proud of his heri-tage, proud enough to wear an Irish claddagh ring as his talisman on patrol. "It's a poor area," he said, describing home. "It's a very good community, except for the projects." He had a hard time seeing himself outside of a world filled with fighting and friends who wouldn't live much past adult-hood, but then the answer seemed obvious: His dad was in the army and had spent years earning several master's degrees, the epitome of a soldier who wanted to better educate himself. Johnson's brother served in the Spe-cial Forces. Suddenly it seemed as if that were a better life goal than petty drug dealer.

"I kind of got a little jealous," Johnson said. "My family's all infan-try: 'You're infantry or you're nothing. If you want to be a soldier, be a soldier.' But I had no idea what the infantry was." He went off the drugs cold turkey, but that wasn't the hardest point. He signed up in May 2001 and left for basic September 18, understanding fully that the world had changed since he had enlisted five months before. "I had a massive au-thority problem going into basic training," he said. "They pretty much destroyed me. I spent the whole time in the sandpit getting smoked. But toward the end, things started popping." He snapped his fingers, and his accent grew stronger as he remembered. "I started feeling like a member of the team. When they started building me back up again, I started realizing I'm not the same guy I was. They'd say, 'We expect more from you.' I'd get off on it. I can't picture doing anything else in the world."

In the army, he moved up the ranks quickly and was known as a problem solver. No one would have known that he had had such a troubled youth, except he was open about that, too. He wanted to show the young guys just how far they could go.

Montenegro and Wood had been there when Johnson fell in love in Samarra, and they teased him about it constantly.

Going out on patrol one day in Samarra, Johnson was told to go to the aid station to pick up the medic. "Fuck," he whined to Montenegro when he found out who he'd be with. "I don't want to go out with a girl. What the hell are women doing out with infantry units, anyway?"

"Dude, maybe she's hot," Monte teased.

"[Like] I give a shit if she's hot. She can be hot in the Green Zone," Johnson said, slamming his gear around as he prepared to go out on patrol.

He spent the whole patrol sulking. Women shouldn't be working with infantry units. Period. On patrol, if they got hit, she'd have to play infantryman: provide cover, keep her cool under fire, protect other soldiers. There's no way a woman was as capable of doing the job as a man could be, and if she were, what did that say about those traditionally male roles? Johnson refused to talk to her the whole time they were out.

But then he started visiting the aid station on his downtime. Suddenly, he developed an interest in learning about basic combat procedures, and she—Jeana—was willing to teach him. He asked her to marry him four months later. Jeana Johnson didn't deploy to Adhamiya: She had just given birth to their second child. But when Johnson called home with war stories, she could instantly relate, and, being a medic, she encouraged him to tell the stories, no matter how bad they got.

In Samarra, Johnson had served in second platoon, but in Adhamiya, he was pulled in as a squad leader for the scouts, so he fell under Headquarters Company like the medics, but, also like the medics, Johnson was attached to Charlie Company. His role quickly changed to that of a peacemaker. All the Charlie Company men—from platoon sergeant to private—felt comfortable talking with Johnson because he fit in a neutral spot by moving to the scout platoon. Normally, the scouts pull reconnaissance, sneaking out ahead of everyone else to see what the infantry units would encounter on a mission. But in Iraq they had been set up basically as infantry units. The battalion sent Johnson, an infantryman, to the scout platoon to retrain them. But he spent all his time with second platoon.

And that essentially meant spending time with the whole company. The platoons didn't differentiate, especially when they were bored.

Several of the guys liked to get together for salsa dancing, and the lessons continued when they got bored in Iraq. Rough at work, then smooth in style and moves on the dance floor, Sergeant Ely Chagoya, thirty-one, danced well enough that the others asked for tips, and he obliged. He'd teach his guys anything they asked. But when Mock asked, Chagoya couldn't help laughing a little. Mock was as white as they come—freckly, even—and looked as if he should be at the local cowboy bar, especially with his "Strength" and "Honor" tattoos. But the man loved to salsa. And all the men loved to retell stories they all knew from home. Talking about being in the club helped them forget about Iraq.

"I'll be dancing with a girl, and he stops me, 'Hey, Gunny! Teach me another step,'" Chagoya said, laughing and demonstrating, Mock grinning nearby, smoking cigarettes. "He dates this girl from Colombia, but he doesn't speak Spanish, so he says it in English and I translate. He's like, 'She said this. What does it mean?' This little white boy trying to salsa dance at the club—that's Mock."

"I'm getting pretty good, though," Mock said, still smiling. "You're just afraid I'm gonna get better than you and you'll have to hand over salsa to the white kids. Just wait until I speak Spanish better than you do. You won't be able to pick up any brown girls. I'll get them all."

Chagoya laughed so hard he lost his step as he demonstrated Mock's dancing moves, using Cardenas as a partner. "OK, man," he said. "You are getting pretty good, but not that good. Never that good."

In Iraq, Mock's Spanish was getting better the more time he spent with his crew, but he still needed help. He'd find Specialist Ernesto Martin whenever he got a letter because Martin gave him the least amount of crap about it. Martin, probably the friendliest guy in the company, with a big happy grin and big bright eyes, had only recently learned English himself, just so he could join the army.

"Hey, man! What'd she say?" Mock would ask, handing Martin a letter, and Martin would laugh his way through the mushy stuff, and then laugh more when Mock asked him to translate a letter back to his girl. "Hey, OK," Mock said one day. "Write this: Tell her I miss her and that her eyes burn like coal in my memory."

"Man, you can't say that. You sound like a pogue," Martin said, as he tried to translate Mock's professions of love. A "pogue" is anyone who isn't infantry. The troops came up with a new acronym for an old word: Personnel Other than Grunts.

"Dude, I didn't ask for a critique," Mock said. "Just write it. She'll like it."

Mock loved the Latin culture, and his Latino friends loved him back.

But the groups of friends overlapped: Agami and Mock, Wood and Montenegro and Johnson. DeNardi and Cardenas. There were no real cliques and as they spent more time together on patrol, anyone could drop into any conversation. As far as they were concerned, they were brothers, and some of them had already proven what they were willing to risk for each other. Montenegro and Wood had been stop-lossed, so even though they had fulfilled their contract with the army, they were forced to stay until the end of another combat tour. Anyone who had three months left in the army before a combat tour began was automatically extended until the end of the company's time in theater, and that could be anywhere from a year to fifteen months. Sometimes units made arrangements for those men to fill a position where they wouldn't have to patrol so much, such as supply or working logistics. But in 1-26, the guys stayed with their platoons. They wouldn't desert their friends.

Before they deployed, Baka talked one of the guys into reenlisting so he could go to Fort Benning as an instructor, rather than being stoplossed again. He tried to help others into college so they would have a reason not to do a second tour with only a couple months left to their enlistments. He and Hendrix had tried to work out the details as soon as they had heard they might head back to Iraq. "You know, they know what they're getting into," Baka told Hendrix as they tried to work the system a bit. "But they're fooled into thinking they'll get one deployment in combat and then they'll get out. It's an internal draft. We're drafting our own."

"We don't even have choice," Hendrix said. "After the first deployment, fifty percent of the formation is gone. And honestly, what would we do without their experience?"

They don't want to lose the combat vets. Those are the guys who will be leaders during the next deployment. But they're really only getting eight months' rest, rather than a full year, after a twelve-month deployment because of all the training.

Baka understood how the deployments affected his soldiers from personal experience. His life had also changed significantly since September 11, 2001. Even though the soldiers know Saddam Hussein hadn't been involved in the terrorist attacks on the United States, they also knew the wartime deployments began soon afterward, so the date would always be connected in their minds. Baka had missed time watching his first daughter grow into a toddler while he was in Iraq for a first tour, and now he would miss the first year of his second daughter's life. He did the same thing his men did: He connected hard with the soldiers. In Adhamiya, he went out on patrol every day.

Baka had taken one year of Arabic in school, just enough to show the locals he was trying, but also enough to know for himself the importance of the Iraqi family. Each day was very much the same: On a typical visit, he walked into a house with Santana, Captain Nathaniel Waggoner, Hendrix and a few of his men, leaving several other soldiers outside to watch for snipers and men with grenades.

The first time Baka went out with Santana, the interpreter lit up a cigarette in the backseat of the Humvee. It never occurred to the Iraqi man that smoking might be verboten.

"Santana," Baka said, "you will not smoke in my truck."

"What?" Santana said, obviously confused. In Iraq, it seemed as if everybody smoked. "Oh, right."

He stubbed it out on the bottom of his boot and tucked the cigarette back into his uniform pocket. At first Baka worried how effective he could be with someone like Santana, who seemed likable enough, but maybe not serious enough. As it turned out, Santana not only interpreted Baka's words, he conveyed the commander's emotions. If the convoy needed to stop, Santana would jump out to direct traffic without having to be asked. Santana was from Basra, and his wife was Lebanese. He'd sent her home to Lebanon with their toddler son, but he wanted to stay in Iraq because he thought he could help. Charlie Company came to trust Santana completely, even while they worried about their other interpreters.

On one mission, they entered a fairly typical home: Low sectional couches lined the walls of a living area, with a television as the focal point. On the walls hung pictures of Saddam Hussein; lots of lamps sat on shelves and were bracketed to the walls; carpets graced tile floors; and plastic flowers wrapped around the arches of the doorways. Baka sat on a couch with the adults in the family and drank strong, sugary, spicy black tea in a tiny cup. A middle-aged man who probably looked older than he actually was with his gray hair and deeply lined face sat next to Baka. Years of wars made the adults look old and the children—who were often malnourished—look younger.

In this house, Baka found a couple about the same age as himself and his wife. The man offered Baka a cigarette, and Baka took it, fearing that if he didn't, the Iraqi man would think him rude. Inside, he always took off his helmet so he'd appear more like a human. He wanted to show a side beyond the American soldier all bulked up with body armor and carrying a gun. But he was also trying to show his sergeants how to interact—to earn people's trust.

As Santana teased the children and handed out candy, Baka pulled out pictures of his girls: Elizabeth, two, and his newborn, Hannah. The Iraqi family had two girls about the same age. As he talked with the family, he found more similarities. The wife was a Shia, and the husband was Sunni. Baka's wife is a Protestant, and Baka is a Catholic. Both the man and the woman worked at the local hospital, but struggled to get home before curfew. By the end of the conversation, the little girls were sitting in Baka's lap, and he playfully showed them his uniform and let them hold his helmet. Baka had been working to make the Americans seem more human, but the girls provided a good reminder of a family not that different from his own.

By the end of the evening, he was trading hugs and handshakes with the couple.

Not all the visits went so well. Another time, as he sat in yet another living room, he asked Santana to translate for him.

"Ask them if they need anything," Baka said.

After a flurry of words and hand gestures, Santana answered:

"They need everything."

They had no clean water. They had no electricity. They couldn't go outside. They couldn't work. Their children needed to go to school.

Baka promised to do his best, but realized the Iraqis had to be thinking, "Can we trust this person? This is the seventh or eighth American we've seen in three years."

So he had Santana ask another question. "What can we do to make things better?"

"I know the solution to all our problems," the man said pleasantly, as if he were having a reasoned conversation with an old friend. "Bring Saddam back."

Baka answered without so much as a raised eyebrow, "I'm glad you have the freedom to say that, that you feel safe voicing your disagreements," he said. "But that's not going to happen, so what can we do to make things better for your children?"

Then they talked about the things the family would like to see: Security. Education. Peace.

Baka asked his normal follow-up question. "Are you seeing any insurgents?" Santana translated.

"No, no," came the reply. "No insurgents here. They're in the next street."

In reality, the neighbors didn't necessarily know who lived across the street. As the insurgents moved in, the homeowners moved out, fearing for their lives. Shiite homeowners were often killed and replaced by new Sunni owners. Those who stayed or moved in quickly learned it was best to let out as little information as possible. And if they did see something bad happening across the street, they knew it was in their best interest to keep their mouths shut. The Americans could not always be there to protect them. But Baka handed them a card with a cell phone number anyway. "If you see anything, call us," he said. "Yes, yes," they answered. Eventually, tips began to come in, but the company had to carefully check to see if they were legitimate.

As Baka sat inside the house talking with the family, the soldiers grew edgy outside, joking nervously, staying away from open entrances, and keeping their weapons pointed up and out, as if an attack would come from above. Once, as Baka, Waggoner, and Hendrix left a council meeting, they were shot at in the street. Anytime they stayed in one place for more than fifteen minutes, someone attacked them. Baka finally emerged, ready to hit the next house and start the questions again.

Baka's closest ally was the Iraqi army colonel, who was a Sunni protectionist, an old Hussein officer. But the new Iraqi army was Shiite. Before Charlie Company had arrived, the Iraqi army soldiers were known for carting off Sunni civilians to jail for no reason, trashing Sunni homes, and smearing human shit on Sunni religious posters. Having the new Sunni colonel helped, but to join the army, Iraqis had to go to Western Baghdad, and no Sunni felt safe going across the river for that trip. The colonel wanted to create a militia made up of people from Adhamiya. "We really can't support that," Baka told him, but he acknowledged that the corruption in the Shiite military was horrendous. If there were more Sunni in the military, they could at least provide a counterbalance to the Shiite. Baka went up his chain—all the way to General George Casey, commanding general of the multinational forces in Iraq—to push for more Sunnis in the Iraqi army.

"The Iraqi army, man, about 80 percent aren't worth anything," Hendrix said, shaking his head in disbelief as he and his soldiers smoked on their stoop at Loyalty.

"It's pretty sad when the Iraqi police and the Iraqi army won't patrol their own city," DeNardi said, standing in front of Hendrix and kicking at stones with his sand-colored boots, the color in his cheeks rising with his frustration. "They set up with us, but they always have some fucking excuse: 'No gas. It's too dangerous. We don't have enough guys.'"

For some reason, when DeNardi imitated Iraqi soldiers, he always used a high-pitched, effeminate voice.

A couple of days before, Charlie Company had to go pick up an Iraqi who'd been killed on Route Remy because the Iraqi army had given them their typical excuse: They were out of gas. "When we were coming back in, they rolled past us," DeNardi complained. "They don't even try to hide it."

"Do you suppose they're just really that disorganized?" Wood asked, and then began doing jumping jacks, but instead of his hands clapping together, one hand would go over his head and the other would hit his leg. When the Iraqi troops did jumping jacks for physical training in front of the palace at Apache, they looked like popcorn—skinny uncoordinated popcorn in too-big uniforms.

"Dude, they can't even march in step," Agami said. "Like ever. And they practice every day."

"I think maybe twenty percent of them mean well," Hendrix said. "But the others are just here for the paycheck."

Hendrix could always tell on patrol who was good and who was bad by who paid attention and actually appeared to be working.

"But that doesn't even make sense," DeNardi said. "They're getting shot at, just like we are. Are they stupid?"

Every single day, Iraqi soldiers on patrol would die in Antar Square. They'd fall asleep in their fighting positions, or light fires to stay warm, giving the enemy perfect targets.

"Part of our job on patrol is to go around and wake their asses up," Hendrix said. "Then again, maybe we should let natural selection take its course."

Hendrix was convinced that there were informants for the insurgents within the Iraqi army, and in the house across the street from Apache. He was convinced the neighbors knew more than they were telling the Americans. He tried to explain to his soldiers why no one would call them with tips.

"What are we going to tell them?" Hendrix said. " 'If the insurgents show up, give us a call?' We can't protect them all the time."

But the soldiers' inability to accomplish anything didn't help morale. If Charlie Company set up generators to help the citizens, the insurgents would take them over and charge for electricity. If they brought in contractors to clean up the garbage and sewage kids at play in the streets waded through, the insurgents would kill the contractors. If they brought food to someone who needed help, that family would be accused of working with the Americans.

Baka tried to help the situation by working nonstop. He'd go out on patrol all day, call his wife, write up awards for his men at night while listening to the radio traffic, and then plan for the next day's missions. He averaged about four hours of sleep a day, and it was usually interrupted by some emergency or some high-ranking visitor who needed a briefing.

Hendrix realized Baka needed a break, even if Baka would not admit it. When they first began spending more time at Apache and less time at Loyalty, Hendrix and Baka shared a room with everyone from their platoon leaders to their gunners. At one point, there were eleven men in one room, including the CO and the first sergeant. Hendrix quickly decided they needed their own space, and by "they" he meant Baka. He sectioned off an area so that only he and Baka shared a room. He blacked out the windows with blankets so they could sleep during the day after night patrols. Then Hendrix left Baka alone. When the first sergeant wasn't at Loyalty, he either hung out in Apache's tiny command area or played video games with his guys in headquarters platoon. Baka would spend his limited downtime in the room, either reading his Bible or calling his wife.

But both Baka and Hendrix, when not sleeping or working, spent much of their time trying to figure out how to get second platoon back to Charlie Company. Back where they could see them. Back where they could be responsible for their safety. Back where Baka could be the one to call their families if they were injured or killed. Where they could watch for signs of stress, and signs of bad behavior, and signs of brilliance, and where they could admonish them and praise them and love them. Hendrix and Baka wanted second platoon at Apache.

Baka discussed with the battalion commander the proper distribution of resources and battle spaces made up of peers and argued that the need to have his company back was more important than those issues, knowing Schacht, a friend, would at least listen to Baka's reasoning. He argued that he needed the extra combat support in the violent neighborhood of Adhamiya, as well as the manpower. Engineer platoons are smaller than infantry platoons.

Baka repeated his pleas at chance encounters in headquarters hallways or after battalion meetings: "Sir, with all due respect, I need my men back."

Baka had known going into battle that a platoon would likely be pulled away from him, and he dreaded it. He had memorized birthdays and children's names, and he had talked to each soldier one-on-one to try to get to know him. Would their new commander know Wood had been stop-lossed and dreamed only of art school? That Martin had grown up in Mexico and studied English for a year just so he could join the U.S. Army? That Agami had given up life as a disc jockey in Miami almost the instant the towers had crashed down in New York?

Charlie Company saw second platoon when they went to Loyalty, but Baka wanted them rotating into Apache. And he wanted to be the one who decided which missions they did, as well as to argue against ill-fated missions. Zone 17 wasn't bad, but second platoon had to commute out for every patrol in Adhamiya. That drive just seemed to be getting worse, and it visibly took a toll on the men.

At Loyalty, Sergeant Derek Halbasch, twenty-three, of headquarters platoon, checked in with second platoon one afternoon after heading to the gym. At 6'5" and 150 pounds, the guys teased Halbasch that he needed to work out even more than the Iraqi soldiers, and Hendrix teased him worse than anybody. Rather than get angry, Halbasch started the "Gun Show." He'd roll up his T-shirt and make a muscle with his skinny arm, flexing anytime anybody rolled by going off to patrol. The guys couldn't help but laugh every time he did because Halbasch looked so damned silly.

Halbasch had been stationed with Staff Sergeant Garth Sizemore, thirty-one, in Vilseck, Germany, before moving to Schweinfurt, so he ended up spending a lot of time with Sizemore's platoon, second. On his way back from the gym, Halbasch stopped in at Sizemore's room.

"What's up, man?" Halbasch said, grinning as he always did when he saw his buddy.

"Man, I can't wait to get home to my wife," Sizemore said, bragging yet again on the woman he'd married just a few months before.

"Dude, we just got here," Halbasch said, rolling his eyes. Halbasch loved to hang out with Sizemore, Staff Sergeant John Gregory, and Staff Sergeant Robert Morris because they had deployed to Iraq before and they could teach him a lot. All three were patient and could explain a complex topic in layman's terms, and all of them had good soldiers because of it. But Halbasch noticed his friend looked tired, the circles naturally under his eyes just a little darker. They'd been running patrols several hours a day after driving to get to their sector in Adhamiya. Halbasch tried to cheer Sizemore up, teasing him about his wife and telling him the year would go by quickly.

Sizemore's wife, Lena, was Russian, and Sizemore was extremely protective of her. When the platoon sergeants asked for contact numbers for all the spouses in case anything happened in Iraq, Sizemore wrote down his own cell phone number. He had decided he wanted to inform her of any emergencies himself. So when the rear detachment noncommissioned officer—the man in charge of the Charlie Company troops who would remain behind in Schweinfurt—decided to call all the spouses a week before Charlie Company deployed as a way to let them know he'd keep them informed about their husbands, Sizemore answered the phone.

"Why in the hell are you calling my wife's number?" he asked. "I want to be the one to tell her if I'm injured."

The rear-detachment NCO called Baka while Baka was in the field in Germany training his men. Baka called Sizemore. He knew Sizemore was stubborn, and knew he was a good NCO.

"If you don't want your wife notified, then you wouldn't have married her into the army in the first place," Baka told him. "I don't have to get your permission to call her: It's her right."

Their argument was over with the phone call, and Sizemore had respectfully agreed that the chain of command could call his wife, but only if Sizemore couldn't. And he apologized for yelling at the rear-detachment

NCO. By the time Baka had reenlisted Sizemore in front of a Bradley out in Hohenfels training area before they deployed to Iraq, they were on good terms.

With Halbasch, Sizemore was a little more relaxed when talking about his wife, and soon Sizemore started teasing back.

"It must be nice to be a single guy who knows he's not gonna get any anyway," Sizemore said, laughing.

"Oh, that's low, man," Halbasch said, glad to see his friend smile. "Them's fightin' words."

As they continued to give each other crap, Hendrix walked into the room, and Halbasch automatically flexed his muscles.

"Yeah, yeah, gun show," Hendrix said, half grinning. "Got it. Get out of here."

Even though second platoon was no longer under Charlie Company's command, Hendrix wanted daily briefings about their missions, and Sizemore could be trusted.

The next day, October 17, second platoon rolled out to zone 17. Second platoon set up a traffic control point as the engineers checked in at a university just south of Adhamiya. As they were getting into their vehicles to go back to Loyalty, a sniper took aim from Adhamiya. The bullet went through a magazine and then entered just below Sizemore's front plate—through the groin protector that hangs down like a codpiece—and then exited through Sizemore's lower back.

"Ouch," Sizemore said as he slumped to the ground, and his platoon sergeant, Ybay, ran to his side. Instead of manning his weapon, Sizemore's gunner, Private First Class Tim Armstrong, knelt down beside Sizemore and prayed with him. Sizemore bled out almost immediately. Armstrong stayed by his side as he died.

The men rushed Sizemore back to Apache. Baka had been sleeping, but someone woke him up. As he walked to the aid station, he saw Ybay and Gregory and the rest of second platoon huddled together outside.

When Baka entered the aid station, Sergeant Terence Kupau, an aid station medic, sadly shook his head. Doc Whelchel said, "He didn't make it." Baka walked to his soldier's side.

Sizemore had recently shaved his head, and Baka brushed his hand over the fresh stubble and said a prayer. Then he walked outside to comfort his men.

Then Baka called Cathy. And cried.

Schacht, the battalion commander, called Sizemore's wife, and Cathy visited her friend often. Lena Sizemore spent those visits holding Baka's tiny daughter Hannah, trying to gain comfort from the baby's brand-new life.

Sizemore's death left the men inert, unable to do anything but patrol and dwell on their loss. Chagoya found himself unable to leave his cot. Mock tried to bring him around. "C'mon, man," he said, hand on Chagoya's shoulder as Chagoya lay on his stomach. "Sizemore wouldn't want you to be like this. He'd want you to laugh, to keep fighting."

But Chagoya said he didn't want to talk about it, to think about it.

"I just need to stay to myself," he said. "It's too much reality too soon."

Hendrix went from room to room at Loyalty, checking in on his men. They had seen death, but they hadn't lost one of their own.

Baka called Colonel Schacht.

"Sir, I think it's time to bring second platoon back to Charlie Company," he said.

"We'll see what we can do," Schacht said, reminding Baka that all companies were expected to give up a platoon to spread resources around. The engineers attached to Charlie had skills Baka's infantrymen didn't have.

Baka didn't care. He wanted his men back.

Five days later, on October 22, second platoon rolled out of the gate of Loyalty to again patrol Adhamiya. Immediately, they sensed that something was wrong. No one walked the street or gathered at the corner to chat. No children played. Dead quiet. And then, too much noise.

One of the Humvees rolled over a pressure plate, setting off a road-side bomb and blasting out the front of the vehicle—not fifty feet from an Iraqi National Police checkpoint. Presumably, someone at the checkpoint should have seen someone setting up the bomb. Maybe the police had been sleeping. Maybe someone had slipped them money to "not see" anything. Maybe they were insurgents themselves.

The blast tore through gunner Private First Class David McIntosh's calf. The Iraqi interpreter, who had been sitting behind Mock, died after shrapnel flew into his head. The blast forced a golf-ball-sized piece of shrapnel into Private First Class James Gmachowski's back. Gmachowski had been sitting behind the driver.

But Mock's injuries scared the hell out of second platoon. The explosion blew Mock's legs off to the hips, and he knew he just needed to make it to the Green Zone. "You've got to get me back to the aid station!" he begged. "I don't want to die."

Gregory helped the medic apply tourniquets to try to stop the flow of blood, but it was coming fast.

Mock's friends, including Gmachowski, promised, hands on his shoulders, trying to calm him. "You'll be OK," Gmachowski said. "We've got you, man. We'll get you back." They surrounded him, telling him they loved him and he was going to be OK as they quickly evacuated him to the aid station at Loyalty. They didn't let on that he was losing too much blood, that his freckles stood out too starkly from the pale of his skin. They tried not to look lower than his face.

Baka and Hendrix were at Loyalty for Sizemore's memorial service. When the news that Mock had been hit came in over the radio early that morning, they were both asleep because they had been out on patrol all night. The radio operator kicked on the door.

"Sir, we've got a bad IED that just hit second platoon," he yelled.

Baka and Hendrix immediately felt guilty for sleeping while the platoon was out working, even though they'd only managed three hours that night. Baka started to pull on his physical training clothes—typical uniform for a Sunday morning when the men were not on patrol.

"Sir," Hendrix said. "We got to put on our ACUs. We can't go to the aid station in our PTs." "ACUs" is short for army combat uniform—the camouflage daily uniform. "PTs" means physical training uniform, or shorts and a T-shirt.

"You're right," Baka said. "Of course."

Baka had been thinking in terms of time, but it only took two more minutes to lace boots and Velcro his uniform top.

As they came out of the door of their hooch, a government contractor happened by in a golf cart. "Get in," he said, and then they rushed over to the aid station.

It was Baka's first time with severely injured soldiers.

Gmachowski walked himself into the aid station and took off his own gear.

"Dude," Doc Gary Pritchett said, after he saw a piece of copper sticking out of Gmachowski's back, "you need to lie down."

Gmachowski, a red-haired giant at 230 pounds and a height of more than six feet, was pure muscle. If he had not spent so much time building up his body, the shrapnel would have gone straight through him. The metal had bypassed Gmachowski's body armor.

When Hendrix stopped by his litter to check on him, Gmachowski grinned.

"I'll be back, Top," he said, knowing he was headed for a hospital in Germany. "And then I'm going to kick your ass in spades."

(After six months' recuperation at home, Gmachowski would volunteer to go back to Iraq.)

McIntosh, at eighteen the youngest man in the battalion, almost lost the bottom part of his leg. But the medics, with Captain David Escobedo in charge, were able to stabilize him. The doctors in the Green Zone and back in the States would save it. He would not return to Adhamiya.

No one even noticed that Mock's driver, Private Tyler Norager, had also been injured. He had passed out during the blast, and a piece of shrapnel had burned his neck. He mentioned it only when he got to the aid station.

Mock was conscious, and the medics had pushed an oxygen tube down his throat, leaving him unable to talk.

Baka and Hendrix moved in closely, with Baka standing right by Mock's head. Baka grabbed Mock's shoulder with one hand, then grasped Mock's hand with the other.

"Look at me," Baka said. "Look at me."

As Mock focused in, Baka kept talking, looking his soldier in the eyes. Mock looked terrified, his eyes wide and his face drawn.

"I'm here," Baka said. "You're doing fine. Strength and honor."

Baka, Hendrix, and the medics continued the refrain Mock's men had begun: You're gonna be OK. Love you, man. We're gonna take care of you.

They carefully delivered him to the waiting helicopter, which transported him to the hospital in the Green Zone, trusting that the docs could save him. Of everyone delivered to the combat support hospitals—even with the war's most horrific wounds—90 percent lived.

After Mock flew off to the Green Zone, 4th Brigade, 101st Airborne Division, Brigade Command Sergeant Major Mark Atchley and Colonel Vail, who had insisted on clearing Baka's area the day Schacht was shot, showed up at the aid station—in their physical training clothes. Baka looked at them, and then at his soldiers still wearing bloodstained uniforms, and then at Hendrix.

"Thanks, First Sergeant," he said.

Then the pair walked outside. Again, they gathered their men in close to offer what comfort they could.

After Mock was hit, Hendrix began to prepare for Sizemore's memorial. He set up Sizemore's boots and weapons in the front of a large room they used for meetings at Loyalty. He took care with Sizemore's dog tags, knowing his men would pay attention to each detail. As he grieved and honored his soldier, more like family than any coworker could be, he heard footsteps. He turned around to see the battalion sergeant major, a man he'd known for years.

"Mock didn't make it," McClaflin said. "He died in surgery."

Hendrix sat down and lowered his head. McClaflin grasped his first sergeant's shoulder, and then left him alone to mourn.

The soldiers attended Sizemore's memorial having lost Mock that morning. Baka sat down next to Colonel Schacht. "Sir," Baka whispered. "With all due respect, please give me second platoon back. They need me and I need them."

That night, Baka made his first phone call to a family. The worst phone call he ever made. He waited until he knew the family had received official notification of Mock's death, and then, because of the time difference between the United States and Iraq, he waited until late in the evening.

Baka climbed the stairs to the roof of Apache in the dark, sat in a chair, and talked to the family. There no one could see him as he cried.

Talking to Mock's family wasn't just a duty to perform. It was a need, a way for Baka to talk out how he felt losing one of his men to someone who loved him even more than Baka did. He asked Mock's mother what she knew. When the men in uniform showed up at Mock's home in Kansas, all they could say was that there had been an explosion. "Do you want to know more?" Baka asked.

Yes.

He told her, but Baka was careful. He thought about each word, hoping not to cause more pain, but understanding the need to know each detail—to try to hold on to a son's last words, to know whether he suffered, to know if he was surrounded by friends.

The second death stunned the men into a numbness that they would never quite rid themselves of while they remained in Adhamiya. Chagoya stayed on his cot, determined to block everything out. He quit playing his guitar, quit listening to music. It all reminded him of Mock.

Cardenas, who had joined Chagoya and Mock for dancing, and considered Mock his best friend, also had a hard time after they lost him. Sitting in the mess hall one day, he heard some Marchata music. "That's Mock's music," he said to DeNardi, and then he started to cry.

DeNardi, watching his friends suffer and thinking about his own loss, became irate, his cheeks turning red and his whole body becoming jumpy. "In combat, you don't cower, and Mock never did," he said, as he and Cardenas huddled together at Loyalty trying to figure out their new world. "That man was meant to be like a fucking Spartan going up against millions, and to be killed by some cheap shot? That's not fair. It should be you facing your enemy one-on-one—not a mile away pushing a button."

Johnson stopped going to the gym. Completely. Without Mock and their daily arguments about the Spartans and the Romans, what was the point? But Agami kept after him. "You gotta get up, man," he said, trying to get Johnson off his cot, where he lay in a numb haze. "Will's laughing at us. We have to do this."

And that did it. He and Agami went back to the gym.

But he didn't think about his friend's death. When Mock came to mind, Johnson thought about him as if he'd gone home on leave or would be waiting for him when he got back to Schweinfurt. He couldn't deal with Mock's loss, so he just didn't.

Almost to a man, the guys had one similar response: They froze up, became numb. It wasn't necessarily intentional; it was more like their bodies and minds reacted in a way that allowed them to continue to try to survive. But it also kept them from dealing with their emotions. Consciously, as a group, they made a decision. If they thought about their lost friends, they thought about laughing and dancing and teasing—or else it was impossible to get back in the Humvee.

Ybay realized he couldn't keep his promise to bring everyone home, and he cried more than anyone, enough so that the sergeant major asked Hendrix if maybe they should bring in a new platoon sergeant. Hendrix stood up for Ybay, and Ybay understood that he'd have to regroup to help second platoon perform their mission. "My job is really hard," he said, his eyes instantly filling as he talked to Hendrix, telling him he could continue in that position even after losing two men. "But God led me here for a reason." He grieved openly for his soldiers, and trained his platoon even harder than before, determined to bring them home.

Schacht watched their misery from a distance, and he thought about Baka's pleas.

On October 25, three days after Mock died, second platoon reunited with Charlie Company.

CHAPTER 5
The Commander's Wife Handles Adhamiya's Deaths at Home

As she makes her way to her living room, Cathy Baka picks up a toy, pulls up the sagging pants of her two-year-old, and talks on the phone. Her home feels comfortable, and so does she, like she wouldn't mind too terribly if someone spilled coffee on her cozy cream couch, and if she did, she would never let on.

Tall and athletic, with heavy honey-colored hair and amber eyes, it makes sense that Captain Baka would have sought her out. Both believe anything can be accomplished after they have decided to do it. They met at West Point, where he studied in the class ahead of hers. "He was cute," she said, grinning a wide, straight smile. "And he treated me like a girl." Based on looks, that would seem obvious. But a strong tomboy streak, as well as a commanding presence, meant that the other students treated her like one of the boys. Cathy walks into a room and takes it over. She fixes things. She doesn't wait for orders, or stand back to see if someone else has another idea about the way the flowers should be arranged or what's next on the meeting agenda, while managing not to step on toes. She moves.

Those qualities made her a great military intelligence officer. "I grew to love the military and the army and that whole service aspect," she said. "But it was a different army when we graduated from West Point. War wasn't even on the horizon." After September 11, 2001, that quickly changed. In eight-and-a-half years of marriage, she and Mike had been separated for about four years as they went through training or jobs or because Mike had deployed to Iraq. Cathy ultimately decided to leave active duty to take care of their daughter, Elizabeth. Mike deployed to Adhamiya three weeks before Hannah, their second daughter, was born.

Cathy's experience in the military meant that she not only understood the basics of what Mike was going through—she understood the acronyms and slang and knew what his job entailed—but she also wanted to know more. There's a deep tradition of protecting family members by not telling them what's going on in the war zone, but Cathy was determined not to continue it. She gently grilled Mike about what he saw when he called her every night from his room at Apache, making sure he understood he could tell her everything. Needing him to tell her everything. Mike obliged Cathy's loving requests for details, welcoming the opportunity to talk. As company commander, he had no peers of his rank with whom he could talk at Apache.

"If we lose that communication, we'll become separate," Cathy said. "There's a void. You can't sum up a year's worth of experiences when he comes home." During his first tour to Iraq, there hadn't been the same fear that he might not make it home. But in Adhamiya, he told her about the days when he had to kick in doors and that the explosive devices scared the hell out of him. "We talk every day without fail," she said.

And every day, she shows her daughters a picture of their daddy. At night, they pray for him.

The first time Mike called, Cathy put him on the phone with Elizabeth. She immediately put her dad in time-out. "You made mommy cry," she accused.

Elizabeth's parents laughed, but it was bittersweet. Cathy did cry—and often. "There were times I think I wish I didn't know so much." But she insisted that he tell her everything. "I always ask him point-blank."

Sometimes she did not say a word. She listened.

During this deployment, she knows much more about post-traumatic stress disorder than she did during the first. As men returned to Schweinfurt with the wounds of war, she and the other wives talked about how the soldiers seemed "different." "It's scary to think about your husband and the other soldiers you love coming back as strangers and suffering so much," she said. So she studied the syndrome, and memorized its symptoms: nightmares, insomnia, flashbacks, an inability to connect with others, distractedness, hyperawareness, a hatred of crowds. From a distance, she watched her husband's every move. "I know he's suffered from PTSD," she said. She knew about the numbing, the inability to feel. She would listen until they both cried.

That helped her in her job as the leader of the Family Readiness Group. She had taken it on thinking it would be a bunch of meetings and maybe baking cookies for the guys, but hoping it could be a true support group for the families. It took over her life. At first, Cathy tried not to get personally involved. "It's not my job to solve people's problems," she said, "which is hard, because I love to solve people's problems." She focused on classroom training sessions about how to read an LES—a leave and earnings statement. Or she'd make sure everyone understood how to contact the American Red Cross in case of an emergency. And she talked to them about what would happen if one of their husbands died: How they would be notified. How they could transport the body to the burial site. How they could seek benefits.

While she had been on active duty, Cathy trained as a casualty notification officer, but never had to use the skill. But that training allowed her to provide relevant information for her spouses.

The wives understood there would be casualties during this deployment, even if their husbands held back the details. As a group, they panicked over things that usually seemed normal—like a lapse in e-mail or a missed phone call. Little things could mean something bad had happened. When someone died or was injured in Iraq, the soldiers weren't allowed to communicate to anyone back home until the deceased man's next of kin had been notified. Their MySpace and Facebook pages would go quiet. No one would call home. And all the wives would know.

Then the phone calls would begin. If Cathy had heard from Mike, she would tell the wives that everything was OK, that there had been a death in another unit at Loyalty, or that their Internet access was down or that they had been running patrols like mad and no one did anything between patrols but sleep; they did not have time for phone calls.

But sometimes she said, "I haven't heard from him either, so let's just pray."

Maryann Slater—Private First Class Justin Slater's mom—watched cars pass her home in a state of abject fear for four hours one morning. Finally, she broke down and called Cathy. "I woke up this morning," she said, "and I just knew. I waited all day for them to show up on my porch."

Cathy comforted Maryann, saying she'd heard from Mike and that everything was OK. But it made her think about how it would feel if a uniformed soldier appeared at her own door.

"It pained me to know she'd sat there and waited," Cathy said. "I've done that. The door rap comes at 8:30 in the morning and it's some kid selling candy." And not a notification officer, wearing dress greens, wondering how he would comfort yet another widow.

In Schweinfurt, soldiers who did not serve as notification officers were forbidden to wear their dress greens purely to avoid scaring those with loved ones in Iraq.

Second platoon was famous for how tight they were. The wives who didn't have children spent their time out together. Before their husbands left, they'd gone out as couples. But soon Cathy started seeing divorces between young people who had barely known each other before one of them went off to war for a year. "It was almost happening before they left," Cathy said. "It's the army. It happens."

But even with a pragmatic view about the normal tragedies offered up by life in addition to deployment, she and Mike worked together to help marriages make it through the war.

If she heard from one of the wives that a soldier wasn't doing well, she'd tell Mike, and he'd try to fill her in from his end. Then she could make sure the wife understood what the soldier needed, and Mike could do the same with the soldier.

The women who stayed in Germany and stayed with their husbands grew even tighter. They met for coffee and movies. Many of them were pregnant, and they started with the baby showers and became birthing coaches for one another because their husbands couldn't.

Cathy started sending out newsletters, making an effort to reach out to the families of the single soldiers and the wives who had returned to the United States while their husbands were in Iraq. Her desk turned into a mini publishing plant. Ultimately, the newsletter spread by e-mail to grandparents and cousins, to church groups and former teachers—anyone who had an interest in one of the boys. As she sent out the news-letters, she got to know the men—all of whom she'd met—even better. She'd gaze at their photos, write up stories of their achievements, and listen to Mike talk about how proud he was of their latest mission.

Somewhere along the way, Cathy realized that, though the immedi-ate families received official notification, the other families in the close-knit Schweinfurt community would have to depend on a script read to the wives over the phone or even by e-mail, notifying them that a mem-ber of the unit had died.

"We weren't going to do that," she said. "As a family readiness group leader, you call your wives. Nobody knew what that looked like, but we just did it."

It would also allow them to be there for each other if the worst hap-pened.

It did.

When Sizemore died, Cathy knew almost immediately. Mike called.

"She's the only person I can talk with or cry with on the phone, other than the moms," he said. "It was difficult to deal with." He rarely talked with Hendrix about his emotions, feeling that his position as commander precluded him from placing his worries on anyone else. There wasn't another company commander at Apache. "After I talked to the mom or the dad, that's when I'd call Cathy."

Lena Sizemore showed up for every Family Readiness Group meeting and was a favorite with the other women. Her two closest friends were also Charlie Company wives, and Cathy would call them after she knew Lena had been notified. First, she called Kristy Gregory, wife of Staff Sergeant John Gregory, and then Grace Maravilla, the wife of second platoon's leader, First Lieutenant Ryan Maravilla.

"How do you mentally prepare yourself to tell someone her husband's best friend has died?" Cathy asked. "I probably cried uncontrollably on two or three phone calls. I was not prepared for Lena."

The three tried to comfort each other, and then Kristy and Grace asked if it would be OK to go to Lena.

"Yes," Cathy said. "Go."

Cathy found someone to watch her daughters, but some of the phone calls stopped her in her tracks emotionally. "Lena was loved by everybody," she said, and they understood that she was going to leave them, and that it was going to hurt to help her through the next couple of weeks. "We were her friends, and we were there any way she needed us."

Cathy would take time before dialing the next number to cry, and then she'd call another friend and cry more.

"The first time you do anything like this you always feel like you did it all wrong," Cathy said. "The Rear-D actually provided a script and we were supposed to read only that, but you can't just read a script and hang up. They always have questions, and you do your best to answer them."

She continued with her calls. She called all of the wives who stayed in Germany, and then all of the women who had returned to the States. "I just don't believe it should come by e-mail," she said.

In the middle of the night, she talked to Mike. He wrote up the speech for Sizemore's memorial, and then for Mock's. Cathy edited them, understanding how important those words would be to the men who listened, and to the man who spoke. She pictured her husband on the other side of the world, sitting on the rooftop watching the moon so big he could trace its progress as it moved across the sky. The same thoughts came whispering back through her mind.

"Feeling alone. Nighttime. Being an ocean away . . ."

CHAPTER 6
Top Keeps Morale High in Hell

After they lost Sizemore and Mock, morale in Charlie Company plummeted. First Sergeant Hendrix tried to combat the fear and misery with the basics: Play Station, Girl Scout Cookies, and poker. But Loyalty would never feel like "home." They had nowhere to gather beyond the gym and the tiny smoking area. The barracks should have been condemned, and nobody felt safe sleeping there because of all the rockets. Captain Baka hated having the company command post so far away that they could only communicate by radio. Worse, if something bad happened on patrol, he wanted the other platoons close by and able to assist.

They had suffered far too many losses on the drive back and forth between Apache and Loyalty, including Mock and Sizemore as well as several nonlethal shootings and blast injuries that had taken men out of the battle, and no one could concentrate on the mission fully after that harrowing drive. And, according to the counterinsurgency theories, the guys should be living in the community, making sure the insurgents knew they were committed to the battle, and letting the neighbors know there were lots of troops nearby.

There was one more little problem. With Hendrix at Loyalty, the platoon leaders and platoon sergeants went to Baka anytime there was bickering among the platoons, or anytime they needed to move a soldier to a different platoon, or anytime someone had a complaint about the living conditions, which was pretty much hourly. Baka couldn't get any of the work of a company commander done.

Captain Baka called First Sergeant Hendrix.

"I can't do this," Baka said. "I can't be a first sergeant. I need you out here. First Sergeant, I need you to move to Apache to get the house ready."

"Roger that, sir," Hendrix replied, grinning on his end of the phone. He'd already started making plans.

The company executive officer, Captain Curtis Brooker, would stay at Loyalty to oversee maintenance as the guys rotated in to take care of their vehicles and to get a break from Adhamiya. Schacht had mandated that Baka take a break every two weeks, and Brooker would head out to Apache on those days to take over.

After Loyalty and its collapsed building, Apache didn't seem as if it could be that bad, and it was too small for anyone to hit with a mortar, though a couple of duds had landed near the fuel truck out by the port-a-potties. But Hendrix had to start from scratch. There was no parking lot in which to keep the Bradleys, and limited space for the Humvees. They had to park the Bradleys on the Iraqi side of the base, where they had to post guards because the Iraqi soldiers kept looting the trucks. The building had eleven MiT team guys from 4th Brigade, 101st Airborne, spread throughout, and it didn't occur to them to make room for the two hundred guys who had been taking turns sleeping in the basement. The MiT team used one of the basement rooms as a minigym, leaving even less room for the Blue Spaders.

Early on, Hendrix housed every lower-enlisted soldier in the basement. After they realized the sewage from the Iraqi army troops leaked through a broken pipe directly into Charlie Company's basement, Hendrix pulled everybody out. He got a contract for a sump pump to suck the sewage out of the basement. It ran 24-7. Staff Sergeant Scottie Magrum, who worked in the Apache command post, ran out to check the pump every morning. If the guys in the CP didn't check it, the guys downstairs would be in a world of, well, shit.

And then it rained, and the water behaved as if it knew right where to turn the corner at the front of the building and pour down the stairs into the basement. After pulling fourteen-hour shifts patrolling the streets of Adhamiya, the soldiers would wake up in the middle of the night to knee-high water that had drenched their gear and sleeping bags. The first time it happened, they began filling sandbags in the dark and stacking them in the stairway to try to keep the water out. The water leaked through anyway. They began storing their gear on pallets and just expected to be wet when it rained—and rained biblically—from December to February.

At night, in the fall and winter, the temperatures would fall below freezing. The wind seemed to take the same path as the water, and Apache did not have heat. Soldiers, including the first sergeant, began buying down comforters. Space heaters filled the areas between cots.

The situation with the morning ablutions—peeing into a tube and shitting into a port-a-potty with the back cut out so they would not swelter—did not immediately improve. Standing outside one morning as his platoon sergeants gave a briefing about that day's mission, Hendrix realized that every face, including his own, had pinched in, as if by screwing up their faces they could keep out the smell of a week's work. "I love the smell of shit in the morning," Hendrix joked, realizing he had much to do to make Apache home.

He decided that stuffing all of his men in one nasty room was unacceptable, and as the old MiT team was replaced by a new MiT team from 2nd Brigade, 2nd Infantry Division, Hendrix commandeered more rooms. He moved the MiT guys to the top level, where they still had five bedrooms for eleven men. Then he started tearing down walls and rearranging living space. He took the gym out of the basement and put it outside on a porch, where the guys could work out in the daylight, rather than in the sauna that the basement would become as the temperatures rose.

Some of the guys suspected the building had been some kind of hotel or guest house, but it didn't look as if it had been in good shape since long before the war began. The outside looked as if a child had pieced it together with khaki-colored Legos, with upper rooms sticking out a bit beyond lower rooms, and each room on the bottom floor defined even on the outside of the building by sharp lines one Lego out from the room next to it. One closet-sized room was unusable: Water damage had caused the ceiling to collapse. The command post—or TOC, as everyone called it, though technically, a TOC is the battalion-level command post—was in an odd room off to the left of the main hallway. To enter, the guys had to step down, sort of like a sunken living room from the 1970s, minus the shag carpeting. The battalion commander spent most of his time in that room when he visited Apache, and that's where Baka could usually be found.

As his men patrolled, Hendrix tried to get contracts to have more rooms built so the guys would not have to be quite so close. None of them got approved. Hendrix knew that, to keep morale up, he'd have to convince his soldiers that somebody cared about them. But they were pissing in a tube, waking up to flood waters, and sleeping in sewage.

After a while, Hendrix worried that his hopes for fixing the place up were, in fact, only a pipe dream—without even the pipes. He always had a project going, and when a soldier didn't have an M-4 in his hand, he likely held a hammer. But the guys couldn't build everything.

After a big mission one day, the whole company passed out cold, leaving behind a skeleton crew to watch the TOC and protect the COP. Hendrix went to his room. He'd had about one hour of rest in the previous twenty-four, and he immediately fell into a coma-like sleep.

Until someone started rapping on the door.

"Who in the hell wants me?" he yelled, baffled that someone would dare interrupt him. It sure as hell had better not be one of the privates. The door opened and he raised his hand to protect his eyes from the light in the hallway. When his eyes had adjusted, he tried to take in all the rank: There stood the Multi-National Corps–Iraq command sergeant major, Neil Ciotola. He had four sergeants major with him.

"I've heard about the rough time you're having out here," Ciotola said, seemingly not noticing the dark circles under Hendrix's eyes or the fact that he was still under the covers. "I just wanted to see what you're doing. Can you show me around the place?"

Rubbing the sleep out of his eyes, Hendrix knew this was his chance. The company had three laptops, all in the TOC, and no way for the guys to e-mail home. They had no satellite phones. They had no space. The few air conditioners they had barely worked. They had no TVs. The guys sat out on the front steps smoking for entertainment between patrols. All of that was pitiable, the sergeants major agreed as Hendrix showed them around. Then Hendrix walked the gaggle of rockers—curved bars beneath their sergeants' chevron stripes denoted additional rank—down to the basement and gave them a quick tour. Ciotola looked at Hendrix quizzically, as if he couldn't quite imagine sleeping in such a place.

"You know what I'm thinking, First Sergeant?" he said. Hendrix shook his head no, but he imagined Apache hadn't made a good impression. "You guys are kind of living dirty."

"Yes, Sergeant Major," Hendrix replied.

"What do you need, First Sergeant?" Ciotola asked.

Hendrix let loose: He wanted phones and computers and Internet. He wanted contracts for additional rooms and someone to fix that damned pipe that was leaking sewage into the basement. He wanted tables and chairs and a kitchen and cooks. Hell, he could tell them the order numbers for the equipment he needed. He'd been studying it for weeks.

The next day, four Humvees pulled into Apache loaded with Dell computers, satellite phones, and TVs. That was just the beginning. The contracts started coming in, and suddenly it started feeling like home. Between patrols, soldiers picked up saws and hammers. They built a dining area and filled the hallway leading to the company command post with desks for the computers and phones. From then on, the hallway served as a gathering area. Some soldiers even set up a makeshift barbershop there a couple of days a week, filling the hallway with puddles of hair and banter about sports teams and movies.

On the wall dividing the dining area and the computer hallway, Hendrix created a memorial for his men. He hung photos in a row: Sizemore. Mock. As the months went on, he would add more rows. Eventually, the wall would seem to sag beneath the weight of all the men whose names graced it, but it also provided comfort—knowledge that their friends would not be forgotten.

Outside, Hendrix had a contractor build an entirely new structure, a big sleeping bay, and then asked Baka what kind of beds he should order.

"Stack 'em three high," Baka said. "I want all my soldiers out here."

Hendrix still had to get a little devious to make things livable, but he'd been in the army long enough to be skilled in acquisition. As in every war, the care packages and equipment addressed "to any service member" stopped at the first person to see them—usually the mail clerk or headquarters people. TVs and video games and personal-hygiene sets filled the Green Zone, where they already had showers and stadium-sized dining facilities and even swimming pools. In the Green Zone, where service members could easily shop for soap or frozen coffee drinks or even Burger King, there was no shortage of Christmas care packages and donated socks or CDs. But even if those gifts managed to make it past the orderly room clerk, no one was going to drive it out to Apache. Who would risk a roadside bomb for a box of homemade cookies?

First sergeant would. He "borrowed" an Armed Forces Network converter from a chapel at Loyalty so they could watch TV that wasn't in Arabic. In the new dining area, Hendrix set up couches and then mounted the TV to the wall so his guys had a place to watch football. Morale immediately improved with access to the NFL. Hendrix ran mail back and forth through those treacherous streets. And anytime he took a platoon to the mess hall in the Green Zone or at Loyalty, he had the soldiers fill their pockets with packets of peanut butter and granola bars.

But peanut butter could not solve all their problems. And neither could Hendrix. He had to depend on his boys.

Under Hendrix's guidance, they hooked up the video games—when they played Halo, Hendrix's moniker was "Richard Nasty"—and organized spades tournaments, but on their own, they brought out the guitars. And then they started making up songs. "Hey, sing 'Achmed, the Left-handed Terrorist,'" Hendrix yelled over to DeNardi as he strummed his guitar while sitting at a table in the new dining area. Muslim culture forbids using the left hand for anything but wiping one's ass. As DeNardi started to sing, Hendrix shook his head. "That kid—"

He didn't finish his sentence. He just laughed.

DeNardi charmed the company, even at his most sarcastic. Everyone could serve as the object—or target—of his affection. Big gray-blue eyes and the biggest mop of hair the army allows, he quickly became the company cruise director. He organized karaoke competitions and computer game tournaments. He carried his guitar everywhere but out on patrol, and he made up songs about his pals, usually foul. In a way, they were love songs: If a guy made it into the lyrics, he was the well-liked subject of a joke. Usually a dirty joke.

Sometimes, when Apache became quiet underneath that giant moon, DeNardi lost the sarcasm. His songs sounded more like lullabies, and the air seemed balmy with the sound of crickets beyond the constant hum of the generators. DeNardi had grown up in a musical family, a family that understood DeNardi's tendency toward moodiness and sudden bursts of song. Even his name came from a history of sadness. Gerry, pronounced "Gary," is Scottish—unlike his obviously Italian last name. His first name came from his mother's clan, but when there were no more male heirs to pass it on, DeNardi's great-great-grandmother had given her son the first name "Gerry." As that Gerry drove his parents home from a New Year's Eve party long ago, he hit a patch of ice and crashed his car. Everyone in the car died, except for his sister. She had a daughter, and the daughter named her son "Gerry." That was DeNardi's uncle.

"As children, Gerry was my everything," said Elizabeth Sanderson, DeNardi's mother, speaking of her brother. "My playmate, my storyteller, my protector, my shield, my provider, my all." Their father left when Sanderson was a toddler, and her mother was an alcoholic. Gerry, who was a year and a half older, took care of the little girl, mostly by telling her stories, usually with an accent to lend credence to Robinson Crusoe or Oliver Twist.

When Elizabeth had her first son, her brother showed up at the hospital with a book written by General George Patton as a gift. She took him to the nursery to introduce him to Gerry Edward DeNardi, Charlie Company's charmer. Elizabeth's brother asked her why she had given the baby such a horrible name.

At first, the name didn't bring good luck to DeNardi. He had fifteen operations by the time he was five because his lungs did not develop properly, and because he had a cranial malformation. "I swear he screamed for the first two years of his life, nonstop," Sanderson said. "But, boy, was he cute—blond and blue eyes and a face that would just light up and shine with his laugh."

Soon, Sanderson and her husband divorced, and she was a single mom, dancing around the kitchen with her children, acting out stories from books, or telling tales from history. DeNardi graduated second in his high school class, but had grown up with a grandfather who had been a hero during the Battle of the Bulge, so rather than college, he started thinking about the military.

And then, Gerry Sanderson, DeNardi's uncle, died in a house fire in 2005. One year to the day later, his nephew deployed to Iraq. He had a name to live up to.

But when someone asked him why he joined the army, DeNardi said he didn't want to spend his life sitting in a hammock, thinking about what could have been. In reality, he wanted to make his mother proud.

Every guy in the unit knew how close DeNardi was to his mother.

Not only did she talk to her son often, she sent care packages to the whole unit for every holiday, including St. Patrick's Day.

But she was also a nurse.

Army traditions often involve pain, and Charlie Company soon developed a little ritual to check each other's reflexes: In formation, they'd turn around and slap each other in the nuts. It started out as a light tap, just a reminder that pain could happen, and it usually involved Derek "Gun Show" Halbasch, DeNardi, and Sergeant Jeremiah Grubb.

One day, DeNardi stood in formation, beefed up in body armor, carrying weapons and ammo, head turned, talking to a buddy, and someone hit him hard.

"Oh, fuck!" he yelled, dropping everything, bending his knees and grabbing where it hurt. "Fuck! Fuck you guys!"

Halbasch blamed Grubb. Grubb blamed Halbasch. Both had been victims of DeNardi's hits, but at this moment, it didn't matter. DeNardi didn't even try to pretend he could take it. He let the tears roll and blamed them both, and both understood they'd done the man wrong.

They felt even worse when, hours later, their friend still couldn't sit. The pain was so bad it convinced DeNardi he had been permanently damaged. The next evening, in misery after a day bouncing around in the back of a Bradley, and after a black bruise had spread where he'd never seen a bruise form before, DeNardi took his case to the expert: his mother.

Via webcam.

After she had examined him long-distance, Sanderson reassured her son that he would still father children. "It's OK, baby," she consoled. "I know it hurts, but it's just a bruise. Just a really bad bruise."

His buddies were just as relieved as DeNardi was, possibly even more so. Now they had something else to tease him about. "You did what?" Halbasch asked in pure disbelief as DeNardi explained why he knew he was going to be OK. "You showed your mother your nuts?"

"What, man?" DeNardi said. "She's a nurse."

By the end of the evening, the whole company was howling. "Oh, honey," Agami said when DeNardi entered the dining room for chow. "Let me take a look at that."

"Oh, sweetheart," Wood chimed in. "Does it hurt when I touch you here? How about here? Oooh, baby, how about here?"

DeNardi pouted for a while, still in pain, but his friends laughed so hard he eventually had to join in.

Sergeant Ryan Wood teased as much as everyone else had, but then, when he and DeNardi had a moment alone, he checked to make sure his pal was OK. Woody usually could complete DeNardi's sentences, and if they sang a song together, the lyrics only got dirtier. He matched De-Nardi in creativity, but Wood had more of an edge. DeNardi seemed innocent still, and Wood seemed to already understand the world. Wispy blond hair above sharp cheekbones, he looked hard and wiry, like the guy everyone knows better than to mess with in the bar. But then he would flash a smile that lit up his pretty blue eyes, bordered with thick, dark eyelashes. Billy Idol without the sneer.

Woody spent his time drawing, and usually his wry sense of politics and war came out in his pictures: In one, he depicted a punk rocker with a cigarette hanging from his mouth, a torn American flag hanging over his shoulders, and a bunch of skulls at his feet. He had designed his own tattoo based on his life and had it inked while he was home on leave. It featured a sorrowful warrior in front of the burning Twin Towers from September 11, 2001, but the soldier stood behind a cop car and marijuana leaves. Underneath, it read, "My war." He had been stop-lossed and didn't want to be in Iraq for a second combat tour. But like the others, he wouldn't leave his friends.

Together, DeNardi and Wood wrote "Adhamiya Blues," but both of them had to be available to play the tune. DeNardi knew the music, and Wood knew the words. Wood wrote them in a notebook he kept with him always. Without both, the song didn't exist.

ADHAMIYA BLUES

War, it degrades the heart
And poisons the mind
And we're tossed aside
By governments' lies
But we continue to grieve.

The rest is in the notebook.

Generally, Wood and DeNardi stuck to lighter fare, like karaoke contests. Late into the evening, their warbling—they sang Britney Spears just as often as they did Dave Matthews—would drift up the basement stairs so that everyone at Apache could hear it. Hendrix stayed away from those sessions, preferring to let his guys have some time without the boss around.

Standing in between bunk beds in a tiny space surrounded by wall lockers and cubbyholes, they almost forgot their surroundings as they sang. Often, there'd be a duet: DeNardi and Wood singing Beyoncé and Jay-Z—and fighting over who got to be Beyoncé. Cardenas singing Michael Jackson. Martin trying Justin Timberlake.

Agami, with his disc jockey background, was always convinced that he would win. For all his brawn, the guys knew Agami quietly took care of them. Once, when Johnson's clothes got lost after he'd sent them out for laundering, clean T-shirts, socks, and camouflage pants mysteriously showed up on his bed. Though Agami never said a word, everyone knew he put them there. Another time, Agami gave up his sleeping bag when he learned one of the guys was doing without. And DeNardi always could count on Agami to give up his last energy drink. Agami was always protective of the younger man.

None of that helped Agami's singing.

Worse, Martin always won—Martin who had grown up in Mexico and had only learned English five years before. "Man, what the hell!" Agami said one night in frustration, throwing the microphone on a bunk. "You can't even speak English!"

Martin—or "Marteen" as the first sergeant called him—just grinned. He had taken English as a second language at a community college just so he could join the army, and he loved being a part of Charlie Company, even when they teased him about being Iraqi.

One night, when Martin was out on patrol, he saw the new MiT team commander, Major Peter Zike, approaching as Martin sat in his vehicle. Martin flashed the lights on his night-vision goggles to let the officer know he was there and friendly, but the officer kept coming.

"Who's there?" the officer yelled.

"Hey, Major Zike," Martin called out. "It's me!"

But Zike kept coming. He wanted to know why there was an Iraqi in an American vehicle. From then on, the guys gave Martin constant hell: "Hey! What are you doing in my truck?"

At Apache, coworkers lost their ranks and last names, except for officers and the first sergeant. Privates became best pals with staff sergeants. Platoon leaders, barely older than Cardenas and DeNardi, participated in the video-game competitions. Everybody shared everything, and it became hard to tell who was in which platoon.

CHAPTER 7
Ladue Earns Three Purple Hearts in Two Months

Sergeant Shawn Ladue, twenty-seven, pushed his lips forward, rather than parting them, when he spoke, a habit that made him seem younger than he was. So did his freckles. Still, the guys called him "Rambo" because he tended to keep coming back even after everybody thought he was down. Earnest and honest, he talked openly about his emotions, seeming not to have the guile—or the need—to represent himself as fearless. That made him a Charlie Company favorite: Everyone knew he could talk with Ladue without being judged.

Ladue joined the army after dropping out of high school, and then left the military to try a trade school. He tried automotive school and community college, and then, after a series of "crappy-ass jobs," re-upped in September 2004. He missed his army buddies, and he figured he needed to get out of Phoenix. In August 2005, he joined Charlie Company's third platoon.

Third platoon seemed to be an insurgent magnet. In some ways, that worked well: If Baka ever needed to find somebody on the high-value target list, he sent third platoon. Somehow, they'd manage to stumble across the bad guys. Often, they found trouble even when they weren't looking for it, and it seemed as if someone had painted Ladue in at the center of a third platoon bull's-eye. It got so he hated going out, but he wouldn't let his men go out without him.

Ladue's bad luck began in October. Most of the time, the guys found bodies, as many as ten a day. So October 14 started as a typical day: Coming off Route Absolut, they found yet another dead person sprawled on the sidewalk. The young man had been shot in the mouth, but he had lived through it. Private First Class Jonathan Hewett, the medic, checked him out, and third platoon decided to take him to the hospital. But even with his horrific injury, the Iraqi man begged the soldiers not to take him there. Beyond being short of bandages, medicine, and doctors, everybody knew hospitals could be death traps. Often, the Mahdi army provided guards, but those same guards would kill anyone who wasn't a Shia. In 2007, an Iraqi doctor was convicted of killing his Sunni patients by putting poison in their IV bags. The soldiers were not allowed to bring the man back to Apache to treat him themselves because, as part of the counterinsurgency plan, the Iraqis were supposed to take responsibility for treating their own people.

Ladue and his platoon dropped the man off at the Iraqi hospital, feeling like they had left the man to die, and then went back out on patrol. As they drove through the streets, they spotted three young men in a car. In a street-smart game of profiling, Charlie Company knew that more than two young guys in a car could mean weapons, parts for making explosives, or even cell phones filled with videos of insurgents going to battle. But as they dug through the car, all they found was a big batch of worthless Iraqi money, so the Americans let the young men go.

As Ladue climbed back into his Humvee, he heard a funny, whizzing noise. It stopped him cold. Then he felt a sharp burning pain in his side. A bullet had hit the side of one of his body-armor plates and ricocheted off into his shoulder. But Ladue didn't react to the pain so much as to the perpetrator. He whipped around and started shooting at a building. Then the little voice of reason inside his head said, "Hey, dumb-ass. You just got shot." The bullet had entered just below his left shoulder. As Ladue started doing internal checks to make sure he was still breathing, Doc Hewitt pulled him out of the truck. "You're OK, man," Hewitt said. "It's just a flesh wound."

But Hewitt recommended getting Ladue back to Apache for treatment.

At the aid station, Hendrix waited for Ladue and quickly realized the bullet had not hit anything important, but it had bored out a perfect circle from back to front. As Ladue sat on a table, Hendrix teased. "Now that's a big-ass gaping hole," he said, playing on Ladue's habit of adding "ass" to every sentence. "Man, you can see clean through your side." Ladue let loose his sheepish grin, relieved that the wound had not caused major damage, but a little shaken that someone had just tried to kill him.

The medics bandaged him up, and he went to the Combat Support Hospital in Baghdad for two days to recover. After a couple of days pulling guard duty at Apache, he went back out on patrol. On breaks, the medics would change out his seeping bandages.

In the meantime, third platoon went back and searched the house Ladue had shot at, thinking that it was the source of the sniper fire. They found nothing, and deduced that the family inside had nothing to do with the incident.

About three weeks later—November 5, 2006—an Iraqi court found Saddam Hussein guilty of crimes against humanity and sentenced him to death for killing 148 Shiites in 1982. As Iraqi television began broadcasting scenes of Shiites celebrating throughout Baghdad, Charlie Company braced itself. In Adhamiya, where posters of Hussein still hung from city walls next to anti-American graffiti, no one would celebrate this verdict.

From across the river, at least seven mortar shells came screaming into the dust surrounding the Abu Hanifa Mosque, as if the Shiites in Kadhamiya wanted to rub in their victory. Within five minutes, AK-47 rounds began ripping off in the distance, and then grew closer as the Sunnis arrived to take out their rage on the Americans. "Those guys are coming out of the woodwork," Hendrix said, gleefully preparing his men for battle. "I guess the verdict motivated them to not be cowards."

On a normal day, someone would set off an IED or throw a grenade from a rooftop or try to snipe them from a tower, and the Americans didn't have a chance to shoot back. They had no target.

But November 5, the soldiers could see the enemy. They arrived in groups and covered their faces with ski masks. They carried AK-47s, grenades, and rocket launchers.

Rounds continued coming in from across the river, and the wall above the porch of Charlie Company's building quickly filled with bullet holes. Hendrix sent his headquarters men—including Halbasch, Osterman, Cardenas, and DeNardi—up to the roof, or "the Alamo," as they called it. A ten-foot wall ran along the edges, and someone had embedded steel sliding windows that the men could open and shoot through. Even higher than the wall stood a tower they called the Crow's Nest where the .50-caliber shooters stationed themselves.

Baka worked things from the company TOC, yelling at someone to wake up Private Chad Darrah and the other sharpshooters. Darrah went straight for the Crow's Nest with his M-14 sniper rifle and began taking down targets.

Someone had to shake Chagoya awake as he slept on his cot in the basement. The noise hadn't even registered because they'd all grown used to sleeping through explosions and gunfire. But when Chagoya understood the insurgents had attacked Apache, he ran to the roof, excited to have a real battle. "This is my happy time!" he said, grabbing gear and grinning at the private who had gingerly woke him up. He and the others ran up in their physical training shorts and full battle rattle—helmets, web gear, and body armor, grabbing rounds and weapons as they raced to the roof. Chagoya climbed up to the Crow's Nest, where he found Sergeant Billy Fielder.

"Dude, there's a sniper taking out IA guys," Fielder yelled. Neither of them could figure out where the shots came from. "Get left," Chagoya said. "I'll get right." Private First Class Michal Cieslak had a 240 and said he'd shoot toward the middle. Soon the sniper fire ended.

"Get him?" Cieslak called out.

"I don't know, man," Chagoya said. "Stand up and see if he shoots."

"Fuck you, man," Cieslak said, laughing.

The sharpshooters would have seven confirmed kills that day.

Hendrix stood in their midst in the brilliant noontime sun directing fire. Baka worked from the sunken CP. Hendrix called down targets to Baka for the platoons that were already out: "I see thirty masked men in front of Abu Hanifa. There's a hundred just to the north. It looks like they're gathering outside the gate."

"Hey," Baka called out to his driver. "Get my vehicle ready. I'm going out with first platoon."

Hendrix realized the insurgents had penetrated the compound. They'd sneaked in through the fences. A group of Special Forces operational detachment guys, who also lived at Apache, were shooting them down from the roof, leaving bodies along the river. The soldiers left the bodies where they lay, knowing if they went down to police them up, they'd be shot.

Hendrix radioed down to Baka that he could see a mass of about a hundred masked insurgents gathering, but their numbers grew quickly.

As the tempo of the battle grew fierce, Hendrix sent some guys down to the Bradleys to shoot their guns across the river. They watched as insurgents fell in Kadhamiya, but then a car would shoot down to pick up the body. "Shoot the flippin' car!" Hendrix shouted. The Americans could not identify the insurgents without the body.

As they fought from Apache, the platoons rolled out into the city. Hendrix ordered some of the guys on the roof to load up in the Humvees, knowing full well they wanted to be wherever the fight was. Second platoon had just rolled into Apache from a morning patrol when the fighting started. "My guys ain't taking a break," Ybay yelled, not that he had to persuade them.

Right away, the platoons—about forty soldiers altogether—encountered men in ski masks toting rocket-propelled grenade launchers. About 250 people had gathered. Second platoon headed for zone 19, and first platoon took zone 18, driving to Antar Square. The Iraqi army and police were already engaged at the square with insurgents carrying small arms and rocket-propelled grenade launchers.

Baka, out with two Bradleys and four Humvees from first platoon and two trucks from headquarters platoon, started hearing noise coming in over the radio. As they headed down Omar, they saw a bunch of people carrying signs:

"U.S. KILLED SADDAM!" and "SADDAM REST IN PEACE!"

The people with the signs started throwing rocks, baffling the soldiers. Then the people started shooting, and first platoon's gunners started shooting back.

Second platoon was out with two Bradleys and four Humvees.

"Where you guys at?" Baka said over the radio, making sure he knew the exact coordinates of all his platoons.

Baka told first platoon to head for the mosque. As they drove, the road split, so he sent the Humvees up the east side and the Bradleys west toward Abu Hanifa Mosque. Baka went west, riding in a Humvee. As they drove, everyone started taking fire, mostly RPGs, which could do a lot more damage to a Humvee than to a Bradley. Santana rode in the seat behind Baka, keeping an eye out.

"RPGs! RPGs!" Santana shouted. A man was aiming right at Baka. Baka's gunner, Cardenas, killed the man with his .50 cal.

Baka called over the radio, "Sweep them north toward the river!"

As they drove, they saw three or four dud grenades just lying in the street.

Then Baka heard Newland come in over the radio from his Bradley: "They're in the middle of the street with AK-47s! Can we engage?"

"Are they carrying weapons?" Baka asked, trying to clear up why there was a question.

"Yes, but are they for real?" Newland asked. "We're in Bradleys!"

"If they want to stand out in the open with AK-47s fighting Bradleys, then kill them!" Baka yelled.

Newland shot, and continued to shoot. Every time he or the other gunners—Woody had the same scenario going with second platoon—saw a man with an RPG, they took him out with a big gun. If they didn't, someone else would just pick up the man's grenade launcher and start aiming for the Americans again.

The only people on the street for this battle were the insurgents.

And one old man walking down the sidewalk.

Oblivious.

Harmless.

"Hold your fire!" Baka barked over the radio.

Walk.

"What is he doing?" Baka asked.

Walk.

Walk.

Finally the old man opened a door and entered a building.

"OK!" Baka yelled. "Fire!"

But then ambulances, marked with the Muslim crescent moon, started showing up. On a normal day, Charlie Company couldn't get the ambulances to come out for civilians injured on the street. November 5 made clear why: The ambulances were running out to pick up the enemy casualties. They were working with the insurgents.

Baka had his Humvees wrap back around west toward the Iraqi police station and the Bradleys head north.

"Hey, we're to your west," Baka yelled to his platoons, working to make sure no one suffered from friendly fire. "Orient your fire!"

An IED exploded underneath a Humvee, but no one was injured.

Then an MiT team showed up out of nowhere, without the Iraqi army troops they were ostensibly there to train. They just followed Charlie Company around, hoping for action.

"Cowboy," Baka muttered.

But they had missed the three-hour battle. Two Apache helicopters showed up, and the insurgents slipped back into the alleyways, taking refuge in the mosque or in people's homes as they always did when the Apaches approached.

As they headed back to Apache, Baka contacted the MiT team over the radio. "Watch out," he said. "There are grenades all over the road."

"We got it," came the reply.

Looking at his passenger's side mirror, Baka saw one of the MiT Humvees roll right over a grenade.

Ka-thump. Ka-thump.

"Oh, man," Baka said. "This is no good."

He had everybody stop, and his men shot the grenades with their M-4s from a safe distance—target practice.

For the rest of the day, Apache took intermittent fire, but Charlie Company didn't have a single injury. As he had run to his vehicle before going out into the city, Baka stuck his head in the kitchen and asked if any of the cooks wanted to come out. Two of them, Specialist Nicolas Garcia and Sergeant William Redding, earned their Combat Action Badges that day.

One Iraqi soldier died. And they counted thirty-eight insurgent dead and ten wounded. Most of their bodies were picked up by the Iraqi ambulances and delivered to the morgue. The drivers piled the bodies up until their families could claim them. Those never claimed were buried in a mass grave. But the Iraqi army refused to retrieve the bodies of the dead insurgents down by the river because they were afraid they would be shot themselves, so the insurgents remained, the smell of rotting flesh a constant reminder of their presence. Eventually, wild dogs carried the bodies away.

After the battle on November 5, the number of shootings went down significantly. Charlie Company was sure most of the enemy snipers had died that day.

As the days grew cooler and the nights cold in the unheated building, Charlie Company grew better acquainted with the Mahdi army, or Jaish al-Mahdi in Arabic. The soldiers called the group "JAM." They were believed to be the ones behind all the killings, including the explosively formed penetrators as well as the mortar attacks from across the river and in Sadr City, two kilometers to the east of Adhamiya. The violence of their tactics stunned the soldiers: Children killed at school or on the playground by mortars. Females murdered for not covering their faces. Students killed for listening to rock music. Usually, when the Blue Spaders went after a high-value target, or HVT, it was a member of JAM.

The soldiers continued to go out on patrol, scanning for IEDs and hoping it wasn't their day. On November 13, the mortar platoon from Headquarters Company rolled from Forward Operating Base Shield— just north of Loyalty—to Apache. Private First Class Daniel Allman II had been the first soldier from 1-26 to shoot an insurgent in Adhamiya. But that day, just outside Adhamiya, an insurgent set off an IED near Allman's vehicle. Allman and Private First Class Jang Kim died in the explosion.

Baka had to rein in his troops to keep them from losing their counterinsurgency skills and going back to pure infantry skills. They had to go back out, talk with the people, hand out candy to the kids, and refrain from excessive force. So when they went out after Allman and Kim died, Baka tried to calm his men down first.

"We're going to do a cordon search, but we're not going to find the guy," Baka told his leaders, standing in front of them in the sunken TOC. "People probably saw it. We got to get the information from them."

But Allman and Kim's deaths set off a series of conversations as the soldiers tried to define their world. Was this worse than World War II where the men always knew how they would fight their battle and usually believed in the cause?

Sitting on the couches in the dining area, halfheartedly watching a football game, Johnson argued that the soldiers in Germany and Japan always tried to move forward, but the soldiers in Iraq didn't move anywhere. They weren't trying to take new ground.

Baka had stopped in just long enough for a cup of coffee and to catch the score.

"You could probably equate our level of combat as similar to Vietnam," Baka mused, thinking back to those West Point history classes. "You have your insurgency, but you don't have a uniformed army. It requires everyone to think, to try to outsmart them."

But sometimes, intelligence left the equation completely, and all the men could do was respond.

Private First Class Carlos Perez got his first bit of action when he wasn't looking for it. He was out pulling security with Private Omar Avila and Sergeant Dequinn Nickerson when Avila said he saw someone coming toward them. Perez shined a laser light on the Iraqi man, but he didn't stop.

So Perez hit him with the laser again.

And again.

But the man kept coming. Fast. Almost as if he were speed walking.

"Fire a warning shot, man," Avila told Nickerson.

Perez fired a warning shot.

The man kept coming.

"Dude," Nickerson said to Perez. "One more warning and then you have to take him out."

Perez fired another warning. The man kept coming.

"OK, man," Nickerson said. "You got to hit him."

Perez fired, but he aimed low, hitting the man in the leg.

The Iraqi man kept limping toward them. Perez felt his heart sink into his stomach, knowing what the next command would be.

"Shoot to kill, man!" Nickerson yelled.

Perez shot the Iraqi man in the abdomen, and the soldiers watched as he dragged himself around a corner. The next day, the hospital reported that a man with a wound to the abdomen died in the hospital.

But Perez would never know what the man had wanted with the

soldiers. That made it even harder to go out. What exactly were they fighting against? Men who did not care if they died?

But it was more than fear for the soldiers themselves. Ladue was devastated when he saw how even children were treated if their religion were found out. On patrol in zone 18, gunner Private First Class Sean Cousino saw a pair of zip-cuffed hands sticking out of a window. Third platoon went inside to check it out, breaking down doors and yelling as they went. Two men—who hadn't bathed in so long the soldiers could smell them before they even made it outside the building—ran to the soldiers' trucks and starting kissing their interpreter. One of the men turned out to be an Iraqi army colonel. He pointed out several people—including an old woman—who he said had detained them. A younger man with the colonel said he hadn't seen his brother for a while, but that he had also been taken hostage. As the guys started piecing stories together, they realized they had horrific news for the colonel.

The day before, third platoon had seen a body in front of the same building: It was a young boy shot in the side of the head. It was the young man's brother and the colonel's son. "It feels good—like we actually may have accomplished something instead of driving around waiting to get blown up," Ladue said that evening, talking to his friends as he fiddled with his dinner. The soldiers had zip-tied a man and the older woman and prepared to take them to the military police in Baghdad. "But you have mixed emotions. We don't know who is who. I know that we don't know anything."

"Roger that," Avila said, shaking his head. The sight of the dead child had upset him more than he wanted to say, and he hoped to end the dinner conversation quickly.

"Man, this isn't what I expected," Perez said, his thick black brows pushed together, and his dimples disappearing. "I mean, I love being with you guys, but this is some shit."

The operation turned out to be a husband-and-wife team set on killing Shiites and sabotaging Charlie Company's work. After the Blue

Spaders set up generators to provide electricity for the locals, the couple would blow up the generators. They lured the Shiite to Adhamiya by calling handymen and telling them they needed something fixed, and then the couple would torture and kill them. Soon, no workers would come to Adhamiya. No one picked up the trash. No one treated the water. No one fixed the sewer lines.

The soldiers had caught the couple by pure luck, and that seemed to be how it worked for third platoon. Another time, their platoon leader, First Lieutenant Matthew Martinez, saw a group of men who he thought just looked suspicious. The soldiers searched their vehicle and found black masks, weapons, and bloody gloves. It was an execution squad.

But some of it was pure persistence. Martinez was known for saying, "Let's make one more go-round," if third platoon hadn't found anything on patrol. Most of the time, the guys loved that Martinez was so gung ho. Most of the time.

On November 20, Ladue earned his second Purple Heart. He rode up in the lead truck, and they'd had another boring night and were about to go back in. "Let's make another go-round," the lieutenant said. They drove past Abu Hanifa Mosque, and then past the new graveyard that had been a soccer field before the war. They drove past a trench. "Man, that would be a good place to hide an IED," Ladue said, just as somebody always said every time they saw it. But this time, somebody had hidden an IED there.

Ladue's mouth and eyes filled with engine oil as the blast took out the front of his Humvee. He couldn't see anything. The explosion had knocked his gunner's 240 off its mount, so the gunner, Private First Class Eduardo Gutierrez, rose back up from where he'd fallen, knocked down the pope shield—a thick glass barrier mounted on the turret that protected him from gunfire—grabbed his squad automatic weapon, and started laying rounds into the mosque.

Ladue, after rubbing the oil out of his eyes, jumped out of the Humvee and was trying to shoot while searching for a grenade he always kept with him. Then bullets started to ricochet off the outside of the Humvee just as Specialist Matthew Yearwood started screaming. The steering column had collapsed on him, causing massive bruising.

Ladue grabbed the radio and screamed, "Hey! Get us the fuck out of here!" He'd been bruised from his ass all the way to the bottom of his calves. Blood came out of his ears. He couldn't focus on anything. And Yearwood was still screaming. When they extricated Yearwood from the vehicle, he had also been badly bruised, but the damage wasn't as bad as he had first feared: There were no crushed bones. The other Humvees rallied around to push Ladue's disabled vehicle back to Apache, where Hendrix and Baka waited for them at the aid station with the medics. Seeing Ladue walk in greatly relieved the first sergeant, but he worried about his future. "Is this guy going to make it through this deployment?" he said to Baka. "Boy's got some bad luck."

Baka immediately went back out with third platoon to start clearing buildings near where Ladue had been hit.

After checking back in at Apache, Ladue's platoon tried to regroup. Everybody walked away from that one, but it scared the hell out of them. The next day, they got back in the trucks. If they didn't, someone else would have to go in their places. Ladue and Yearwood were terrified, but they could see everyone else getting ready to roll. "Ah fuck," Ladue thought. "I can't puss out."

So he went out again on Thanksgiving night. Another boring night. He asked Staff Sergeant Christopher Cunningham to take the lead, and he and Yearwood rolled out in the middle of the convoy because they were both pretty spooked. Usually, IEDs hit the first vehicle. Between the two of them, Ladue and Yearwood felt like ducks at a fairground shooting range.

For the first three hours of patrol, they drove past the spot several times where Ladue's Humvee had been hit. Each time, he pulled back into himself, preparing for the explosion, going out of his mind with fear.

They drove to Apache for a break. Staff Sergeant Juan Campos, one of Ladue's buddies, gave him a hard time, mostly trying to rile him out of his fear. "Quit being a pussy," Campos said, punching Ladue in the arm. But Ladue wasn't in a place to be teased. Instead, the ribbing hurt. They didn't talk to each other again for the rest of the break.

Third platoon went back out and was getting ready to head back to Apache again. But while they were sitting at Antar Square, the lieutenant said, "Let's make one more go-round." Ladue tried not to see it as an omen. They drove into the market area, usually a calm part of the route where everyone allowed himself a bit of a breather.

Then it hit.

"Not again! Not again!" Yearwood screamed.

The insurgents had hit them with another roadside bomb. Ladue didn't feel hurt at first. At first, he didn't feel anything at all. The blast had blown his door open, and he stuck his M-4 out, looking for the enemy. Almost every time an IED went off, someone would be hiding in the bushes or behind a car waiting to shoot at the soldiers in the confusion. Ladue got off one round before the pain hit him. "Oh, I'm fucked up! I'm fucked up!" he yelled. Somebody pulled him out of the vehicle, and Campos was the first one on the scene.

"Oh, God, I didn't mean it, man," Campos said, kneeling at Ladue's side. "I'm so sorry."

They loaded Ladue into a good Humvee, Campos at his side, and took him back to Apache. The bomb had blown through his foot, leaving it a mass of formless mush. At Apache, they loaded Ladue on a helicopter. He arrived at the Green Zone in a fog, only able to think about how cold he was.

Gunner Private First Class Joshua Reyes was slightly wounded in the attack, and the explosion deeply bruised Yearwood's legs. But rather than allow the soldier, whom everyone liked, to spend Thanksgiving in the Green Zone hospital, Baka sent the scout platoon to fetch him back to Apache. Yearwood arrived on crutches, and was thrilled to see his friends so soon after such a traumatic event.

But Yearwood blamed himself for hitting the IED that injured Ladue. After Yearwood spent about a month recovering in the hospital, Hendrix moved him to Headquarters Company, deciding his soldier had seen too much. Yearwood had no choice in the matter, and continued to go out on patrol with his new company.

If the bomb had exploded a foot later, it would have killed everyone in the vehicle. The soldiers tried not to think about that. Instead, it lingered at the back of their minds, yet another factor to ignore as they loaded back into the Bradleys.

Ladue had made his final patrol: The army shipped him to Walter Reed Army Medical Center for treatment. He sent Campos an e-mail telling him he loved him, and that he knew his friend had been trying to help. And then he attempted to explain why he had lived through three attacks while so many others had died.

"I think surviving three instances like that is random dumb luck," he wrote, and Campos read it out to his platoon. "I'd like to think someone was looking out for me, but I don't have any good conclusions on that."

CHAPTER 8
McGinnis Earns a Medal of Honor

Conversations at Apache always went back to comparisons.

As young soldiers, most of them hadn't traveled far in the world before landing in the army, so they compared what they knew. Staff Sergeant Ian Newland offered up his knowledge from beneath a furrowed brow as he thought carefully about each sentence. He made his contributions more as something for his soldiers to consider than as mandatory truths.

He knew that Samarra—his first deployment—had changed the way he looked at the world, the way he looked at his wife and his baby daughter. He knew just how easily life can be lost. But as they talked, the guys who had deployed to Samarra realized they couldn't even use what they'd learned in Samarra in Adhamiya. Yes, it was horrific. Yes, they had lost friends. Yes, they had had their first experiences with combat stress.

Newland had seen members of the Iraqi police gutted and set on fire. He had seen children killed as "collateral damage." But this time he watched as the insurgents matched skills with the Americans, as if Samarra had been only a training ground for the Iraqis. When the guys stopped standing in open doorways and began using Bradleys to block entrances of homes as Baka talked to people inside, the insurgents moved from bullets to grenades. When the soldiers deflected grenades with pope shields, the insurgents used IEDs. When the guys started sending Bradleys out to lead the lineup of trucks, the insurgents set off the IEDs remotely so they'd go off under Humvees.

But the guys who had fought in Samarra also faced another problem that they hadn't foreseen: Combat stress appears to be cumulative. The army had conducted studies that show the more often a person deploys—especially those who deploy for a year or longer—the more likely that person is to develop PTSD. In Adhamiya, the war veterans couldn't help but be haunted by what they'd seen in Samarra.

On the night of Iraq's first elections in January 2005, during his first tour in Samarra, Newland's platoon responded when another platoon started getting hit on a particularly bad day. At 9:30 P.M., someone set off an IED in a school. The soldiers started getting hit from every direction. By the time Newland got there with first platoon, the battle was over and Newland was detailed with cleanup.

The guys thought the excitement was over for the night, but as Newland, the gunner in a Bradley, rounded a corner, a 300-pound man with a shotgun kicked open his front gate. Newland hit him with a 25 mm Bushmaster round. The man's face split in two, and he began puking out of his neck as Newland watched, horrified but unable to look away.

Inside the house behind the gate, the soldiers gathered forty more Iraqis, including a little girl. The soldiers put the Iraqi man Newland killed into a body bag. When Newland put on gloves and opened up the body bag to have the family identify it, the man's head rolled out with a mass of blood, puke, and flesh hanging in strings from his neck.

The man's daughter—she was maybe five—saw it. Like Newland, she stared. One of the soldiers quickly moved in front of her to block her view as a family member grabbed her and pushed her tiny face into the front of his shirt. Newland scrambled to push the mess back into the bag.

But he dreamed about it for months, thinking of his own tiny-faced little girl.

After four months in Samarra, Newland had found himself becoming distracted—violent even—on foot patrol. His squad leader moved him to the gunner position, where he would not have to leave the vehicle as often. The guys had never heard of PTSD at that point, but then one of Newland's friends was separated for mental health reasons. It made more sense than staying sane: They were getting mortared every day. They were living in plastic huts. A guy playing video games had his throat blown out one night when a mortar landed on the roof. Another guy was sleeping when the mortar landed, and he never woke up. Iraqi neighbors ratted each other out for money. Adults hid behind their children. Children placed IEDs.

The soldiers found babies lying on dirty floors by themselves, naked and covered with bugs.

Newland's squad leader probably did exactly what Newland needed when he made him stay in the truck. Newland needed to get his head back together.

Military leaders considered Samarra a success, and Newland still loved being a soldier, but he did not want to go back to Iraq. Not ever. But he knew better.

When they returned from the tour, they immediately began training to go again, and Newland got a new platoon sergeant: Sergeant First Class Cedric Thomas. Newland instantly felt drawn to Thomas, and he never left his side. He loved that he was squared away and smart—possibly smarter than Newland, which would be difficult.

Thomas pushed Newland to win the soldier of the year competition, and he encouraged him in his leadership efforts. That's how Newland got to know Campos, who had also been put in for soldier of the year. Campos said he had a soccer game, lying so that Newland would go to the U.S. Army Europe competition. Their platoon grew tighter and tighter, encouraging each other in everything.

Thomas also encouraged Newland to stand his ground when he wanted to go to school to become a better soldier. Newland had reenlisted in Samarra, mainly to go to airborne school. Then unit leadership told him they didn't have the money to send him. Newland pleaded breach of contract, hot-faced but calm, and eventually went to Fort Benning, Georgia, for training. But in training, he hit the ground hard on his second jump.

Newland assumed he would die as his body hurtled toward the ground. But after his trainers raced toward the piece of earth where he had landed, they discovered he had merely sprained his knee. He earned his airborne wings after jumping three more times and then continued on for ranger training. Before training started, he went on a run with one of the instructors, but eventually fell down with the pain. A medic looked at his knee and sent him to the hospital. No more ranger school.

The worst moment came when his four-year-old daughter, Haley, heard the news. Newland had spent months explaining why he was leaving and what exactly "ranger" meant. By the time he left, Haley assumed her dad could do anything. When Newland returned home, she quickly summed up the situation.

"So you're not a ranger," she said, crestfallen, her big brown eyes lowered above the same dimpled chin her dad claims. She heaved a heavy sigh.

Newland, caught by surprise, tried not to laugh at being so harshly judged by a child whose head barely reached his damaged knee.

"You're four," he teased. "Go to your room."

Then he gathered her in for a fierce tickling session.

The twenty-seven-year-old had made staff sergeant in four years and earned instant respect from his men and his leaders. But it took some work to get there. He had married young, and he and his wife immediately started a family with the birth of Haley. Both came from poor families, and after they got married, they struggled to end that cycle. Newland worked two jobs, but the family still needed Women, Infants, and Children assistance to get by. Neither Newland nor his wife had graduated from high school, and the prospects for good pay were slim.

But then Newland's older brother, Justin, sent Newland a copy of *Band of Brothers*. Newland found it so inspiring that he went to see a recruiter, eventually making his way to first platoon.

Soon after Newland's platoon returned from Samarra, Private Ross McGinnis showed up in Schweinfurt with a wave of new guys who needed to be trained up for deployment. Newland got "stuck" with him and his constant questions. "Hey, Sergeant Newland, how does this work?" "Hey, can you show me how to change the tire on a Humvee?" "Hey, Sergeant Newland, what's it going to be like in Iraq? Does it ever get cold? How do you know who the bad guys are?"

McGinnis never stopped, and while Newland appreciated the kid's need for knowledge, he couldn't understand how this guy was always "on." He never seemed to need downtime or quiet. Busy. Fingers in everything, even if he didn't know what he was doing. Newland couldn't blow his nose without McGinnis wanting to emulate his style.

One of his squad's favorite phrases became "Shut up, McGinnis." McGinnis would just grin and go on asking questions as if he were on a constant sugar high.

He even looked like a kid. He weighed maybe 125 pounds, and he had the biggest, softest brown eyes—and that grin. Always a grin. When Newland had his squad over for dinner or barbecues, his daughter Haley would walk straight to McGinnis, take his hand, and lead him off somewhere to play.

Eventually, Newland started to relax and enjoy his new charge. After all, McGinnis couldn't help but make a great soldier with all he wanted to learn, and as McGinnis got more comfortable with the group, it turned out his 125 pounds was pure, silly fun. McGinnis had been a bit of a goofball in high school, and he had joined the army to find a sense of direction. With Newland, he got it. Newland was known for pushing his men, but he tried to be smart about it. If McGinnis answered a question incorrectly, Newland didn't tell him to drop and do push-ups; he had him write a paper about the first carbine. If he forgot to do a chore Newland had given him, Newland made him write a paper about Audie Murphy. And after living through Samarra, Newland quizzed his guys constantly about first aid. McGinnis loved it.

McGinnis also had two unusual attributes: He was ambidextrous and qualified sharpshooter with both his left and right hands.

And he shared his birthday, June 14, with the U.S. Army.

Before they deployed, Newland started inviting McGinnis over for poker games with the guys, but McGinnis usually ended up off playing with Newland's kids. He was, after all, only nineteen.

By the time they got to Adhamiya, McGinnis more than fit in. He was a favorite.

But his sergeants made sure his training continued in Iraq. Sergeant Chagoya also worked with McGinnis, but usually ended up on the receiving end of his antics, which made no sense at all. Newland could be intimidating, but Chagoya was a former Marine with an imposing height and mass. He didn't look as if he could be moved with a bulldozer, not for size, exactly, but more because he's so stubbornly square. Chagoya would grab the youngster whenever he had something new to teach, which was often. He hated seeing the guys standing around smoking cigarettes or playing video games when they could be training. The guys learned to scatter when they saw Chagoya coming.

One day, he dragged them all down to the basement to train on night-vision goggles. Sometimes the training seemed more like busy work, but Chagoya wanted his guys to know everything by muscle memory so they could act quickly in bad situations. That day, he wanted them to break their night-vision goggles down and put them back together while blindfolded.

Sitting at a table, Chagoya wrapped an olive-green bandana across his eyes and started to demonstrate. But he sensed that something was off. He could hear the guys swallowing giggles, letting out choked-off snorts. "C'mon, guys, this is important," Chagoya said. Normally, that would have been enough. Then he saw a flash through the edges of his blindfold. After that, the laughter came full force. "What the hell?" Chagoya said, ripping off the bandana. The guys were laughing so hard they couldn't even stop long enough to tell him what was funny.

Someone just handed him the camera.

Chagoya's flashbulb-lit face filled the right half of the screen. McGinnis's bare ass filled the other half. Chagoya couldn't help but laugh. "Where in the hell do you come up with this shit?" Chagoya said. McGinnis grinned, thrilled that he'd made his tough sergeant laugh.

McGinnis spent the rest of the lesson haranguing Chagoya with questions no one else would think to ask.

Because he was the new guy, McGinnis got stuck as the platoon armorer, which most people think of as the most annoying job in the company. Basically, McGinnis had to keep track of everyone's weapons—and fix them in an atmosphere that promoted jams. Sand crept into every opening, slithered in through cracks and worked its way into any part with even a hint of oil. The 203s bounced around in the backs of Bradleys. M-4s went out in rainstorms and sandstorms. Everyone, always, worried about his weapon. But rather than complaining about it, McGinnis embraced the gig, happily challenging himself to keep the weapons spotless and using the position to get to know the rest of the company. And he loved his .50 cal. He had a buddy record that with a video camera.

"This is your round," he singsonged, holding up a pinky-finger-long M-4 round. Then he proudly displayed the hand-long .50 cal round. "And this is my round."

He held up the little round.

"Your round."

And then the big round.

"My round."

But for all of his playing, McGinnis would cut the sarcasm and the joking long enough to make sure he could be there to take care of his men if—and when—a bad situation arose. Soon after the company medevacked

Ladue to Germany, the men began intensive grenade training. On patrol, grenades constantly rattled off the sides of turrets or bounced off the roofs of Humvees. On November 29, first platoon saw a kid known for throwing hand grenades riding on a scooter. They chased after him in their vehicle until he ran inside a house. Then someone threw a grenade.

"Grenade!" yelled Private First Class Brandon Waugh, as he bailed out of the truck. Newland heard the ping as it landed inside. "Get out of the fucking truck!" Waugh screamed.

Everybody dived for the ground around the Humvee.

Then nothing.

"Are you sure it wasn't a rock?" Newland asked. "No, man, it was a grenade," Waugh said. "I saw it." Then Newland remembered the six cases of Mark-19 40 mm explosive grenades inside the Humvee. The grenade should have gone off by then, so Newland ran over to check while everybody else stayed flat on the ground. Newland saw the grenade lying on the floorboards. The kid who threw it hadn't pulled the pin. If he had, even if the blast of the grenade hadn't killed Newland's crew, the Mark-19s would have. Instead, their only injury came when Waugh scraped a knuckle leaping from the Humvee.

When the guys got back to Apache, they filled the first sergeant and commander in on what had happened. "Holy shit," Hendrix said. "We need a new plan."

That week, they started practicing with tennis balls. Someone would toss a ball at a Humvee or Bradley, the guys inside would hear it thud, and then they'd open the doors and flop out on the ground.

McGinnis, of course, immediately started giving Chagoya a hard time based on his background as a Marine. The guys talked about what they would do if they saw a grenade and knew their friends wouldn't have time to get out of the truck.

"Marine! You will jump on that grenade!" McGinnis said in his best drill instructor voice, back straight and finger jabbing the air, but still unable to hold back that grin.

And then McGinnis, losing the drill instructor shtick, said, "Fuck that! I'd be like, 'See ya!'"

But it sparked some serious discussions, too. "You never know how you will react," Chagoya told his men. "You come over here all tough, but you will never find out who you really are until you are in that position."

On December 4, they all went out on patrol as usual, McGinnis silly-excited because Baka had just signed a waiver at McGinnis's eighteen-month mark so he could promote McGinnis to specialist; he would officially lose the "Fucking New Guy" status. Only two people per company can get a waiver to be promoted six months ahead of their peers. Newland went out, even though it was his day off. If he stayed behind, he'd just think about someone being out there in his place, and he'd be bored. In Adhamiya, it's hard to de-stress, to find a place that's calm and quiet. Newland found it was better for his mood if he just worked every day. Besides, he would be with his favorite sergeant, Thomas, and his favorite private, McGinnis. They rode through the streets of Adhamiya, with Newland's crew riding last in a string of six Humvees. They were looking for a place to put a new generator to try, yet again, to provide the locals with electricity. McGinnis, of course, manned the .50 caliber machine gun as they rode back toward Apache. First Lieutenant Travis Atwood led the company mission and rode in the second Humvee. Baka rode in the fourth. They stopped for a minute, about a mile away from the COP, near a two-story building.

McGinnis yelled over the Humvee's intercom system: "Grenade!"

The insurgents had lobbed so many grenades at the team that the guys reacted calmly, looking around for the offending weapon.

"Where?" Thomas shouted.

McGinnis yelled again: "The grenade is in the truck!"

Then Newland could hear it ricocheting around the turret, a heavy metallic drum. McGinnis tried to grab it so he could toss it back out before it blew, but he missed. He stood as if he were going to leap out of the top of the Humvee, but instead he dropped down from his fighting position into the truck. Newland thought McGinnis was trying to escape the grenade. But he wasn't. McGinnis had realized that his teammates hadn't spotted it, and so he was chasing it. Newland couldn't move quickly enough to get out of the truck with its combat-locked doors, and none of the guys quite understood what was going on because McGinnis hadn't dived out.

Then Newland saw it, a fist-sized black bullet of metal. He heard McGinnis say, "It's right here!" And it was. Right on the radio mount in the front of the Humvee between driver Sergeant Lyle Buehler and truck commander Thomas. Newland froze as his brain processed this information. It was there. It was live. It was going to blow.

Then he watched as McGinnis threw his back against the radio mount, against the grenade. McGinnis wasn't going to bail. He knew his friends didn't have time. Newland could see the determination in his friend's face.

Newland watched as the grenade immediately blew McGinnis toward the back of the truck, but he couldn't yet comprehend what had happened. The truck filled with black smoke. The explosion knocked McGinnis's machine gun off its mount and blew open the doors. All Newland could think about was the pain. A steady stream of blood poured from the inside of Newland's thigh—dark, dark blood. He grabbed a tourniquet, but only managed three turns before the pain overwhelmed him. Private First Class Sean Lawson, a new medic who had yet to prove his abilities to the men, had also been riding in the back. The blast knocked him cold for a few seconds, but when he came to, Lawson ran around to Newland's side of the truck. "I need a tourniquet," Newland told him, as Lawson froze up. Every medic tells the story of that moment of inaction the first time they encounter an injured friend. Lawson quickly shook himself out of it and adjusted the tourniquet.

But then Newland realized they were being shot at, so he grabbed Lawson and pulled him back into the truck. Lawson checked the driver,

Buehler, who had shrapnel in his right thigh, right shoulder, and right side of his face. Thomas, sitting in the front passenger seat, had lacerations to his left shoulder and neck and a massive bruise on his back.

Thomas, who had also been knocked unconscious for a few seconds by the blast, saw a guy on the roof of a building and started shooting.

Newland looked over to see how McGinnis was doing. His friend's eyes were moving around, so Newland grabbed his hand. "I gotcha man," Newland said. "We'll get you out of here." He held tight to McGinnis's hand and began to pray.

But Newland soon had to release McGinnis's hand to deal with his own injuries. His jaw throbbed, and he was going into shock. He couldn't focus on anything but the pain. A four-inch piece of shrapnel had embedded itself in the bone. He used his hands to try to hold pressure on the wounds, but blood poured out between his fingers and shot up toward his face. More than fifty pieces of shrapnel had entered every part of his body except his chest, which was protected by body armor. As he pulled off a glove, he thought his hand would come with it, so he left it for the medics to deal with. Shrapnel had cut through a tendon.

Newland could hear people nearby and worried that someone would pull him out of the truck and he'd end up a hostage, videotaped and exploited on the Internet for his wife and kids to see. Then he realized he had passed out. He could hear Thomas screaming, and then he passed out again.

Thomas continued to shoot, and Newland thought, "If I don't get to the aid station, I'm going to bleed out." He looked at Thomas. He felt light. "I'm going to die right now if we don't get back to the aid station," he said. Thomas started yelling at Newland to keep him awake, to keep him alive.

Two Humvees ahead of them, Baka had heard the blast, then looked back to see McGinnis's truck with the doors blown open. He had his driver whip their vehicle around and quickly had his men provide security for the disabled team. Sergeant Patrick Cramer took Buehler's place at the wheel, but he couldn't close the doors to the Humvee. As he followed them back to Apache, Baka could see the doors flapping.

As Cramer drove, Thomas tried to talk to McGinnis. Cramer drove over a median, and Newland's M-4 fell out.

"Don't worry about it," Baka said over the radio. "Keep moving."

Baka had his driver stop and grab the M-4.

Immediately, the scout platoon went out to look for the person who had thrown the grenade. Sergeant Keegan Swope and his men passed first platoon coming back in the gate. About a dozen men from Charlie Company spent the next five or six hours kicking in doors and searching every car. But they didn't find anything. They never did immediately after an incident.

Newland saw the gate, and then he passed out. Buehler walked himself to the aid station, bleeding from the head. Thomas needed help walking, and soldiers carried Newland in.

Baka and Hendrix ran to the aid station, staying with their injured men and making sure no one but the medics came inside. But they couldn't protect the wounded men from seeing each other's pain.

A double-doored ramp led into the aid station at Apache, with two stands for litters. Newland lay with his head close to the door, while McGinnis's feet were toward the door. Doc Whelchel stood checking McGinnis for a heartbeat. Blood poured out beneath McGinnis's litter, but Newland couldn't see that. Baka could, from where he stood next to Hendrix near Newland's head.

Buehler sat in a corner in shock with his shirt off, not so much watching the situation as gazing through the scene. Thomas stood between McGinnis and Newland as the medics checked them out. A huge bruise ran up Thomas's side. Lawson had come in with his platoon.

Newland was in the most immediate danger, and he knew it.

As Baka held him down on a table, Newland started yelling. "Don't mess with me!" he shouted, convinced he was dying. "Did it hit the artery?"

Baka pushed him back down on the table. Aid station medic Staff Sergeant Branden DeSersa filled him up with morphine.

"You're going to be OK," DeSersa said. "It's under control, and you're going to be fine."

Baka and Hendrix needed to hear it, too.

Newland had a big hole under his lip where the shrapnel had entered. He started to break down a little, the shock setting in. Baka stood over his head, hand on Newland's shoulder.

"Hey," Baka said. "Open your mouth for me."

Newland did, and Baka leaned in for an inspection.

"You got all your teeth, man," Baka said. "You're good. But you've got a big-ass hole in your chin."

Newland laughed, that half cry, half giggle of emotions too close together. Baka knew he had to get his soldier to focus on himself.

Inside the building at Apache, Chagoya had the day off. He laughed as he watched a video on his laptop that McGinnis had made for him. McGinnis pretended he was a newscaster, reporting on a friend's minor injury, a paper cut requiring a Band-Aid. "So, how does that make you feel?" McGinnis asked, playing off the reporters who had come through and asked them silly questions. As Chagoya watched, someone burst into the room. "They're taking Ross to the aid station!" Chagoya went cold, and then ran outside. Hendrix wouldn't let him in the aid station, but Chagoya quickly realized no one seemed hopeful.

Inside with the medics, the knowledge was just catching up with Newland.

Before the morphine took over, Newland caught sight of McGinnis lying on the other litter.

"Sir?" Newland said. "What's wrong with Ross? Why isn't anybody working on him?"

Baka squeezed Newland's shoulder and gave him the answer straight.

"He's gone," Baka said.

The knowledge collided with the wave of morphine, allowing Newland a reprieve until the doctors in the Green Zone could help him.

When the helicopter arrived, the soldiers evacuated Newland and Buehler to the Combat Support Hospital in Baghdad, both with Purple Hearts pinned to their blankets. From Baghdad, Newland flew to Landstuhl Army Medical Center in Germany.

As his friends had lifted McGinnis out of the Humvee and onto the litter, McGinnis let out a massive exhale, as if he had been holding his breath, thinking of nothing but saving his friends. A breath of relief.

At dusk, a second helicopter would arrive for McGinnis.

He had died instantly in the blast. His soldiers conjectured that the exhale was merely air leaving his body, but their hearts held onto that last sigh.

A few days later, Hendrix helped question the fifteen-year-old boy who threw the grenade that killed McGinnis. They had captured him three times before, but they never had enough information to keep him. If they took him to the MPs and said, "We found him with explosive-making material," the MPs would say, "You have to give us more." Hendrix remained proud that his soldiers were careful not to use excessive force, but that day, it took everything he had to keep his bearing, to not destroy the kid who had killed McGinnis. "These guys are no one," he vented to Baka after the hero flight had taken McGinnis away. "They don't represent anyone. It's not an enemy force. Most of them are doing it for the money."

McGinnis's death earned the Iraqi kid $50.

It earned McGinnis the Medal of Honor.

CHAPTER 9
The Mission Continues at Home

When Newland arrived at the Landstuhl Army Medical Center in Germany and found himself still alive, he figured all he had to do was work on getting better. That was not the case. After all he had faced in Samarra and Adhamiya, his treatment in Schweinfurt ended his love affair with the army.

Newland's wife, Erin, had flown home to the United States for Christmas. When she left Schweinfurt, she called the rear detachment, the 26th Infantry unit element that stayed behind when the rest of the unit left for Iraq, and gave them a phone number for every place she would be for the next month, as well as her cell phone number. But nobody called her with the news that her children's playmate—McGinnis—had died saving her husband's life, and that her husband had been wounded.

From the hospital, rattled with a brain injury from the explosion, Newland couldn't remember his wife's phone number, so he called his dad.

That day, Erin had gone shopping in a big box store. Walmart may not seem like a treat to people who drive past them every day, but Erin hadn't seen one since she'd gone to Germany, and she looked forward to stocking up. As she shopped, her cell phone rang. It was Newland's aunt.

"He's been in an accident," she said. "You have to call his dad."

"Wait!" Erin said, panicking, her two toddlers sitting in her shopping cart next to stacks of paper plates. "What happened?"

"Erin, honey, I don't know," Newland's aunt said. "You have to call his dad."

She did, and he couldn't offer any more information—just that she needed to go home.

Soon after, Newland called. "I'm OK," he said. "I need you to come home." He tried to explain what had happened, but he couldn't form complete sentences. He tried to tell her what had happened to McGinnis, but the words wouldn't come out right. On Erin's end, it didn't sound as if Ian's injuries were life threatening, but she knew she had to get home quickly.

His unit finally called her the next day, but it still didn't sound as if Ian's injuries were that bad. Even Captain Baka had been more concerned about the gaping wound in Ian's jaw than any of his other injuries. But no one had seen Ian. Cathy Baka talked with Erin, telling her to give Cathy a call if she needed anything—and that she needed to hurry. On her end, Cathy was beginning to understand the extent of McGinnis's sacrifice.

"All I know is I gotta go home," Erin said. She immediately called to see if she could travel Space Available, a privilege that allows military members and their family members to travel cheaply. Less-than-one-hundred-dollars cheap, but only if there is room on a military flight for an extra passenger. Army officials offered her no help. Air force officials said she could fly Space A if she had a note from Newland's commander. When she priced tickets on civilian flights, she discovered it would cost $6,000 for the three of them to get new tickets from Minnesota back to Germany. She could not afford that.

Erin had attended all the Family Readiness Group meetings, and she knew exactly what was supposed to happen if her husband was injured or killed. But going home for the holidays had thrown the process completely offtrack. So Erin called the rear detachment. But Newland's unit never sent the paperwork she needed to fly Space A. Unknown to Erin, Cathy had the paperwork on her computer at home; all she had to do was print it out. And had Cathy known Erin couldn't find cheap tickets, she would have pooled her resources—called the airlines and support groups to try to get cheap or free tickets. But Erin thought she was going through proper channels and did not realize she could ask Cathy for help with paperwork. In her mind, asking the rear detachment for a slip of paper should have been a simple solution. As Erin's husband arrived at Landstuhl Army Medical Center, she was stuck in Chicago, and then in Washington, D.C. Finally, she received permission to fly Space-Available.

But not before her husband was released from Landstuhl Army Medical Center.

Two days after Newland arrived at the hospital in Germany, hospital administrators booted him out. "We called your unit to pick you up," they told Newland. "We're sorry. We need this bed." They gave him a bag filled, he presumed, with prescription information and a referral to see a doctor. Still heavily drugged on pain medication, Newland arrived home in a haze.

He didn't have a key to his apartment. He had arrived at Landstuhl with only the clothes he had been wearing, and his house key was tucked deep inside a duffle bag in Baghdad.

A buddy called the fire department to let him in. Then the fire department charged him for the service. He spent his first night alone, in pain and barely able to walk. He had shrapnel in every limb of his body. His leg had been badly damaged, shrapnel ripping through nerves and forcing him to walk with a cane. He had been diagnosed with a traumatic brain injury, but nobody bothered to tell him. Shrapnel had cut through his wrist, leaving him with the use of only three fingers. His jaw had been broken.

After a restless night alone and in pain, Newland opened the bag hospital staff had given him as he left, hoping to find pain medication.

Nothing.

No instructions. No phone number to call.

When Newland realized he had been given only a shaving kit, he wept, alone and unable to help himself.

As Erin struggled to get home, Newland quickly sobered up from the pain meds he had been given at the hospital.

When the pain became intolerable, he made his way to the clinic with the help of one of the rear-detachment soldiers. The administrative clerk at the front desk said, "There's a phone right there. You need to make an appointment." When he called, he found out there were no appointments for a week.

That's when Newland pulled the administrative clerk through the window with his good hand and threw him on the floor. "They said I had mental health issues," Newland said. "But there was no psychiatrist. I was like, 'I'm bleeding in your clinic here,' but no one would help me."

Eventually Newland made enough noise that a doctor agreed to see him and prescribe pain medication.

When he returned home, Newland called the company rear detachment sergeant, Staff Sergeant Raja Richardson, who had been shot in the arm in October and had been assigned to look after the Charlie Company soldiers who had remained or returned to Schweinfurt. Richardson had been slow to move into the slot because he hoped to return to Adhamiya. But Baka and Hendrix, after briefings from Cathy Baka, realized they needed a good noncommissioned officer to take charge back home.

When Richardson and the other wounded troops realized Newland had returned and no one was helping him, they rallied around him. But they could only do so much. In fact, many of the other soldiers were in wheelchairs and had no way to get in and out of the barracks—accessible only by staircases—without help. No one was checking up on the single soldiers who lived in the barracks. No one helped them make appointments. No one made sure they had the care they needed.

The married soldiers—the ones whose wives picked them up at the hospital and took them home to constant care—did not realize the single soldiers were suffering because they had their own physical and mental wounds to look after.

When Erin arrived home a few days after her husband, she found a man who resembled her husband, but who didn't act like him at all. She held Ian for hours, kept his children—thrilled to see their daddy home—from jumping in his lap or grabbing his hand, and helped him figure out what to do next.

Because he could not control his own situation, he took care of the injured single soldiers living in the barracks.

He set up a dry-erase board to keep track of them, instantly taking care of the first problem: The guys who had been hurt in Adhamiya believed that no one cared about them. Ian sat down with each of the nine men and talked with them about their injuries and what they still needed, keeping careful tab in his notebook. Then he started making phone calls. He set up appointments. He made sure their household goods—packed in storage before they left—were returned to them. He called commanders to make sure someone addressed their mental health concerns.

Still not understanding what was wrong with his brain, Ian took notes. He wrote down what doctors said to him, and he wrote down what he needed to do the next day, all the way to what he needed to say to people. If he didn't write it down, he would forget. Erin tried to help him keep track, figuring he was still discombobulated by the sudden shift from Iraq to Germany, or that his pain medications made him off-kilter.

If that were the case, Ian thought, a couple of hundred men would be returning to Schweinfurt with similar problems. All of them, he knew, would face the heartbreak they didn't allow themselves to deal with in Adhamiya. At home, they would think of nothing else.

Ian went straight to the battalion commander, bleeding through his bandages. "You know you sent my guys into a high-conflict area," Ian said. "You've got guys in the barracks in wheelchairs. You've got to take care of these guys. You need more mental health workers. You need someone to look out for them in the barracks. You need to make sure no one comes home and wraps his car around a tree."

By the end of his speech, Ian cried tears of frustration and anger. The commander listened, and what Ian said made sense. Battalion leadership had missed a key part of the mission, and they would work to remedy it.

But Ian still didn't know about his moderate brain injury, and though he had reason to be angry, the head injury meant he had no filter to help him process when he had gone too far. He said whatever came into his head. As he struggled to get medical appointments or watched his injured men carry other injured men up and down the staircase to get into the building, Ian could not contain himself.

He made calls. "You better take care of this or I'm going to blow up the clinic!"

He repeated the threat, as well as others, every time he hit a hurdle, which was daily. He wasn't receiving any counseling. He still couldn't get someone to treat all of his pain. He attended to his men with a useless claw for a hand and a bum leg that dragged behind him as he walked.

"I had no idea what had happened to me, or internally, what to do next," Newland said. "I decided that was unacceptable."

Because of the brain injury, the trauma of the shrapnel wounds, and the combat stress he'd faced, he had been diagnosed with depression, confusion, migraines, and flashbacks. Some of the bits of shrapnel embedded in his limbs worked their way out, feeling like thick needles tearing through his flesh. The doctors had removed some pieces. Some, the doctors told him, would remain trapped in his limbs for the rest of his life. His jaw had been broken, he had nerve damage in his wrist, and he walked with a cane because of the damage to his thigh.

Every day he would call someone in the chain of command and explain why his soldiers needed someone to take care of them. And he warned them that if they didn't have a better mental health system in place when his battalion returned home, there'd be trouble. He worried that marriages would end, people would drive while intoxicated and take other risks, and that someone would commit suicide. Based on his own experiences, he had no doubt of that.

He made sure people listened.

"Ian's actions were very appropriate," said Major Daniel Ducker, the health clinic commander at Schweinfurt. "We thought, 'Let's take action.'" Ducker said they changed all the processes for handling wounded soldiers after Newland's complaints. They had focus groups with family members. They created the "Sentinel Working Group" to make sure the hand-off of injured Blue Spaders went smoothly, and that their commanders back in Baghdad knew exactly what was going on. Within weeks of Newland's arrival home, case managers began to be assigned to wounded warriors to make sure they got their medical appointments and kept their paperwork straight. Several months after the scandal at Walter Reed Army Medical Center in February 2007, Schweinfurt also stood up a Warrior Transition Unit, a place specifically designed to take care of the casualties of war.

None of that mattered to Newland, who had been left in charge of his own care. That care—the basics—should have been obvious, and he was livid that the army he loved had treated him so poorly. Even after he complained, Newland still had a hard time getting what he needed: appointments, a mental health therapist, and someone to tell him what was wrong with his head.

In January, the doctors tried to fix Newland's hand, but said they would worry about his leg later. "I'm staying until you get done with me," Newland said. He still didn't know about his brain injury. A cat scan showed that the blood vessels in the front of his brain were leaking plasma. He began having mild seizures and stuttering, but he did not know why.

He had shrapnel inside his knee, but the doctors said it was inoperable. He had twenty pieces of shrapnel in his left leg. "I was really scared," Newland said. "I was shaking every day. I couldn't pick up a glass of water. I lost all of my short-term memory, so I wrote everything down."

The doctors kept him on Zoloft and sleeping meds, but that didn't help the physical aspects of his pain, and it didn't help him sort through his guilt or sadness at the loss of his friend. Ian dreamed. He had flashbacks. He obsessed about how he could have saved McGinnis. Four months later, he went to see an occupational therapist, Captain Patricia Strange. "You need help," she told him. "You need help now." And she worked with him, seeming to understand just what he needed and trying to get him to other doctors who could help.

"She was the best therapist," Newland said. "She devotes her life to helping soldiers. She's the only person in Schweinfurt who took me in. I was able to trust her, and that was hard to do after what had happened to me."

His other treatments did not go as well. He'd show up for an appointment with a neurologist at Landstuhl at 9:00 A.M. and wait until 5:00 P.M. because there were so many soldiers who needed help. Doctors then recommended a nerve graft study on his leg to see what still worked and what needed fixing. "They electrocute you with what looks like a Taser," Newland said. "The second time, the technician hit a nerve, shocked me, and I had a flashback. I threw her on the floor, fell on my face, and my legs have been worse ever since. Now I have pain that wasn't there before. That's when something hit."

"He called me that day and he was stuttering," Erin said.

"I was shivering and I was shaking," Newland said. "I was in pain."

But Newland found some peace with another family. He traveled to Virginia with Thomas and Buehler to attend McGinnis's burial at Arlington National Cemetery. Thomas and Buehler felt like family, and Newland thought they were the only ones who would understand what that day had been like. But McGinnis's dad had also replayed the actions of his son over and over in his mind.

"When I met his family, they were so loving and compassionate," Newland said. "I thought it was hard losing my soldier, but this was just too much."

At the funeral, McGinnis's dad, Thomas McGinnis, pulled Newland in for a hug. A long hug.

"You don't owe my son anything," he said.

Somehow he knew what Newland had been thinking, that he could have done more to try to save McGinnis. That he needed to live each day in a way that would honor what McGinnis had done for Newland. That Newland should have died, too. In Thomas McGinnis's mind, his son's friends had been worth saving. And he was so proud of his son.

Though McGinnis's father helped Newland deal with a lot of the pain, Newland couldn't let it all go. He went back to Germany, but as Charlie Company's tour continued in Adhamiya, he got nothing but bad news about his friends. "I was so depressed," Newland said. "When I got back from Arlington, I was suicidal." He called the mental health clinic and asked if he could check himself in. The clinic staff told him to go to the emergency room at the German hospital. Instead of trying to explain his situation to a doctor whose first language was not Newland's, he continued to replay the day McGinnis died over and over in his mind. "I thought I could have done more," he said.

"Every second I was reliving it. All of a sudden, I'm in the Humvee and the grenade goes off."

He couldn't sleep. He had flashbacks so real it was hard to ground himself in reality. "I called the mental health commander and I went nuts. She called back and wanted to talk to my wife."

They sent Newland to a civilian social worker who specializes in families and kids. Newland started by telling her about the bodies they'd found in Adhamiya. His social worker started to cry, and Newland felt too guilty to tell her the rest. He stopped going.

At home, the stress of the unaddressed psychological issues, as well as the anger that comes with a traumatic brain injury, worked its way into the crevices of his marriage. "Our marriage was about to fall apart," Newland said. "I came from an alcoholic family, and I was drinking. I was messing with Erin really bad. I thought I was the one who should have died that day."

Erin did not know how much longer she could expose her children—or herself—to this man.

"I said, 'I can't handle this,'" Erin said. "'I'm done. I just really can't take this anymore.' I'd move something and he'd flip out. I couldn't understand what was going on."

Many service members who suffer traumatic brain injuries also develop obsessive-compulsive disorder, and Newland needed to have everything in its place, as if he had to have control over some portion of his world.

"I'd been battling every day, screaming at officers," Newland said. "And then I'd come home to Erin. After what I saw happen in that truck, it took a pretty hard toll on my life, my family. And then the brain injury crashed down on me. If I wasn't in a strong marriage, I have no idea where I'd be right now."

Erin scanned the Internet looking for help and talked with Newland's social worker, who, though she did not do well with Newland's combat trauma, did wonderfully helping Erin and the children try to cope with the man who had returned home different from the man they had sent to war.

Erin remembered the man she'd married, the man who bragged about his pretty wife and brought his soldiers home to meet his family. She remembered the hard times they'd had before, when Newland had worked two jobs but they still had gone on welfare to make ends meet. Newland might be stubborn, but he'd met his match.

"Instead of getting into it and getting mad, I'd just let him do his ranting and raving," she said. "The social worker couldn't help him, but she helped me."

"Erin was able to identify when I was getting angry, and she would back off," Newland said.

Erin also began talking to Cathy Baka about ways they could improve wounded soldiers' return to Schweinfurt, as well as how they could better prepare wives for their changed husbands. Cathy began calling wounded soldiers when they arrived in Germany. Erin opened her home to her husband's new charges, trying to make them feel comfortable, trying to talk them through the pain they felt at not being in Iraq with their friends, and offering her silly little girl and her grinny baby boy as beacons of hope.

In the evenings, Erin and Ian lay on the floor together, and Erin helped massage and move Newland's leg. One tiny piece of shrapnel worked its way out of his thigh. "The rest is in—I can feel it now," he said. "I can't even describe the pain." As he talked, the remote control fell off the couch. He blinked hard, stopped, and stuttered before resuming. "I can feel them all. I have three or four pain attacks a day. I have to stop everything I'm doing it hurts so bad."

The army gave him 80 percent on the temporary disability retirement list, and 30 percent of it comes from a post-traumatic stress disorder diagnosis. "I didn't even want to argue," he said. "I just signed it." He receives $800 a month. "If they treated me like they should have, I would still be a soldier."

"You? A pogue?" Erin teased. If he had stayed in, Newland would have been a desk sergeant.

Newland eventually began going to therapy by himself. "Both of my psychiatrists would listen, not say anything, and then they'd give me a prescription. Group therapy consisted of me and one other guy."

The other guy couldn't relate to Newland's experiences at all; he hadn't been in combat. Newland stopped going. The army said he was noncompliant. "They don't have therapy and they've tried to cover their ass by saying I was noncompliant," Newland said. "That's when I went to the Fifth Corps Commander." He explained the situation again, making noise about the injured men in the barracks, unable to hold back anything.

He initially went because he wanted to make sure McGinnis received a Medal of Honor. But he also went because he wanted to make sure his friends had the help they needed when they returned home. As soon as he got that promise, Newland started working more on himself.

More than anything, he wanted to be with his men. More than anything, he wanted to feel worthy of McGinnis's loss. More than anything, he wanted to feel normal. And then he received another gift of life.

Using the last of his savings, he flew from Germany to Fort Carson, Colorado, to start looking for a civilian job. He'd never been to Colorado before, but had heard it was a good place. "It was somewhere I could find work and that was beautiful," Newland said. "As soon as I saw the mountains, I was sold." The director of civilian job services at Fort Carson said he'd help Newland find a job, but the bank shot him down on a loan for a home.

Twice.

And then he couldn't find a job that would earn him enough money to ever move forward.

"At that point, I realized things were going to hell."

Newland went to the chapel at the Air Force Academy in Colorado Springs. As he walked out, he ran into Dennis McCormick from the Army Wounded Warrior Program. Mike Conklin, a realtor, had watched what McCormick went through when McCormick had been injured, and he began Sentinels of Freedom. McCormick said Newland should apply for help, and Newland said, "Well, the army's not taking care of me, so . . ."

He applied, and then flew home to Germany. A month went by. And then six months went by. "I said, 'You know what? I can't rely on a dream,'" Newland said.

But McCormick called on Father's Day. They would buy Newland and his family a five-bedroom house. They would furnish it. They would supply him with a job and a scholarship for school. He would have mentors, including a retired army colonel.

His children could go to school and play in a yard and try to be part of a normal family.

"I've never had anything given to me," Newland explained, leaning on the cane that helps him walk. "I've had to work for everything. But I cannot accept an uncertain future with my children."

He tried hard to change his feelings about the day McGinnis died. He wanted to mourn his soldier, to show respect by thinking about him. But he realized McGinnis would have been miserable if he could see how Newland now lived his life. Newland knew that McGinnis didn't save him so that he could spend his life mourning the happy-go-lucky, silly, courageous young soldier.

"Us grunts, we're always making comments," Newland explained. "You look someone square in the eyes and say, 'I would take a bullet for you,' and mean it. We all consider it. We always think about it. You don't want to watch a friend die if you could have done something. But to be faced with that? Will you actually go through with it? Ross did. He knew how quickly he could exit that vehicle, and he chose not to.

"Every day of my life is a gift from Ross McGinnis."

CHAPTER 10
Charlie Company Tries to Play Nice with the Neighbors

After McGinnis died, no one seemed able to talk about anything else. They all wondered if they would do the same thing. And they wondered if the first grenade—the dud that had landed next to Waugh—had given McGinnis time to think about it, even while he teased that he'd be the first one out of the truck.

It hit Waugh particularly hard. He had done exactly what he should have: yelled "Grenade!" and jumped out with his buddies.

But as they sat smoking one evening at the picnic tables set up outside their building at Apache, Waugh said he should have been like McGinnis. In Waugh's case, the grenade didn't go off.

"That almost makes it worse," Waugh said. "Like I could have been courageous and showed you guys how much I love you, even if it was a dud. Like I'm even less courageous because it turned out to be a dud."

"Man, you guys had different sets of clues," Chagoya told him. "You can't second-guess that. Your brain told you everyone had time to jump out. McGinnis knew there wasn't time."

"You can't beat yourself up," Thomas, who had been in the truck with McGinnis, told Waugh. "We're learning. Every day."

Waugh wasn't the only one who felt guilt. After December 4, First Sergeant Hendrix and his men set about finding a way to deflect the grenades. They tried using camouflage netting, but when they threw tennis balls at the turrets, the netting wrapped itself around the balls like a catcher's mitt. So they tried Hesco baskets, a metal mesh that caused the tennis balls to bounce away as if they'd hit a trampoline. They spent an afternoon welding the baskets to the turrets of all their vehicles, leaving a spot open in front for the gunner to escape in an emergency. Finding a solution didn't stop the second-guessing.

As Baka ran laps around Apache one night with Waggoner, both of them carrying pistols because of the wild dogs and because they never quite trusted the security on the Iraqi side of the COP, Baka tried to clear his head.

"Why in the hell didn't we think of the baskets after Waugh?" he asked. "Why didn't I see this coming?" Waggoner tried to comfort Baka that thinking differently doesn't come automatically. "In the old war movies, no one comes up with a way to evade grenades. Some hero grabs it and throws it back at the enemy, you know?" Waggoner said. "You don't even think about other options. In training, troops learn to dive for cover, not to figure out ways to prevent the grenades from landing in the fox-hole in the first place."

"But it's like a dog I used to have," Baka said. "That dog would chase cars every single day, until one day she got hit. She never chased cars again. I really like to think I'm smarter than that old dog."

At some point, the men had to understand there would be pain they could not escape—safety nets they would not think about, bullets that would slide past body armor, bombs they would not see. That was the reality. But the conversations would always concentrate on what they could have done, or what they would have done had they known. And talking about what McGinnis had done—how much he had loved them—provided some comfort. Going out was never easy, but they understood that the men of Charlie Company would give their lives to save each other, and that meant more than anything they had encountered before in their lives.

Trying to relieve some stress, Agami and Johnson made their way to the weights set up on the porch. As they worked biceps and triceps,

Johnson unloaded his thoughts. "We all say, 'I don't know what I would have done,'" he told Agami. "But McGinnis—he proved it. Every single one of us is willing to die for somebody else."

"Strength and honor, man," Agami said, in tribute to Mock. "I'm there for you. And you know Mock's still looking out for us."

Their moods and morale ebbed and flowed depending on the day's mission. Sometimes, they felt as if they were making progress. Some days, they felt as if they were starting over. One exasperating sign of progress was that they didn't see as many bodies on the streets of Adhamiya. They went from two hundred fifty a month when they first arrived to about thirty a month by winter. Instead, the violence seemed focused on the American soldiers, as if the insurgents had figured out shooting children for violating decrees against play or women for wearing makeup wasn't winning over the citizens of Adhamiya. At about the same time, Prime Minister Nuri al-Maliki stopped backing the Mahdi army, which is Shiite and had been attacking Sunnis. But nobody seemed to mind that they attacked the Americans, and the insurgents' methods were improving.

The Americans had to be smarter, too. After the first roadside bomb, they started rolling the Bradleys out at the front and rear of convoys, figuring the bombs wouldn't do as much damage to the tracked vehicle as they did to the Humvees. Some of the soldiers, such as Chagoya and Staff Sergeant Rick Hamblin, insisted on taking the lead vehicles, because they had the most experience. Both carefully monitored their men to make sure the squads were well balanced and that the best men filled gunner or truck commander or driver positions. And every time Chagoya went out, he tried to say something to each of his men. He didn't know if he'd see them again. Events in Adhamiya constantly reminded him of that possibility.

The guys started thinking creatively to try to better their odds. Sergeant Keegan Swope, a straightforward brunette who talked so fast his sentences felt like radio announcements, was in the scout platoon. When they went out on patrol, Swope's mission was to make sure his men got to spend yet another night bitching about Apache. He tried to guess where they might be least likely to find a sniper or a roadside bomb. But from the very start, the drive from Loyalty, where they still had to travel for vehicle maintenance, to Apache always seemed to be about luck—and timing. Garbage that hadn't been removed for months, broken-down cars, and rubble hid insurgents and bombs all along the route. On the evening of December 10, Swope carefully plotted how he would bring his squad back from Sadr City, where they were helping Special Forces troops by pulling security during special-operations missions. He had based his plan on logistics and history—and gut. They all tried to follow their guts.

But while they were out, Swope heard an explosion.

"Oh, man," Swope moaned to his men, the gut feeling hitting hard, and then sinking. "Somebody got hit."

Later they heard that Charlie Company, 3-509th, 25th Infantry Division out of Alaska had traveled back using the same route Swope had mapped out. An explosively formed penetrator—the most-feared weapon in Iraq—had hit a truck. EFPs could burn through anything. They formed a molten bolt that could penetrate armor. Charlie Company—and Swope—rushed in to help. Body parts were strewn all around the truck, and they could smell meat and copper and human waste. That was the first time many of the men had seen death up close. Most of the men still believed that, at age eighteen, they were invincible. That day broke down some of the expectation that they would all live long, fulfilled lives.

The EFP had continued another hundred meters after running through the Humvee to penetrate a nearby home. The burning mass of copper landed in a bed, burning a hole through it. A retired Sunni general from Saddam's regime lived in the house. When Swope, First Lieutenant Matt Waite, and Baka cleared the house, they found that no one inside had been injured.

But Americans inside the Humvee had been.

That day saw two badly wounded men and three men killed in action, and because they were on the boundary of zone 19 and zone 20, second platoon and Swope with his scouts headed out with Baka to secure the area. The wounded men, including a man who would later die, were evacuated to Apache.

DeNardi stayed back at Apache that day, and he and the other guys heard about the explosion over the radio. As they listened, the color washed up to his high cheekbones, as it always did when something excited or scared him. He'd never seen a dead body before, and he sort of wanted to see one—just to have the experience—and sort of wanted not to. He had a reputation for a fierce curiosity, which was part of the reason the guys liked him so much, even with his sarcasm. That curiosity made the other guys feel that DeNardi was genuinely interested in them. He liked to listen. He remembered things and brought them up later, like whether someone's kid was sick or a girlfriend hadn't called.

But that day, his curiosity got the better of him.

After Charlie helped the unit evacuate back to Apache, DeNardi waited outside. The men opened the trunk of a vehicle, and DeNardi froze, unable to breathe. Just half a man had made it back. Half a dead man.

DeNardi rushed off to the side as the contents of his stomach pushed up into his throat and out into the sand.

After that, he saw bodies everywhere when he and Cardenas were moved from headquarters platoon to second platoon to fill in for casualties and began going out on more patrols. DeNardi would never have the same visceral reaction to a body again.

At the attack site, Baka and his men waited on Mortuary Affairs and a wrecker to pick up the demolished vehicle. Baka and the other company commander checked for sensitive items inside the truck, making sure their soldiers would not have to see the bodies. Then Mortuary Affairs soldiers dug through the remains to find ID tags and name tapes, and then the wrecker crew covered the vehicle with a tarp and transported it—remains and all—to Forward Operating Base Rustimiyah.

Baka wanted to better the odds of survival, and decided to start putting soldiers used to living in the city—the kids who grew up with street smarts—in the first vehicles out on patrol. They picked up on unusual activity the others had missed—a shifty glance, an odd posture, out-of-place clothing—but didn't necessarily know why someone was suspicious. Baka learned to trust it when someone said, "That guy's just bad. Let's stop him." Inevitably, they'd be right.

With the uncertainty of their effectiveness, Baka and Hendrix continued to make sure the platoon leaders and sergeants understood the goal. Every day, all the leaders would sit down to talk about the next day's mission. The routes would be mapped out and changed up often so the insurgents couldn't expect a routine. Then those leaders would go back and brief their platoons: Here's the task. Here's the preparation. And every day the sergeants would remind the men that they were there to help solve the people's problems, even if the Iraqis didn't yet trust the Americans. And even if the Americans didn't trust the Iraqis.

They soon realized McGinnis's death affected the Iraqi civilians, too. Kids—thirteen or fourteen years old—could make $50 tossing a grenade at the Americans, and when the Iraqis heard about McGinnis's heroic action, his loss saddened them. They found his story courageous, and mourned the loss of a good man. On patrols, Baka found himself trying to comfort the Iraqis, who were upset that their children could be so easily lured by money. "We have troubled kids in the United States, too," Baka told families, with Santana translating. But internally Baka seethed. Fifty dollars. Everything is motivated by money.

So Charlie Company tried to find the people who were financing the operations. Detaining the kid holding a hand grenade got them nowhere, because there were more kids and more hand grenades, and always the military police in the Green Zone would glare at Baka's men if they didn't bring in hard evidence. Sometimes, they just couldn't catch them. Bradleys aren't fast enough to keep up with a moped, and they certainly couldn't follow them through a back alley.

However, First Lieutenant Matt Martinez quickly gained a bit of a reputation for his prowess against a scooter. Usually, the guy on the moped would end up crashing, and then someone from the lead truck would leap out and chase after him. But the soldiers wore full body armor and helmets, and carried heavy weapons. Even as athletic as they all were, they had to forget it. Martinez, however, could move, and he'd launch himself at the running perpetrator, catch the tail of a shirt or the leg of a pair of pants, and take the kid down, Charlie Company cheering behind him.

But First Lieutenant Matt Waite, platoon leader for the scouts, held the record for the fastest capture. On patrol, two guys on a moped sped past the convoy. The soldiers saw the Iraqis had a pistol, but the Iraqis became so nervous at seeing the soldiers, they immediately dumped the moped. Waite jumped out of the vehicle, immediately grabbed both Iraqis and then led them to the Bradley.

The quick capture meant the scouts got to come in from patrol early to bring in their captives. But then when they went out for the second patrol of the day, Waite caught another guy within fifteen minutes.

One chase didn't go as well. As a moped flew by, the rider tossed a grenade under Baka's vehicle, and it exploded beneath Baka's seat. The grenade blew out three tires, but didn't hurt anyone inside the Humvee. Baka realized they would never catch the guy, but just in case, the platoons spread out through the nearby houses. Private First Class Michal Cieslak considered himself Baka's protector, and the attack infuriated him. He stormed into a house, kicking in doors and throwing people to the ground, and then headed to a second house to kick in more doors. When Baka walked in the first house, members of the family were cowering in a corner. Baka stalked over to the second house to see what was going on and witnessed Cieslak in action. Baka grabbed him by the body armor and dragged Cieslak out of the house.

"What the fuck do you think you're doing, Cieslak?" Baka demanded, livid at what he had just seen and refusing to allow Staff Sergeant Vincent

Clinard, who had followed them outside, to take over disciplining the soldier.

"Sir, these people are trying to kill you," Cieslak said, his eyes watering with anger and frustration. "They're trying to kill our commander."

Baka calmed down a bit at Cieslak's words, but was still pissed. His soldiers had to maintain control.

"This is war, Cieslak," Baka said. "They are trying to kill us and we are trying to kill them. The good news is the enemy blew his load tonight and no one got hurt."

Baka told Cieslak to get in the truck, and that he wouldn't be going back out on patrol until Baka cleared it.

"You're done," Baka said. "You need to go monitor the radio."

"But, sir—"

"Done," Baka said. "Go. Now."

For the next two months, Cieslak monitored the radio while his platoon went on patrol. Then Baka moved him to second platoon, where Ybay took him under his wing, and second platoon's gruff silliness made Cieslak's world make sense again. Second platoon would let him complain, but then they would pull him back in and remind him of what was acceptable.

Cieslak wasn't the only one frustrated by the rules they felt held them back. As Cardenas sat in the hallway with the computer tables one day, he and DeNardi started swapping gripes.

"We're pretty much just policemen," Cardenas said, absently running his hand back and forth across a table. "They don't let us do what we need to do. They can tell us all they want at the higher level, but we're not seeing any progress."

DeNardi nodded along and added backup vocals: "Man, I don't trust anyone," he said. "I don't even trust our 'terps. They know more than we do, but they don't say anything."

And the surge?

"What surge?" DeNardi asked. "You have two hundred men patrolling where a battalion should be—a brigade, maybe."

Pretty much everytime soldiers sat down together, that same conversation would start.

It wasn't just the younger troops who felt things would be better handled with force, but Hendrix reined them all in with reminders that they did not want to bring dishonor to the company: no unauthorized force. The frustration still led to some problems, and Cardenas complained that it was too easy to get into trouble. A week after McGinnis died, second platoon saw two guys on a moped, so they peeled out after them in the Bradleys, sending rocks flying from beneath the tracks. The moped crashed, as usual, and Cardenas and Staff Sergeant John Gregory caught the men. Cardenas saw a cardboard box sitting next to the moped, so he kicked it over. Inside, he found a grenade filled with nails. As Cardenas and Gregory loaded the men into the Bradley, the detainees "hit their heads."

A week later, Cardenas and Gregory had to go to the Green Zone to talk to a major about detainee abuse. They explained that the detainees had hurt themselves getting into the vehicle, and the soldiers made it out of the Green Zone with a heavy lecture. Eventually, they were called back in to testify against the two Iraqis.

But Cardenas came back from that meeting hot. He went down to the basement, and he threw his gear on his bunk. "They're lucky those guys didn't kill us," he complained to anyone who would listen. "Am I the bad guy? Are they going to send me to jail? That just pisses me off. They were harshly detained, and all of a sudden we're the bad guys?"

The tour in Adhamiya had gone better, behavior-wise, than the tour in Samarra. That first tour let Hendrix know his men had ethics—especially Sergeant Ryan Wood—and would do the right thing.

In Samarra, Sergeant First Class Jorge Diaz headed up second platoon, and he seemed motivated by making his men miserable. When the other platoons had four-day weekends before deploying, Diaz made his men work even on their days off rather than spend time with their families. In Samarra, he made the guys look for IEDs on foot. He forced them to pray—they didn't have a choice—before each mission.

One time, the platoon sergeant took all his soldiers to the pool for the first time since they had been to Iraq. After walking around in 100-degree-plus heat in full gear, they imagined wearing shorts and soaking up some rays. Instead, when they arrived at the pool, Diaz said, "You will participate in a fun day."

He made second platoon jump in the pool, and then instantly ordered them back out of the water. Then he took them right back to their unit, without explanation. Apparently he had been told to take his men to the pool, but didn't believe they deserved the fun time.

In October 2004, the platoon got a tip from an old woman that there was a weapons cache. "The guy next door is bad," she told them. When the platoon went to check it out, Diaz threatened a teenager with a 9 mm, blindfolded him, and cuffed him to the grill of a Humvee. He pointed the gun at him, hit him, and choked him, and then forced him to hold a smoke grenade with the pin pulled—with the boy believing it was an explosive grenade, according to court records. The soldiers eventually released the boy, but the platoon went back a second day on another tip. The elderly woman identified Thaher Khaleefa Ahmed as the leader of the local insurgency. Diaz ordered the platoon to detain Ahmed, his father, and a different kid. The soldiers bound everyone in zip ties with their hands fastened behind their backs, and then Diaz and his men searched a courtyard. They found a rifle, a machine gun, ammunition, technical manuals for Humvees, and anti-American posters.

They questioned Ahmed's father, and then Diaz told Sergeant Fernando Alvarez to help Ahmed stand up.

"Step away," Diaz told Alvarez.

Then Diaz shot the man in the face, according to witnesses. He took the man's zip ties off, reattached the zip ties so the Iraqi man's hands were secured in front of him so the man would have had more freedom of movement. Diaz later claimed the man lunged at him, and that's why he shot him.

Wood turned Diaz in.

Wood talked to CID, saying he did not witness the actual event, but he did hear a gun shot.

"I've heard both sides of the story, and one doesn't add up—at all," he told investigators.

"If he had been a different person, any of the NCOs now in the platoon, no one would have said anything," Osterman said, as he talked with Wood and Chagoya one night at Apache. "The guy he shot was a genuinely bad dude."

Diaz had served in the army for seventeen years, but during his court martial, he was reduced in rank to private and dishonorably discharged. He was sentenced to eight years in prison.

Now, in Adhamiya, Hendrix was determined not to have any more incidents like that, but he knew stress could promote aggression. At the same time, he knew men like Woody, author of "Adhamiya Blues," had the courage to keep things in check, and that made Hendrix prouder than any weapons prowess ever could. Wood was quiet about the incident, not even telling his parents. But second platoon would remember his example of moral courage.

As tensions grew, Hendrix tried to maintain Apache as a place where the guys could forget what happened outside the gates, if only for a little while. But with McGinnis's name recently added to the memorial wall, it was hard even for Hendrix to imagine a Merry Christmas. Apache still felt like a construction project. They now spent their recovery days at Forward Operating Base Taji, rather than Loyalty, because the drive wasn't as treacherous. At Taji, they slept two to a room, had a couple of dining facilities to choose from, could eat all the Burger King and Pizza Hut they could handle, and could even stop in and talk to a mental health counselor if they needed help dealing with stress. But at Apache, they didn't have heat, and at night, the temperatures dropped to freezing. And it was hard to get motivated to do much more than grieve on most days. But Hendrix wasn't one to give up, and his boys needed a break. They needed a day off. They needed good food. And they needed presents. Lots of presents.

On Christmas Eve, Hendrix grabbed headquarters platoon and rode into Taji on a mail run and to pick up Captain Edward Choi, the battalion Chaplain. Christmas morning, the guys knew something was up long before Hendrix hit Apache.

"Ho! Ho! Ho!" he yelled over the radio as they rode back in. "Merry Christmas!"

He arrived wearing a Santa Claus beard and a silly grin over his uniform. Once again, he had begged his relatives and every organization he could find for care packages. Headquarters platoon had filled the Humvees with presents and food, and not just any food. They had shrimp, turkey, crab legs, and steak. Hendrix went into full-on Bubba Gump mode: "We have pecan pies, apple pies, pumpkin pies, potato pies . . ."

They spent the day with religious services, spades competitions, video games, and singing. Hendrix went to each of his men individually.

"Merry Christmas," he told them. "I'm proud of you."

Four days later, the company again received bad news. Private First Class William Newgard had been a member of Charlie Company before the company deployed to Iraq, but had been sent to Headquarters Company after he was selected to drive for the battalion commander, Colonel Schacht. As he and Sergeant Lawrence Carter, also a member of Headquarters Company, drove in a neighborhood near Adhamiya, an IED blew up beneath their Humvee, killing them both.

Hendrix hung Newgard's picture up on the memorial wall. "He was one of ours," he told the soldiers who gathered near him.

Through the holidays, the operation tempo never slowed down. But the men started taking more risks, their attitude changing almost to a dare.

Adhamiya: Come and get me.

Late on New Year's Eve, Chagoya and his platoon were out on patrol when a daisy chain of three IEDs went off under their vehicles. The bombs did no real damage, but the insurgents immediately began hitting the soldiers with rocket-propelled grenades. The guys got out of their trucks, and Chagoya, Private First Class Edmond Leaveck, and Chief Warrant Officer Khan Rassovong crept through a palm grove to look for the enemy. The thick old trees rose up to their telltale bushy tops, leaving nothing but shadows and scrubby plants at the bases. Chagoya and the others scanned the area with their night-vision goggles. Chagoya was convinced that if there were three IEDs, there were more, and he would rather find them intentionally than accidentally.

"I see an antenna," he said. "Right there. Oh my god, that's it. That's it."

He sent the others back to the trucks. "What are you going to do, Sergeant?" Leaveck asked.

"Don't worry about it," Chagoya said. "I got this."

Chagoya didn't think about his next move, exactly. But something broke through the numbness that had been defining his days. If he allowed himself to feel, the pain of losing his friends overwhelmed everything else. Mock, his dancing partner. Sizemore, a sergeant who worked just as hard to protect and train his men as Chagoya did. And McGinnis. Every time Chagoya gave a lesson, he waited for a question from his grinning, silly private, but the questions never came.

Chagoya had put away his guitar because he could not play music without emotion. He had decided not to feel at all—not good, not bad.

Not fear.

Take me. I dare you.

After the others had walked a safe distance away, Chagoya grasped the antenna with both hands. He winced as he pulled it out of the ground.

It didn't go off.

"What the fuck are you doing, man?" Rassovang yelled.

"I figure if it's there, you may as well piss it off," Chagoya said. An insurgent had set up a dud.

"Jesus," Leaveck said, after Chagoya walked back to join the other soldiers. "Please don't do that again, man. We can't lose you, too."

Chagoya just shrugged.

"I think it's time to get back to Apache," Rassovang said. The enemy had disappeared, and Chagoya obviously needed a break: Sometimes he thought too much about the friends he had lost and not enough about the ones who remained.

When they got back to Apache, the guys had gathered in the dining area. With no heat, the cooks kept coffee, soup, and hot chocolate constantly at the ready. But that night seemed colder as they spent the holiday patrolling angry streets just after losing yet another friend.

It didn't feel like New Year's Eve.

Baka walked into the dining room to grab some coffee, but as he surveyed his men, he felt their misery. "Hey, First Sergeant," he said. "How about a little fireworks display? I think we have some weapons that need testing."

Hendrix grinned and gathered up the guys with their M-203s and rocket launchers, and they all went to the back porch. Charlie Company sent star clusters and parachute flares and tracers up into the dark, bringing back memories of home as sparks arced out and flares left streaks of red.

"Remember last New Year's?" Chagoya said, feeling somehow more alive after his encounter with the antenna. "We all met downtown and the Germans almost blew our asses up with the M-80s."

"They just go crazy with that shit," Montenegro said, grinning and remembering a plaza filled with music, people, and booze. "That was a drunk night."

Woody sent a star cluster up into the night, and they all smiled when they heard the Iraqi soldiers hooting and hollering from the other side of the outpost. DeNardi and Richardson got out their guitars, and they played sweet, soft music that reminded them of home. No shooting tonight. No explosions. Just Wood's happy grin as he moved his head from side to side, ear almost touching his shoulder as he relaxed into the music.

Private First Class Thomas Leemhuis sent another parachute flare up, and they heard their Iraqi neighbors clapping their hands. Even they had gathered as the soldiers filled the night over Adhamiya with something lovely. For a moment, the soldiers sat silently in the cold, thinking of New Years' past—of resolutions and kisses and friends.

Wood, sitting on a step, looked up at Baka.

"Sir?" he asked. "What's a star cluster for, anyway?"

CHAPTER 11
Charlie Company Continues the Battle, but Faces More Death

The men had been itching for a mission, a pure cowboy mission. So far, that was the only thing they had seen work—violence. Guns and breaking down doors and pure infantry. Everything else was pure crapshoot. Sometimes, talking to an Iraqi leader seemed to create a strong understanding. But then a known insurgent would walk through an Iraqi army checkpoint. Or the American MPs would let an insurgent go because Charlie Company hadn't collected videotape of him in the act of doing something wrong. Or a child would toss a grenade for fifty dollars.

The soldiers wanted a mission. They didn't want to drink tea; they wanted to catch insurgents. But the intelligence about where those guys were hiding often came to Charlie Company's command post after the insurgents had left their most recent house, or the mission went to the Special Forces teams to conduct in secrecy. If that happened, all Charlie could do was provide security: spread out around the target and keep the SF guys safe until their mission ended.

Most of the time they weren't invited to take part at all. Instead, Baka would go out the next day and try to explain to the mayor of Adhamiya why a couple of his houses had been ransacked by U.S. soldiers. Baka would tell him it wasn't Charlie Company, but then, one time, the mayor brought pictures to prove it was U.S. troops.

"You're right," Baka told him, knowing it was either Special Forces or SEALs. "They were Americans. I'll talk to the commander of that unit." Then he helped him with the claims process to pay for the damages, all the while trying to hold on to the trust it had taken Baka months to build.

But January 17, Charlie Company got the call to capture a leader of the Mahdi army, the Shia insurgent group, and they knew he was responsible for Mock and Newgard's deaths, as well as the recent deaths of three soldiers from another unit. For whatever reason, Special Forces couldn't perform the mission that night, and headquarters wanted it done right now. As Charlie Company cleaned weapons, gathered more ammunition, and went over the maps again and again, they raved that they would finally be able to go after people they knew were bad.

"Dude, the EFPs are made in Iran," Johnson explained to Swope as the scouts prepared to go out. "Iran is Shia. The Mahdi army is Shia. The Iraqi government is Shia. Tell me they're not all in bed together."

"OK, I get that," Swope said, strapping a knife to his calf. "But what's going on with our government? Are they in bed with them, too?"

Not exactly, Johnson explained, but if the Iraqi government were to gain control of its country so the Americans could hand over the mission, the Americans had to play some delicate politics. Both the Shia and the Sunni had to be made to feel they held the future.

But not that night.

Baka gathered his leaders. First, third, and scout platoons would go out. Second was at Taji for their usual break and maintenance activities. Baka had to make sure each man understood the importance of the mission, as well as the danger: They would drive north of Sadr City into an area not occupied by U.S. troops, a no-man's-land.

"To get this guy, we're taking three platoons," Baka told his men. "En route, if a platoon gets hit by an EFP, you're on your own."

He registered the shock in their faces—What about no man left behind?—and continued. "This mission is too critical for us to have a change of plans en route to evacuate casualties. We have to get this guy."

He did not have to push the issue. Not a man in the company could stomach the thought of Mock's killer running free. Major Zike, commander of the MiT team, would keep a quick reaction force ready at Apache in case anyone needed help.

In the middle of the night, they rolled out of the gate in a string of Bradleys and Humvees, each man on high alert. Third platoon navigated, leading the company to their target in total darkness on unmapped roads. When they arrived at their target neighborhood, one of the platoons wrapped around a block of about a dozen one- and two-story houses to provide security. The company was too far out to call into Taji with the radios, so Baka used a cell phone to call Major Don Padgett at the battalion TOC. In Baka's other hand, he held the mike for the radio to communicate with the men in his company.

As soon as his men reached one of the target houses, Lieutenant Waite, leading scout platoon, had his driver ram down the gate with his vehicle. Inside the gate, they knew several insurgents had gathered inside a building. Unknown to the scouts, the Mahdi leader had heard them breaking down the gate and scurried to the roof with his bodyguard.

Around the corner, "Gun Show" Halbasch climbed over a fence and opened a gate to let third platoon into another building south of the scout platoon.

When the platoons started entering buildings to the sounds of dogs barking and people scrambling, Padgett monitored the Mahdi army target using the unmanned aerial vehicle feed that was being sent to a large television screen at battalion. The scouts expected to find the insurgent inside the first building, but then Padgett called in with news from above: The target wasn't inside the building. He was on top of it.

"There are two guys on a roof!" Padgett told Baka over the cell phone. "He's bounding from building one to building two!" Baka repeated it to his platoons over the radio, trying to relay the message calmly, but his heart pumped wildly beneath his body armor. Back and forth over the roofs, the radio-to-cell-phone system worked like a clock. Better, each team leader had a "quarterback sleeve" attached to his forearm with

Google Earth aerial imagery. Baka had mapped out each house and given it a number so the guys would know exactly where to go during the mission.

First platoon continued to clear houses on the ground.

The other platoons raced back and forth among the houses for about an hour as the Iraqi man leaped from rooftop to rooftop. Padgett watched it all from the images the unmanned vehicle sent to Taji.

Halbasch and third platoon—Lieutenant Martinez leading them— headed up to the roof of building one, but they couldn't see anything. There was no moonlight, and with no electricity, no lights throughout the city. Through his night-vision goggles, all Halbasch saw were sheets and dishdashas and burqas hanging out on laundry lines.

In the meantime, third platoon had cleared the roof of building two. As third platoon raced back downstairs, the insurgents leaped from building one back to building two. Campos, a squad leader in third platoon, heard the call over the radio that the suspect had returned and yelled to his men, "Let's go back!" So third platoon raced back upstairs to the roof where they had just been. Private Omar Avila ran right; Private First Class Chad Chalfant went left. The guys had been teasing Chalfant all night about not being able to find anything: His eyesight was bad because of cataracts, and he had to use refrigerated eye drops every day. To go to Iraq, Chalfant had to get a medical waiver because it's difficult to guarantee refrigeration in a war zone. But if he wasn't good at spotting the details, he made up for the problem by paying attention to shapes. And one of the shapes on the roof didn't look right the second time he went up. He noticed the air-conditioning unit on the roof looked different from the way it had five minutes before.

"He's over here!" Chalfant yelled. "Hey! I've got somebody over here!"

There were two men: the Mahdi leader and his bodyguard. Campos rushed over from the corner of the roof and stuck his pistol in the insurgents' faces before the bodyguard had a chance to react. As Chalfant and

Campos held the men prisoner, they heard the rest of the squad's boots thudding across the roof to their position.

"Is this the guy?" Campos asked, his big frame towering over Chalfant and the insurgents cowering next to the air-conditioning unit. "Hey, check out the picture. Is this the guy?"

"How the hell would I know?" Chalfant said. "I can't see shit."

Avila shone a light on a photograph.

"Yeah, yeah," Avila said, laughing, as he kept his weapon up. "That's him."

They called it in to Baka and loaded the captured insurgents into a Bradley, keeping the leader separated from the other ten prisoners. The other insurgents thought he had gotten away, but the insurgent leader had sprained his ankle during that last jump to building two, third platoon's assigned building. That left him with no choice but to hide, so he had crept behind the air conditioner. As third platoon drove back to Apache, they asked Chalfant how he had found the two men.

"You were running around and you tripped over him, huh?" Avila teased. "How is the blindest guy in the unit gonna find him?"

"Fuck you, guys," Chalfant said. "I got him, didn't I?"

At Apache, they proudly handed over their find to Baka and Hendrix, who had already arrived at the outpost. The two leaders beamed at third platoon.

"Now that was an outstanding mission," Baka said, breathing freely again. A lot could have gone wrong with the night's work, but everything had gone smoothly, and in a war zone, that never happens.

But they still had work to do. Baka wanted to make certain they had the right man before they called in their accomplishment to headquarters, but all they had was a photograph of their target accepting a flag from Muqtada al-Sadr, the founder of the Mahdi army. There wasn't a lot to distinguish their target from all the other men with brown beards and white robes.

Santana, Halbasch, and Johnson were with Baka, pulling security, and all of them tried to help figure it out. As the man stood before him, Baka noticed a scar on his arm. The man in the picture seemed to be holding the flag oddly, as if he couldn't quite turn his palm up to receive it properly.

"Hey, Santana," Baka said, "ask him how he got that scar."

The man said it came from a gunshot during the Iran-Iraq war.

Then Baka had a brainstorm. "Santana, tell him we're going to play a game of Simon says. Tell him to do exactly what I do."

Baka stood in front of the man, who sat on a cot with his swollen ankle. Baka raised his hands up to his sides. "Follow him, do what he does," Santana told the man in Arabic.

The man lifted his arms.

Baka brought his hands straight out in front of his chest, palms together.

The man followed suit, seeming to believe Baka was some kind of doctor conducting a physical.

Baka brought his hands to his face, the man following exactly. Johnson snapped a picture at just the point where the man's hands would be if he had been accepting a flag from al-Sadr.

"What do you think?" Baka said, holding the digital photo next to the paper photo for comparison.

Halbasch immediately started laughing. "Yeah, that's our guy," he said.

The photos were identical.

Within an hour, the prisoners had been picked up by helicopter and delivered to the Green Zone for interrogation.

But within days, the soldiers' good mood had passed, and life had gone back to the "one step forward, two steps back" pace they had grown accustomed to. As always, they patrolled with the knowledge that they would lose more men. It always felt inevitable.

Private First Class Ryan Hill had been especially down since losing Mock and Sizemore, and he could not seem to shake the sense that they weren't accomplishing anything in Iraq, even after capturing Mock's killer. He understood the arguments from command, but his heart held on to his losses, even as he earned a reputation as a favorite with the other guys, especially Agami. Before they left Germany, the two updated their MySpace accounts daily with "Your mama's so ugly . . ." jokes until Hill's mother found out and called it off.

At that point, Agami thought he had won. But a couple of months later, when his girlfriend flew in from the States for a visit, he found out otherwise.

"I can't wait for you to meet Ryan," Agami told his girlfriend as he drove her from the airport to the barracks. "He's one of my best friends."

But when they walked into the barracks, he noticed one of the guys was wearing a jacket just like Agami's. And then someone walked by wearing Agami's pants. And favorite sweater. And hat. When they got to Agami's room, his mattress was missing.

Agami ran down to Hill's room, where he found his buddy wearing five of Agami's winter jackets. The rest of his wardrobe? Hill had sold Agami's clothes to the rest of the company. Agami had to run around the barracks for the next couple of hours buying his clothes back.

Hill had won.

He had been a bit of a troublemaker as a teenager, but like many of the others, things clicked when he joined the army. He loved making sure people were squared away, and he loved his friends.

But he still did not understand war.

Throughout the deployment, the guys told their families what they thought about Iraq on MySpace. Hill wrote, "It is walking on that thin line between sanity and insanity. That feeling of total abandonment by a government and a country you used to love because politics are fighting the war . . . and it's a losing battle . . . and we're the ones ultimately paying the price."

On January 20, Baka sat near the radio at Apache in the middle of the night as he deployed platoons and checked on missions. Then he heard the worst: There were casualties. And it was second platoon. Again.

The Humvee Hill was driving had rolled over a deep-buried IED, exploding under Hill's seat and causing him massive injuries. It severely injured Private First Class Albert Grose. Sergeant Derrick Jorcke suffered a traumatic brain injury in the explosion, and his left elbow swelled up as big as a softball. Montenegro was in a truck behind Hill's, and he immediately ran to their Humvee to help. He grabbed Grose's M-240 machine gun, set it up behind a concrete barrier, and established suppressive fire so the rest of the platoon could treat their injured men. Private First Class Timothy Ray, the platoon medic, rushed from his vehicle to Grose to stabilize him for the trip to Apache. Ybay, after a quick triage, realized Hill wasn't going to live and that Grose needed to get back to Apache immediately. He told the guys to load up Grose first.

But Jorcke, his ears ringing, his vision blurry, and his elbow firing off hot needles of pain, along with Cardenas, Sergeant Billy Fielder, and private First Class Ron Brown loaded Hill, rather than Grose, onto a litter as Ybay yelled, "One, two, three, lift!" In the confusion of the moment, both soldiers barely recognizable through blood and gear, Ybay didn't realize there had been a switch.

Baka and Hendrix ran to the aid station to wait for their men. One vehicle pulled in, and Ybay jumped out, and ran around to the back of the vehicle to get Grose. But at the aid station, Ybay found Hill inside his Humvee.

"Where's Grose?" Ybay yelled when he looked into the Humvee, sounding baffled and scared. "Where's Grose?" The men had decided on their own to load Hill into the first truck.

Realizing he hadn't another choice, Ybay helped carry Hill inside, where Sergeant Terence Kupau immediately began CPR. He continued for twenty minutes, refusing to let Hill go. As second platoon brought Grose into the station a few minutes later, Baka told Kupau to keep working on Hill, but he needed the others to help Grose, who had a hole in his chest the size of a fist from exploding shrapnel. He had a collapsed lung. The bones in his upper left arm had been shattered, leaving it as limp as a noodle.

After second platoon laid Grose out on a table, Baka and Hendrix immediately went to his side.

Shrapnel had pierced Grose's lung.

"Hold him down," Doc Whelchel told Hendrix, and Hendrix did, holding his breath as he pushed down. Grose screamed in pain and tried to get up. He started spitting up blood on his first sergeant as Hendrix pushed him back into the table. Doc Ray ran over to help hold the soldier down.

"I need to punch this guy's lung open," Whelchel said. But he couldn't get it. He forced a chest tube deep inside Grose's chest, his big hand inserted as if he were kneading bread. The lung had compressed hard, like a balloon sucked free of air, and Whelchel had to push the tube through the ribs into the space between the inner and outer lining of Grose's lung. Hendrix took another breath and pushed Grose down with all his strength. Somehow, Hendrix would need more courage to witness the blood and almost violent handling of his soldier's body than he ever needed on patrol.

Whelchel reached farther inside Grose's chest, the soldier crying out in pain.

But they all heard a whooshing of air as Whelchel reached the lining, draining the space of blood, fluid, and air, and allowing Grose's lungs to expand. The sound caused Hendrix to lose all his own breath and almost pass out, woozy from the blood and from watching the medic manipulate Grose's body. "Are you OK?" Doc DeSersa asked, staring the first sergeant down with eyes full of concern.

"I just need some fresh air," Hendrix said, and went outside to get some, thinking about the skill that emerges off the battlefield without a trace of bravado. He would always admire his medics.

As Whelchel finished up, Grose was conscious and in pain. Baka grabbed his hand. "Who do you want me to call?" he asked. He'd learned from Newland's experience that it was often best if he called the families of his wounded soldiers himself. Sometimes, army officials didn't call the correct people, and sometimes they made the injuries out to be much worse than they were, scaring mothers into thinking they would never see their sons again.

"Don't call anyone," Grose said. "I don't want to scare anyone."

Baka didn't press the issue, instead saying, "Do you mind if I pray with you?"

As Baka prayed above him, Grose immediately began to calm down. Baka figured the morphine had begun to course through his system. Grose asked if he could have some water, and Baka gave him a little to slosh around in his mouth. When Grose spit it out, his blood splattered on Baka's uniform.

"Sir, I'm so sorry," he said. "I'm so sorry."

"Grose, Grose, don't worry about it," Baka said. "It'll wash. Let's take care of you."

Baka continued to pray and to reassure his soldier after Whelchel had finished closing up his chest and stabilizing him for the trip to the Green Zone. Grose lay still the entire time.

"I'm so tired," Grose said. "I just want to close my eyes."

"Promise me you won't close your eyes on the helicopter," Baka said, getting right next to Grose's face and demanding that the soldier look at his commander. "Promise me."

As the medics took Grose off to the helipad to await a flight to the Green Zone, Baka turned to Whelchel. "Man, I'm glad you got him the morphine when you did," Baka said. "He looked like he was hurting bad."

"We couldn't give him morphine," Whelchel said. "His heartbeat was too slow."

Grose had calmed down just as Baka had placed his hand on the soldier's shoulder and began to pray—"spiritual morphine," the men liked to call it. It could have been a placebo effect of a soldier sure he would receive morphine, or perhaps purely the calming effect of having his commander standing nearby, ordering him to fight. Baka, however, felt certain it was the prayer itself.

Grose made it to the Green Zone, and would wait for the Blue Spaders back home. Hill, despite all the life Kupau had breathed into his lungs, died. He was the first of twenty service members to die that day, the deadliest day in Iraq to that point.

"IEDs have no names on them," Wood said in the dining room the next morning, as the guys tried to console each other. "They just happen." Beyond having their hearts broken, once again, that particular IED shook the men. Before, the blasts had blown out tires or, in Ladue's case, hit the engine block and destroyed his foot. But the blasts were getting bigger, and by burying them rather than hiding them in garbage, the insurgents could place a bigger bomb. With snipers, the soldiers had a chance. Even in battles with men dressed as civilians, Charlie Company's soldiers could make decisions based on behavior. But the deep-buried bombs on roads didn't offer the soldiers a chance to evade based on intelligence, agility, or attentiveness. Every time the men went out of the gate at Apache, they knew their lives depended on chance. With IEDs, there would be no opportunity to fight for each other.

Ultimately, the blasts happened to every man in the company, though the majority of the bombs just shook them around or blew out tires. Some guys were in vehicles that hit IEDs as many as a dozen times. Most of the men had already been blasted at least twice. Beyond the usual blown tires, a more sinister, silent injury—just beginning to be understood by the men—could affect the rest of their lives. Often, after a blast, the guys would jump from their Bradleys or Humvees with bleeding ears, headaches, and fuzzy vision, the classic symptoms of a head injury. Even if they didn't slam into a windshield or wall, the blast waves would travel through the brain, causing burst blood vessels. In football, the guys knew the injuries as "concussions." In the military, they call them "traumatic brain injuries." Most people heal within days, but still should not go back out on patrol until given the go-ahead by a doctor. This is because a second injury—especially for a young brain, because they don't fully develop until age twenty-four—could kill them. In some people, headaches and vision problems may follow for months. Others, like Newland, would stutter, have seizures, and suffer short-term memory loss, possibly for the rest of their lives.

But even if the soldiers of Charlie Company knew the risks of the IEDs, they refused to stop going back out because of a little headache. After every explosion, a medic took the shaken through a series of questions and a quick short-term memory test. But all the guys had memorized the test. All of them continued to go out unless they were so obviously rattled that others could see the symptoms. They would not let their friends go out alone.

Baka allowed second platoon some time to recover from Hill's death, and Jorcke needed time to recover from his concussion, which had been so obvious even a memorized test couldn't put him back on patrol.

For Hill's memorial, Hendrix once again carefully arranged boots and dog tags and helmet, and then gathered his men to honor another friend.

Several of Hill's friends stood in front of the rest of the battalion to tell their stories, funny stories, usually. They tried to celebrate the lives of their friends even as they mourned them. But all of the memorial speeches concentrated on how much they loved each other.

"I know that right now he is in a better place," Agami said, his eyes bright with tears and determination. "A place where he's watching over us with Staff Sergeant Sizemore, Sergeant Mock, Specialist McGinnis, and Private First Class Newgard, making sure we are all safe and we get home to our families without a scratch or any harm. Hill would want us all to be as careful as possible: Don't lose hope and keep our moral high. If we lose our bearings now, then more tragedy will happen. Hill always thought we had the best company in the battalion, so let's show Hill and the other brave soldiers we have lost that we will continue our mission until mission complete.

"I love you, Hill. You will always be in my heart forever."

The men didn't have much time to process loss or fear. They simply did not have enough men to take time off. Baka's platoons were shrinking: Four men had died. Four were being treated for combat stress. Six had gone home wounded. And each platoon had to give up four men for the new Iraqi joint security stations, where they would work with the Iraqi police.

The mission, however, continued. Baka met with the Iraqi army colonel, a Sunni who had worked hard to improve the relationship between the citizens of the town and the Shiite soldiers under his command. Hill's death angered the colonel, and as he and Baka sat in the colonel's office on the palace side of the COP, he fed Baka information he hoped could be used to investigate Hill's death. Baka always felt he could trust this man, but how could he pass that feeling back to his men? How could he convince them they were still dealing with just "4,000 shitheads" in a town that wanted nothing to do with the insurgents?

Many of the young men had joined the insurgents because they couldn't find a job. Those same men later found work with the Iraqi army or police, and that was part of the counterinsurgency plan: Bring them over to the American side. That didn't lead the Americans to trust their Iraqi counterparts any better. But if the motivation for picking one side over the other were truly money, and the former insurgents had jobs, new uniforms, and respect from their families, then there should be less of a problem, the soldiers reasoned. Surrounded by Shiite neighborhoods, the Sunnis fought everybody, including the U.S. Army. At some point, Baka told his men, the insurgents would grow tired, and even more of them would join the ranks of the Iraqi army and police.

Baka knew his best defense against pure helplessness was the children. Hand a soldier a box of soccer balls and send him out to talk to the kids, and he's going to have a good day.

He told Charlie Company they needed to convince the children to go back to school. The soldiers spent several days with the teachers—all women—at the local elementary school. "Tell us what you need," the platoon leaders asked them. School supplies, security, they were told. This stunned the soldiers. All they needed was supplies? The school's windows had been broken, and the trash had piled up. A mortar had hit the school early on and killed a couple of little girls, reminding the soldiers of other little girls in mismatched clothing who followed them on their patrols, begging for candy, learning army slang, and giggling. But the teachers refused to leave the school while there was a chance the children would return, even as they received death threats from the insurgents for daring to work with the Americans.

One of the soldier's wives organized a school-supply drive. Soon, backpacks full of pencils, paper, and teddy bears filled a small room at Apache. The children began to return to school, new backpacks in tow, which fed the soldiers a much-needed mark of accomplishment. Better, if the insurgents told the children not to go to school that day—a clear sign that there would be an attack nearby—the teachers would call the cell phone at the company command post.

As the children returned to school, the parents became more hopeful, too. School speaks of the future, of a time when those children will grow up to be lawyers or sheikhs or teachers, but not insurgents. Not suicide bombers. Not victims.

When the platoons went out, they handed out tip cards with the cell phone number on them, and told the locals they could call anonymously if they saw something happening. Usually, the tips came from somebody pissed at a neighbor, who then enjoyed watching that neighbor woken in the middle of the night and his house searched for naught. But sometimes, Charlie Company received good information.

As the insurgents continued to fight for control, street gangs made up of small-fry thugs began to spring up throughout Adhamiya. They wrestled for control of power supplies or of who could walk down which street. Or they took captives hoping for ransom money. Eventually, Charlie was able to get rid of a lot of the gangs, but even that came with mixed feelings: Was it a success for the Americans or for the insurgents? One step forward or two steps back? As the local bullies grew powerful, the insurgents would go after them because the amateurs were bringing the heat down on everybody. One particularly virulent thug led a group that robbed and kidnapped people and took over their homes. Charlie Company looked for the gang leader everywhere, and then put out the word: We're going to lock this city down 24-7 until we find him. Within a week, the soldiers received pictures of the thug. He'd been shot through the skull.

Though the Americans didn't promote vigilante activity, no one was disappointed to see the body count go down even farther by February.

Sometimes, as Charlie worked to promote good relations with the locals, outside units would come into their sector either looking for trouble or without doing their research. One day, Lieutenant Waite heard some MPs on the radio as he and Lieutenant Martinez sat in the company command post with Baka. The MPs, based in the Green Zone, were conducting hospital checks throughout Baghdad, and had found themselves in Adhamiya. "Do they know where they are?" Martinez asked Baka, incredulously. Within seconds, they heard that the MPs had a casualty, and then nothing. A soldier had been shot in the leg and the bullet lodged in his testicle. Within twenty minutes, MPs had brought the injured soldier to Apache, but they came in through the Iraqi army side, rather than the side closest to the aid station. They had to carry the soldier to the aid station. Baka and Waite didn't find out the MPs had decided to bring their casualty to Apache until he showed up in the aid station, where the medics stabilized the terrified young man and then called in a medevac flight to the Green Zone.

A few days later, a Stryker platoon rolled in, seemingly random but probably pogues looking for action they couldn't find in their own sector; they said they were there to clear a section of houses. "They're just bebopping around the streets," Waite said, again sitting next to Baka at the command post. "No way did they check this neighborhood out first."

Baka took another sip of coffee and shook his head, maps spread out on the plywood table in front of him. "I didn't ask for this help," he muttered. "Cowboys. I need to put up No Trespassing signs."

About thirty minutes later, they heard that a grenade had been tossed into one of the Strykers. "I told them, man," Baka said. He'd told everyone—brigade-wide—every chance he had. "They need turret shields made out of Hesco baskets. People just don't get it until it happens to them." Then he wondered if the platoon leaders and truck commanders had reconned the aid station at Apache, as Baka had advised, or at least checked their position on a map. The Stryker unit had eight people injured in the blast from the grenade. One truck commander drove right to the front gate of Apache and straight to the aid station. He had checked a map before he went on patrol. The other Strykers all went to the back gate, where the Apache medics actually had to drive out to the helipad to work on the injured men near their vehicles because the Strykers couldn't get to the aid station that way. When the medevac crews landed, the Apache medics worked as debris flew from the rotor wash and was embedded in open wounds.

But even when Charlie Company had learned a lesson and come up with a solution, circumstances seemed to pile up against them. Specialist Chad Marsh had joined the Junior Army Reserve Officer Training Corps while he was in middle school, and knew early that all he wanted to do was be with other soldiers, even though he caught constant hell from them. The man had no common sense, but his sense of humor was so quick that his platoon mates couldn't help but laugh even when Marsh made ridiculous errors.

Staff Sergeant Christopher Cunningham sent Marsh on a simple task one day when the platoon was recovering at FOB Taji: Go get us some pizza. The platoon had to inventory their equipment, and the platoon leaders stressed about missing gear and broken vehicles. But pizza, they were sure, would fix everything. And Taji had a Pizza Hut.

Marsh happily set about his task, ordering up several pizzas, and then walking back over to their living area. He walked with the pizzas stacked sideways—vertically—under his arm as if he were carrying schoolbooks.

"No fucking way did you just do that," Cunningham said, as he watched Marsh walk in the door of their hooch.

"Man, what the hell's wrong with you?" Staff Sergeant Jeremy Rausch asked, hands palms up in disbelief.

They all watched as the knowledge dawned on Marsh's face.

And then he grinned.

"What?" Marsh said. "Didn't you all want your toppings on the side?"

The guys could not help but laugh loudly at Marsh's humor and his silly lack of common sense. They knew it was not intentional, but sometimes it seemed that Marsh might be better suited as a bumbling college professor. As they tried to reconnect strings of cheese with slabs of dough, Rausch looked at Marsh and shook his head.

"Man, you're so lucky you're funny," Rausch said. "You had about two seconds before someone kicked your ass."

Marsh laughed, pieced together his dinner, and knew that—even with his boneheadedness—he belonged.

On February 17, Baka flew into Baghdad International Airport after going home on leave to meet his new daughter, Hannah, who had been born the day Charlie Company moved to Adhamiya. As Baka sat at the airport waiting for a ride back to Taji, Marsh rode out on patrol as gunner in his platoon sergeant's Humvee with third platoon. Someone tossed a grenade at Marsh, and it went straight for the Hesco basket. But the welding had come loose during all their trips on rough roads and over IEDs. Instead of bouncing away, the grenade lodged between the turret and the basket, and then it exploded.

Rausch hadn't been on patrol that day, so he rushed to the aid station to wait for Marsh's truck after he heard the call come in over the radio. Sergeant First Class Widmark Quashie, Marsh's platoon sergeant, flung open the back door of the Humvee when they arrived at Apache. He gently picked up Marsh as if the young soldier were a child. Blood poured down Quashie's uniform.

"Wake up!" he yelled at his soldier. "You have to hang in there! We've got you, Marsh. We're back at the aid station. Please wake up?"

Rausch watched as the medics tried to stop the bleeding, to breathe life back into Marsh. They pumped his chest over and over, getting a pulse, and then losing it.

Marsh had lost too much blood after the blast. He died at Apache with Hendrix at his side.

Newland waited for his friend's body when it arrived in Germany so he could escort Marsh home to his family. Newland used his cane, and the scar on his jaw still showed vivid and red and raw. Shrapnel wounds ran up his arms. But he was proud to escort his friend. The sad journey marks one of the greatest honors a soldier can perform, and no one understood better than Newland what Marsh had seen during his tour in Iraq. Newland made sure every second of Marsh's trip home was perfect, and every chance he got, he sat with his soldier's coffin, making sure Marsh was not alone, talking to him as if he were alive about their friends and the love they shared and how much Newland would miss him. At the end of the trip, Army officials told Newland he could not escort any more friends home. A broken soldier, he no longer presented the correct image. That's when Newland decided he wanted to leave the army.

At the end of February, the rain slowed. It had come down in sheets, leaving the sand a slimy, living mass that covered their boots and stiffened their uniforms. Patrols morphed into exercises in keeping weapons dry and searching out the enemy from beneath dripping helmets and behind drenched goggles. Hendrix had his men build more rooms that they attached to the house near the porch, hoping the hard work—and added privacy—might help them through their grief. Hendrix checked in on them daily and continued to play video games and organize card game tournaments. He listened when they needed him and offered advice to his sergeants about lowering stress levels in the men. But some days it felt as if things couldn't get worse. On those days, they assumed it would. It was as if they were all waiting for the day when they would suffer a catastrophic loss, when an explosion would take out an entire vehicle and kill everyone inside. Every time they left Apache, the thought rode along with them.

As the men of Charlie Company continued to try to build connections, a platoon from the 630th Military Police Company began working with the Iraqi police at the joint security stations in zones 18 and 19. They also had come from Germany—Bamberg—and they saw Charlie Company often out on patrols and when they went into the bigger bases. And some of Charlie's men had been assigned to help man those security stations.

On the night of March 3, the MPs pulled patrol on Route Absolut. Baka had traveled the same route three hours earlier that afternoon on a trip to Taji to meet with the battalion commander. But within an hour of his trip, something had changed. As the MPs drove from the Iraqi police station to the Iraqi police checkpoint, one of the Humvees hit a deep-buried IED. The truck flipped and immediately caught on fire. The soldiers in the other Humvees could do nothing more than watch because the flames were too hot, and because it quickly became apparent that the three soldiers inside hadn't survived. Numb, they watched, trying to get closer, trying to save friends they had lost, needing to do something, anything.

Charlie Company rushed in to help, but there was little they could do beyond provide security and help recover the bodies. Baka, Hendrix, Major Padgett, and Sergeant Major McClaflin rode in to help, trying to pick up pieces in the dark so the insurgents would have nothing to claim as trophies. Baka and Hendrix found a hand in the rubble, and Baka turned to the MP platoon leader. "Your soldiers don't need to see this," he said gently. "Why don't you let us take care of it."

The scenes were always horrific, but the Blue Spaders couldn't close out the smells this time—engine oil, gasoline, and the raw scent of a meat market. Baka sent most of his men to clear houses nearby with the MPs, while others formed a circle around the burned Humvee so Charlie Company could continue to work. The MPs hadn't had any losses to that point. They theorized it was because they didn't live in the neighborhood and weren't considered a threat. Baka's men wondered if the IED had been meant for Charlie Company. They tried not to think about the work they had to accomplish that night. Charlie Company gathered intelligence about the blast. At four in the morning, Baka helped dig through the ashes for any last remains.

Eventually, Baka assigned Charlie Company men to guard the scene and called in a personnel recovery team to finish gathering the remains in the morning.

Sergeant Brandon Parr, Sergeant Michael Peek, and Sergeant Ashly Moyer died that night. Moyer's grave lies next to McGinnis's at Arlington National Cemetery.

CHAPTER 12
A Change of Command Brings a Taste of Progress

Captain Baka knew when he left Germany that he would leave his men midtour. After twenty-one months in command, he would have to let someone else have a turn, a situation he found repulsive. He had more command experience than any other captain in the battalion, and that's why his company had taken the toughest sector. Now, not only would Charlie Company lose a leader they knew, understood, and trusted, they would gain a captain who had never served as a company commander.

The thought left Baka feeling sick at the core, and he talked about it often to Hendrix and Maravilla. "Captain Strickland has got to get his twelve months in before he heads off to Colorado to be a rocket scientist," Maravilla teased.

Baka smiled a little at the reference. Cecil Strickland was Baka's replacement, and in reality he wasn't a bad match. He had come up through the enlisted ranks, earned all the tabs—airborne, ranger, air assault—and then went to Officer Candidate School, just as he had planned to do since he joined the army. He had served tours in Iraq and Afghanistan, and he saw command of an infantry company in the sandbox as a dream tour. He had even gone through basic training with First Sergeant Hendrix. And he was, in fact, an engineer interested in aeronautical engineering, which was exactly what Baka had majored in, as well.

But Strickland's qualifications weren't the point. Baka had bonded hard with his men, and they would follow him anywhere. He knew their families. He had called their parents. He had answered questions from mothers who always started right at the top with the company commander instead of following the chain of command.

Just as important, he knew Adhamiya, had made connections with the city leaders, knew who could be trusted, and understood exactly what his men faced every time they went out on patrol.

The idea of leaving midtour was ludicrous. At the battalion level and above, the army had rules mandating that commanders stay with their troops for an entire tour with exceptions only for emergencies. But at the company level, the rules seemed more about making sure every captain had combat command experience to add to his résumé.

Baka continued a campaign he had begun a month after he arrived in Adhamiya: At every opportunity, he made his way to Lieutenant Colonel Schacht's side. He made the same argument to his confidants, and Hendrix heard it as often as anybody else. But Schacht could take it to Colonel J. B. Burton, the brigade commander.

Schacht forced Baka to take a one-day break at Taji every two weeks, realizing that Baka would work every day if left to his own devices. At Taji one day, on one of those breaks, Baka spotted his boss eating lunch at the D-Fac, or dining facility, and sat down next to him.

"Sir, you've got to let me keep my men," Baka said, the words coming out before he had quite settled into his chair.

Schacht smiled as if he had known it was coming. "Now, Mike, you know we've been over this," he said, taking another bite of burrito. "There's nothing we can do about it now. Besides, I need you at battalion."

Baka would be working in the S-1 shop, taking care of awards and promotions and unit citations. "But, sir, you don't take the coach out in the middle of the game. My men have fought too hard to start over with someone who doesn't know the field."

"I understand, Mike," Schacht said. "But Strickland needs the experience."

Baka had almost not come to Iraq with Charlie Company. Its

deployment date kept getting delayed, and at one point, it had even been canceled. For his personal career, he had worked to get into graduate school, had even lined up a gig teaching math classes at West Point, if he could just get that master's degree. If he got into graduate school, he had permission to remain behind when the company was deployed, since he was due to give up command of Charlie Company in December 2006 anyway. But in July, while in the field, the battalion was notified that it would deploy within two weeks. Three days before he was due to ship out, Baka found out he had been approved to go to Georgia Tech. By then, he had already talked Schacht into letting him remain in command of Charlie Company until December, only part of the way through what they believed would be a ten-month tour. So he turned down Georgia Tech and deployed with his men and persuaded Schacht to allow him to stay until the spring.

Now Schacht tried to reassure Baka: After Baka left Charlie Company in March, it would only be three more months, and then they'd all be home. Baka would be nearby to offer assistance to Strickland if he needed it. And Baka could still, occasionally, see his men.

Baka went back to Apache prepared to say his goodbyes and to try to boost his men's confidence—and morale. He spent his last week sleeping two or three hours a night as he finished up recommendations for Bronze Stars and promotions. When Strickland arrived, Baka introduced him to his men, showed him the routes, took him out on patrol, and tried to prepare him for the worst.

He tried to prepare his men for the best.

On a sunny March day during his last week in command, Baka went out with first platoon. The patrol had been unusually quiet, and Baka felt as if he were taking one last look. Children giggled on their way to school. Women in *abaya* swooshed toward the market square. Men rode bicycles to work. Much of the garbage was gone from the streets. The platoons had gone down from one hostile encounter per patrol to about one a day—still high, but it felt like progress. They saw fewer bodies with each passing week.

Baka had his men stop so he could say goodbye to the head of the Adhamiya District Council, Mudhafer al-Ubaidi, and he found himself getting choked up. Baka would miss these people.

If the people of Adhamiya seemed sad to see Baka go, his men mourned openly. The mood on that patrol was dour, and Baka didn't want to go out that way. Usually, they rode in their vehicles to an area and then dismounted to knock on doors and talk to the neighbors and then got in their vehicles for the ride back to Apache. Walking any more than necessary invited trouble—or death. But Baka needed his men to understand how far they'd come.

He gathered them around him.

"First platoon!" he said, eyes bright and jaw set. "We're going to walk it back in."

Baka would have said it again just to get another look at the stunned faces and complete silence that followed his statement.

"Ah, sir?" Halbasch said. "We're going to *run* it back in?"

The guys laughed nervously, hoping Baka would join them and say he was kidding.

He wasn't. Walking would make them more vulnerable, but they could react quickly. And it would boost their confidence. Baka had his driver radio in to Apache, "Open the gate! We're walking in."

At the command post, the platoon leaders immediately assumed something was wrong: Were the vehicles blocked? Blown up?

"Follow me!" Baka shouted, and headed up the street, a street that had seen battles and blood and bravery. Suddenly understanding, the men strutted after him. The vehicles followed behind as first platoon grinned at kids, waved at women in windows, and kept a wary eye on the alleyways.

As they entered the gate, chests out, weapons raised in the air in triumph, the rest of Charlie Company gathered to watch. Men stood on Bradleys and in the roadway to the motor pool, cheering and yelling out, "Hooah!"

Baka's guys gathered around him, slapping his shoulders as he grinned in the midst of his soldiers. "Good work, men," he said, laughing at their excitement. "No one can get up on that."

On Baka's last night in Adhamiya, he still hadn't written his change-of-command speech, and bags had formed under his eyes for lack of sleep. They'd been conducting clearance missions every night since March 3, when the MPs had lost their three soldiers, and because Baka always went out with his men, he went out again that night. They'd had a tip: A young man had called and said he had information he wanted to share with the Americans.

When they arrived at the house, the human intelligence team and an interpreter went into a side room with the young man. He had already told them his father was upset with him for giving the soldiers information because he feared it would bring trouble for the family. The young man figured the family already had trouble—the whole neighborhood did—and there was no chance for a better future if the young people didn't start stepping up. Hendrix, Baka, and a couple of the soldiers remained in the living room with the father, who sat scowling on a couch.

The family was Sunni, and the father probably a former Ba'ath Party member. The soldiers had a choice: They could sit there in silence, trying not to look conspicuous with their M-4s and body armor while the man glowered at them. Or they could try to connect.

Baka's Arabic had improved since his one year college foreign-language class because of the practice he'd had in Iraq. "Good evening," Baka said, tossing out basic phrases as if he'd been doing it for years. "My name is Mike Baka."

The man's eyebrows flew straight into the air, and he leaned forward a bit. He responded with his own name. Baka asked him about the pictures of family members on the walls. The man got up, grabbed a couple of frames, and sat down closer to Baka. He immediately started talking about a son who had been killed in the war against Iran. As he spoke, Baka translated for Hendrix and his men. They each talked about their own families, with Baka pulling out pictures of Cathy and the girls. For forty-five minutes, they laughed and told stories, all in very basic Arabic, but that was part of the appeal: Baka had clearly taken the time to learn about the man's culture.

Soon, the man told Baka he was worried about his son, that he was young and would take risks that would get him killed. Baka reassured him that no one would find out he had talked with the Americans. The company went to different homes every night, and even those not willing to help received a visit, so the Humvees at the front door wouldn't give anything away.

When his son appeared in the doorway, after talking with the human intelligence team, his father stood up, smiling and arms widespread.

"Come, meet my friends," the Iraqi man said. "Captain Baka studied Arabic in America. There are good people there."

Before they left the house, Baka and the Iraqi man exchanged contact information.

"Come back in a couple years when things are good," the man said. "Please bring your family."

"I hope for a day that Iraq will be safe to visit as a tourist and not as a soldier," Baka replied. "Inshallah."

God willing.

CHAPTER 13
Charlie Company's Leaders Look for Signs of Combat Stress

When Hendrix returned to his bunk after Baka's chain-of-command ceremony, he found several condolence cards spread out across his comforter. "What the hell?" he mumbled, a little emotional from the ceremony.

He—and everyone else—had teared up during the battalion commander's speech.

"There is an intensity about this company," Schacht told Baka's men as they stood in the sunshine at Apache in front of country and company flags flapping in the wind. "It's focused; it's all about business; and it operates with a mind-set that no mission is too difficult, no sacrifice is too great. A company doesn't just get this way by chance: Mike has set the right command climate and tone in this team.

"He is a leader who cares about soldiering, lives it every day, and more importantly, does something about it. His personal presence on the battlefield, his mentorship, coaching and team building can be seen standing in the ranks today."

Baka had cried in front of his men for the first time as he gave his own speech, leaving his soldiers with no choice but to follow their leader with their own chorus of sniffles. In his room, Hendrix tried to regain control of his emotions.

As usual, his soldiers were there to help.

Hendrix picked up an envelope and tore it open. "First Sergeant Mom," it read. "We're sorry you and dad couldn't work it out. We promise to tell the judge we want to live with you if Captain Dad fights for paternity rights."

Hendrix chuckled as he sat on his bunk to read the rest of the messages, figuring DeNardi must have been the one with the foresight to hit the Hallmark section on their last run to Taji. He guessed the others: Sergeant Jeremiah Grubb, Wood, and Cardenas. He could hear the conversation at the PX now: "What's he gonna do to us?" DeNardi would have said. "Make us do push-ups?" The men did push-ups out of pure boredom, and they all knew Hendrix enjoyed the ribbing. This time, they'd picked a good day for it.

Hendrix would miss his captain, and he knew he had to be the one to provide continuity to his men. He would have to step in to make sure the new CO understood personalities when he made decisions. He would have to speak up if Strickland wanted to send the guys into an area without realizing they'd need clearance operations to come along and look for bombs. He'd have to remind the officer fresh from a battalion office when the guys needed a break.

Strickland had told Hendrix their whole mission was about to change, and the men would be restricted by new policies coming down from Big Army—that's what the soldiers called the policy makers at the Pentagon—and the fledgling Iraqi government. Everything was changing, and Hendrix would have to act as mortar in the bricks to hold everything together.

But some situations were out of his control. Back home, things were starting to unravel for some of the families. Bills didn't get paid. Women moved back to the States. Children had ear infections, cars had dead batteries, and toilets needed plunging. And everybody was lonely. Unlike past wars, the guys could communicate with their families instantly, rather than waiting for weeks for a letter. If that letter was late, blame it on the military mail system. But in Adhamiya, if someone missed a daily phone call or e-mail, the folks back home assumed the worst had happened.

Those phone calls could cause a jarring disjointedness. In the hallway one day, DeNardi and Cardenas typed up e-mails while one of their sergeants talked to his wife. They had just gotten back from patrol, and they'd hit a small IED that knocked out a tire. No one was injured, but a couple of them had headaches, and they'd had to replace the tire on the Humvee when they got back in, leaving them with much less time to rest between patrols.

The sergeant's phone conversation started off easily enough with the usual "sweetie" and "miss you" and "everything's fine." When his wife asked what the sergeant had done that day, he told her it was the same thing as the day before.

"You guys don't really do anything, do you?" she teased.

"You know what? Let me tell you about my day," the sergeant said, and then proceeded to give details about almost getting blown up.

"I can't listen to this," she said from the other end. "You know you just scare me. Please don't tell me."

They had all experienced the "shutdown" where they needed to talk about the horrors they'd seen, but either the person on the other end said she couldn't take hearing it, or the soldier decided he didn't want to burden his family with the details.

"God, honey, I'm sorry," the sergeant said, elbow on a table, forehead in his hand. "It's been a bad day."

She moved on quickly, from bombs to taking care of the baby to cleaning the house that morning to an accident with the family pet.

"You know what?" the sergeant said. "I really don't give a shit that the dog pissed on the carpet."

DeNardi and Cardenas, single and beholden only to their mothers, snorted as they tried to hold back laughter, and their sergeant shot them a nasty look—causing only more laughter.

"I'm out here in the middle of hell and you can't take care of that crap yourself?" he yelled into the phone. "What the hell do you want me to do?"

The conversation devolved from there, and even DeNardi stopped laughing. Without face-to-face interaction, it grew harder to recover from emotional phone calls, misinterpreted e-mails, or unreasonable suspicions.

So Charlie Company started the Wall of Shame—a place to honor the women who had cheated with other men, stolen combat pay, or moved out while their husbands were at war. Metaphorically, the wall had been created during their tour in Samarra when two soldiers checked out the webcams that a club back home in Germany had featured on its Web site. "Dude, isn't that your wife?" one of them asked, pointing to a woman dancing too closely with another soldier.

With only one year between rotations, the men often married hastily because they wanted the stability of a relationship while they were in Iraq. But those quickie relationships didn't have much to fall back on when things got tough. Or the marriages had already been rocky before they left home. Sometimes the loneliness just seemed too hard to overcome after six or seven months.

Staff Sergeant Jacob Richardson, twenty-six, could act as Charlie Company's poster child for things that could go wrong on a deployment. Undeniably gentle, his spirit slumped with each bit of violence until his brown eyes always looked down and his smile only came with raw, sad irony. Part of it was because his wife had been added to the Wall of Shame.

He had married her at the end of 2005, after meeting her while on leave back home in Arizona. He tried to make a call from the hallway, but she didn't answer. Pulling out the pictures Richardson always carried in his wallet, he explained why he liked her to Osterman and the others waiting for the phone. "She was really nice, real patient, with a sweet attitude," he said, tucking a bit of chew into his lip. "She was a little shy at first." After eight months, they decided they wanted to be together, so they got married. She moved from Arizona to Germany. The day she arrived in Germany was the day Charlie Company got notice they would deploy to Iraq within two weeks. Richardson flew through sheaves of paperwork and a flurry of appointments to make sure she had a home and a car and knew people who could help her.

But things quickly fell apart after he left Germany.

He had called home in September, but he got a message in German saying his phone had been shut off. Then he started to get letters from the bank: His account was overdrawn. He'd written his wife several checks for $300, expecting that they would last through the deployment. She'd crossed out "$300" and written in "$900." By Christmas, she had moved back to Arizona. "Now my account's dry, the electricity's off, and I owe eight hundred euros for utilities," Richardson told his friends. But he refused to say anything bad against her, hoping only that she would be there when he got home.

His friends had no problem denouncing her. "Man, you have to take care of yourself," Osterman told him. "She's taking everything you have and it's stressing you out. How are you going to do your job here if you're thinking about what she's doing back home?"

"I can do both, man," Richardson said, and then laughed a little after spitting into his chew bottle. He quickly changed the subject away from his wife. They'd talked about this before, and he always came away angry at his friends for talking bad about the woman he loved. So he switched to a safer topic: trying to take care of soldiers.

"Remember when that combat stress team came out here?" he said.

For the first time in the history of the U.S. Army, medical command had begun sending out three-person teams to the smaller COPs to try to talk to the guys about stress. The idea was that the team would stay with the unit long enough to get to know them, which would, in theory, allow the guys to feel comfortable asking for help. At Apache, the mental health team taught the guys deep-breathing exercises and had them place their hands on each other's stomachs to make sure they were inhaling properly.

"Yeah, me and Halbasch do that all the time," DeNardi said, not bothering to turn around from the computer. "Honey, I'm stressed out. Would you touch my belly?"

Not only were twenty-year-old infantrymen not going to get into any metaphysical woo-woo bullshit, they were convinced that nothing as simple as breathing in through the nose and out through the mouth could free them of their fears and nightmares and grief.

"That was worthless," Richardson said, shaking his head. "Those guys don't deal with the stuff we deal with. My guys see a lot of stuff they don't want to see or don't want to remember: Picking up body parts. Seeing blood on a wall after an explosion. Seeing a bloody handprint where somebody tried to escape. Remember when they asked if we get yelled at a lot by our sergeants?"

"Yeah, 'Hey, how 'bout every five minutes?'" DeNardi said.

"Dude, you know you beg for it," Halbasch said, punching DeNardi in the shoulder. "Not everybody gets yelled at every five minutes."

Though the soldiers dismissed the yoga tactics, they all tried to look out for one another in other ways. They had to. For all the talk of getting rid of the stigma associated with combat stress or PTSD, they knew what happened to the guys who fell out. Most of the men called them quitters, and the emotion ran close to hatred: How could you desert us? If you don't go out, somebody else has to take your place.

And a lot of old-school leaders believed that if they sent their soldiers to the mental health team, they were going to lose a warm body. There would be one less person to pull guard duty and slip into the patrol schedule. But in this war, stressed troops went to the unit for only a couple of days—"three hots and a cot"—and then straight back to their company.

In Charlie Company, Hendrix watched to see who needed to be moved or pulled out for a while and then made the changes without letting on that it was because a particular soldier had seen too much. He made sure everybody knew he had made the decision, not the soldier.

According to the army's own statistics, one out of five combat veterans deals with depression or symptoms of post-traumatic stress disorder: nightmares, flashbacks, insomnia, inability to be in crowds, inability to focus, inability to reconnect with friends and family. And it makes sense. When they're in combat, the soldiers have to focus fully on the immediate danger, which doesn't leave time for thinking about all the positive things in their lives. They grieve for their friends and worry that if they stop focusing on that grief, they dishonor their dead. They replay each situation over and over, trying to figure out what they could have done to get the grenade out of McGinnis's truck, or spot the sniper who hit Sizemore, or change the route to avoid the IED that killed Hill.

Some men won't go to their leaders because they're afraid they will be called wimps, or they might be too intimidated to approach someone who holds more rank and seems fearless in any situation. But Richardson, though he knew his job well and his men respected him, did not intimidate. He encouraged his men to talk. If they came from a rough patrol, he'd say, "Man, that was gross. Did you see that?" He tried to talk mental health in terms that felt right to a kid who had to go back out the next day and see another body.

He watched for signs of stress in his first platoon squad. Some men were normally quiet, but when they grew frightened, they talked a lot. Others who normally moved quickly suddenly slowed down. On one patrol, Richardson noticed a soldier frenetically tapping his foot. He pulled him out for a couple of days, had him pull guard duty at Apache instead of patrolling. When Richardson put the kid back in, he was back to his normal, cheerful self.

The medics took on the brunt of the mental health work, and they watched out for each other. Most of the men tried to create some sort of privacy in their living areas, but the medics did the opposite: They tore down the walls. They had a room inside the aid station, and they pushed their bunk beds up against the walls, leaving a communal middle area where they played card games, cleaned their weapons, and talked about what they'd seen that day. They couldn't talk about it with anybody else without hurting them. The medics dealt with more blood and death and pain than the troops did, and the grunts tried to make up for that in the best way they knew how: constant teasing.

Without that gentle ribbing, the medics might not have made it through, either. Doc Ray—"Outlaw Stitches"—probably caught it the hardest. A hard-nosed older soldier at twenty-seven, Ray would grin and shake his head or shoot back a sarcastic remark, but he seemed like the best man in the company for letting the jokes slide right off. If he missed a turn going out because he had a day off, the guys called him "Nurse." But when they found out he considered "Nurse" a promotion, they stuck with "Bed Pan."

"Doc, you're harder than woodpecker lips," Staff Sergeant Gregory told him one day out on patrol. Doc grinned, his sideways smile popping up a dimple beneath cool blue eyes. But it was just a joke. Everyone knew that though Ray stood strong emotionally, he had the best shoulder to cry on. The guys tended to go to Doc Ray before talking to any of their other buddies about nightmares, emotions, and death.

One of the soldiers crept down to Ray's cot after a late-night patrol. "Doc? You awake?"

"What? Yeah," Ray said. "What's up?"

The soldier told him nothing was up, and that was the problem. His friends had died, but he couldn't feel anything.

"If you keep it bottled up, it's going to overflow eventually," Ray told him, trying to persuade him to talk about it. One thing could trigger an emotional release—a funny moment from the past, a detail from the day of the friend's death, a reminder about taking care of the friends who remained—and if Ray hit it, the soldier might lose the numbness, at least for a while. But if his emotions overflowed, or if he could not move away from that numbness, the soldier would stop thinking about the mission, and that could get him killed, or worse. "It's OK, man," Ray told him. "We're all feeling it. Talk to me."

Maybe it was the dark, or the unusual quiet. Maybe it was having a soldier known for being tough say, "It's OK to cry." Whatever it was, the soldier opened up. When he apologized for getting emotional, Ray convinced him that listening helped Ray, too. They had seen the same stuff, and the medic was dealing with it, too. Ray led the soldier through a series of stories—good stories—about his dead friend, and let him cry. Ray asked if the soldier needed anything to help him sleep and if he was still feeling alert on patrol. Then he sent him off to bed, knowing that sleep could often cure more than the medics could.

The next day, at a picnic table set up on the side porch, Sergeant First Class Chad Smith, twenty-eight, and a medic like Ray, sat ready to hit the aid station if anything happened. He worked for the Special Forces but tended to spend his time at the aid station with Charlie Company. He'd been in for ten years, and told a story similar to many about why he joined: At eighteen, he'd been working construction and already married. He needed to support his family, and he wanted to be a medic. When the guys came to Smith there on the side porch, he talked to them in a voice so deep and soft it was difficult to hear him, but with a manner that exuded the calm the men at Apache needed. On this tour to Iraq, his mission expanded to the local Iraqis because he was part of a four-man civil affairs team that went out daily. He'd been in Iraq before, and he worried about the medics at Apache more than he had worried about medics on previous tours because they weren't seeing simple gunshot wounds. They saw burns, head injuries, and blast injuries. And they had to figure out how to deal with the mental health injuries that had become much more prevalent.

As the medics sat in the center of their aid station living space, a card game devolving into a bullshit session evolving into a serious discussion about how they could better take care of their men, they expressed frustration. They felt their biggest job had become dealing with mental-health issues, but they didn't have as much Big-Army support as they needed. Mental health, Smith said, took a backseat to everything else that had to be done before deploying. "Army-wide, the attitude is, 'We don't have time for that,'" he said, but he was preaching to the choir. "The army is choosing not to acknowledge that it's a problem because they couldn't deal with the repercussions of acknowledging it. It's obviously really hard on the men—the things they see and go through. If you started to acknowledge that, it would be combat-ineffective. There would be too many people who would need help."

All of the medics understood that getting them help back home might be a challenge, especially because every soldier reacts differently to combat stress. Smith, who had been ordering and reading books about post-traumatic stress since he arrived in theater, tried to explain it to the other medics, who, while they understood the condition was real, hadn't had much training on the subtleties. They liked to listen to Smith. He spoke precisely and thoughtfully and intelligently, and they felt they could trust his knowledge. Being Special Forces didn't hurt his credibility, either.

"It's definitely a case-by-case thing," he explained, intense brown eyes locking on each face. "The threshold for one person will be totally different for another. But just being associated with a tragedy—even if you're not right there—can be just as real. But in the army, to prove you have PTSD, you have to show how you were involved in a traumatic situation. It's ridiculous. Whether you believe it or not, it's there. It's just like somebody saying, 'My back hurts.' They could be making that up, too. There are plenty of people who could be malingering. We just have to educate ourselves more about those who aren't."

If someone said he wasn't well, the medics took it at face value. In early 2007, the suicide rate in the army was 17 out of 100,000, and army officials made a point of saying that was still less than the civilian rate of 19 per 100,000 people adjusted for age and gender to meet military demographics. But in the army, it was higher than it had been since the 1970s, and the numbers were growing. Smith told the medics they couldn't think of it from the public relations perspective.

"You have to put it into context," he said. "You're screened before you join. That sorts out a lot of the mentally ill to begin with. But it's insulting, too. We're America's fighting force and your reply is 'It's lower than the civilian rate'? Suicide is a direct reflection of how we're dealing with stress, plus the backlogs and the delayed care. When you stop trying to defend everything and just look at it for what it is, it becomes obvious. They need to spend more time trying to fix it and less time trying to defend it. Otherwise, it looks like excuses and lies."

The medics understood that none of them would go home the same as they had arrived. In fact, it would be crazy if they didn't change. How could a person go through what Charlie Company had seen and go home the same?

"I don't think it takes a very educated person to figure that one out," Smith said.

"But, Doc," Ray said. "If you're infantry, aren't you crazy to begin with? I mean, maybe we'll all go back normal."

Everyone laughed. That's how the medics dealt with their own stress. Gallows humor ruled at the aid station, and even the injured men joined in as they came through bleeding and hurting.

But Doc Ray had a serious question, too. He had noticed that often the same guys came back over and over to talk about bad dreams, worries, and fears. But they didn't ask to go to mental health, and they didn't talk about "combat stress" specifically. "Their attitude is, 'If there's no solution, why bring it up?'"

Smith agreed. "'If you can't get me out of it, I'm going to suck it up and drive on.' This unit has been through so much. Are they dealing with it? Absolutely. But it's at a lot of different levels. You've got the guy who's hanging on by his fingernails, but he's still hanging in there. The only option you have is to tuck it away and become numb. But eventually you're going to have to deal with it."

He advised the medics to help the guys deal with it now, just as Doc Ray had been doing, by offering an emotional release. And when it got hard on the medics? When they'd listened to the details of yet another horrific story and packed those images deep inside their psyche, how could the medics remain strong enough to hear yet more stories?

"There's inspiration in those stories," Smith said. "It makes me not take anything for granted. It inspires me to see just how much an individual can overcome. The guys who are going out all the time? It amazes me that they're able to deal with it. But it's up to you to make sure they're well enough to stay safe out there. That's inspiration, too."

From the sidelines, Hendrix paid careful attention to his medics. He witnessed every injury and wondered at the strength of this team of guys barely out of high school who grew steely-eyed in the aid station or in the middle of a battle and then reverted to video-game-playing kids in their downtime. He understood that, ultimately, his medics were pushing more pain down inside themselves than any of his other soldiers.

CHAPTER 14
Charlie Company's Mission Changes

As soon as Strickland arrived, he briefed his men about the change in mission. Standing outside, the men at ease in formation, Strickland told them more troops had arrived in Baghdad as part of the surge. The guys couldn't help but grimace every time they heard the word. "The surge ends at the perimeter of Adhamiya," DeNardi said quietly, causing muffled laughter from his platoon. "You've got thirty thousand troops in the surge, and they're not doing a damned thing."

In Adhamiya, the same two hundred or so men patrolled the ancient streets. But spring brought more talk of "counterinsurgency" initiatives, and new rules meant the Iraqi government wanted the Iraqi army to handle fighting the war while the Americans provided support. The idea was that letting the government create its own laws and fight its own wars meant the United States could pull out sooner. And if the Iraqi government failed, it would no longer be the Americans' fault that the war had been lost. At least, that's how the guys took it.

For Charlie Company, that meant more battalion operations. When Baka had been in charge, he decided what to do next and reported up to battalion. But Strickland, because of the change in mission, had to get approval for his plans. And because the operations tempo increased, the new CO, through no fault of his own, spent more time at the company command post than out on patrol. Not only did he have more raids to plan, he had to be available if something time-sensitive came up.

To prepare for taking over, Strickland had tried to get to know Charlie Company, but he'd been based in Rustimiya, too far away to interact on a daily basis. Instead, he usually saw the men at memorial services or when there was a battalion-level operation in Adhamiya. Still, he came out a couple of weeks early and asked Baka about everything from operations to how to console a mother who had just lost her son. He had never—since he had joined the army in 1991—seen a company as tightly knit as Charlie. It was hard to tell who was in which platoon, and the bonds seemed to grow stronger daily.

Strickland immediately began to lean on Hendrix.

On his first night as the first sergeant's new roommate, he decided to clear the air.

"You know, there's always going to be a tight bond between Captain Baka and Charlie Company," he said, taking a moment from trying to unpack and organize his gear. "I'm a fool if I think I'm going to walk in and say, 'Cut ties. You're mine now.'"

"Roger that, sir," Hendrix said, as always holding his tongue until he knew where the conversation was going.

"There are a lot of changes coming," Strickland continued. "You guys have been separated from the whole battalion, and now we're going to be working with them every day. But we're going to have to play the game and do what we're supposed to do."

"They do like being far away from the flagpole, sir," Hendrix said, realizing Strickland needed some reassurance. "My guys will get the job done. They may bitch about it, but they're too proud to give you anything but their best."

After the change-of-command ceremony, the battalion moved civil affairs, psychological operations, and explosive ordnance disposal teams to Apache. But they lost the scouts as they moved to support the MiT team. And they were short on leaders. Not only had they lost Baka with all of his experience in the area of operations, they watched as platoon leaders moved into battalion slots or good NCOs went home injured or dead. Ybay served as second platoon's platoon sergeant and platoon leader, earning him the title Sergeant First Lieutenant.

Members of battalion set up shop at the Apache command post, meaning Charlie Company lost some autonomy, and Strickland felt as if he had a leash keeping him at Apache, though he did try to go on several night raids a week. But the men saw the changes as a shift from a commander who loved to go out with them to a commander who loved to look at maps and come up with plans, even though that's what battalion demanded of him. No one could replace Baka, and he and Strickland had different personalities. Where Baka continually pulled guys aside to see how they were doing, Strickland felt there should be more distance between enlisted troops and officers, even though he'd been enlisted and therefore felt a bond with his NCOs. Strickland also tended to focus intensely on the moment's task, rushing from place to place without acknowledging a "What's up, sir?" because he simply didn't hear it. His mind was always on the mission.

Too quickly, Strickland would realize that sometimes the mission had to come second.

As Richardson tried to take care of his soldiers, he felt particularly drawn to Specialist Alberto Garcia. Shy and sweet, Garcia represented the army anomaly. He carried his Bible everywhere. If someone needed help with guard duty, he offered his services immediately. One day, he showed up late for patrol and got stuck washing dishes for a week. He acted as if he enjoyed it.

But Garcia had a crazy creative streak, and he and Richardson bonded when Garcia asked Richardson to teach him how to play the guitar. Within a week, Garcia had bought a guitar. One week later, Richardson heard music coming from the picnic tables at Apache. His face brightened as he recognized the music. "Hey! They're playing Johnny Cash!"

He grabbed his guitar, figuring Chagoya or DeNardi was outside. Instead, he found Garcia playing "Ring of Fire."

"Seriously?" Richardson said, stopping short as he arrived at the porch. "How did you learn so quickly?"

Garcia grinned and shrugged.

"Will you teach me?" Richardson asked, and then spent the afternoon learning a new tune.

On March 13, five days after Strickland took command, first platoon rolled out on patrol, Chagoya in charge. Chagoya always tried to follow his hunches. All of the guys had had enough bad premonitions to know to pay attention. Sometimes it was a clue that hadn't quite registered, a bush that didn't look right or a night that was too quiet. Sometimes it was just experience setting off internal alarm bells. Sometimes someone would say, "I don't feel right going down this street," or, "I know this mission, I'm not going to make it back." When more than one guy was picking up bad vibes, Chagoya tried to figure out why—and usually changed his route.

But on March 13, first was rolling with three other platoons out in sector, so Chagoya didn't have a lot of leeway. March 13 felt bad. Chagoya rode with Garcia and Doc Lawson in a casualty evacuation truck. When they hit the IED, it surprised no one. The explosion had gone off beneath Garcia. Lawson rushed to his side, doing his best to stanch the bleeding, but it came from everywhere. Chagoya yelled out orders, "Hold on, Garcia! We'll get you back. You're gonna make it!" They carried him to another truck, then sped back to Apache, where First Sergeant Hendrix waited for him at the aid station. Strickland desperately wanted to stand by his soldier, but he still had four platoons out. He knew his first sergeant had the aid station covered, so Strickland decided to take care of his other men.

At the aid station, the medics surrounded Garcia as Hendrix told first platoon they would have to wait outside and then closed the door. He stood by Garcia's side, loving his soldier, holding his shoulder, telling him he just needed to hold on until the Green Zone. He told him to fight and offered him hope, knowing there was none.

Garcia died in the aid station.

Hendrix cleaned himself up, gathered his emotions, and walked outside to talk to his men. When the guys standing in front of the door saw Hendrix's face, they understood they'd lost another friend.

"It's not right," Richardson repeated over and over. "It's not right."

Not only did they grieve for Garcia, they understood he wouldn't be the last. They saw IEDs on almost every patrol, usually with the ordnance team doing route clearance. But the insurgents always seemed one step ahead.

Strickland made his first phone call from the rooftop, talking to Garcia's dad after the family had already been notified of Garcia's death. As Strickland struggled to find the words, Garcia's father comforted him.

The next day, the men were back out on patrol. Strickland and the company executive officer, Captain Waggoner, divided each sector down until there were two or three city blocks in each subsector. Strickland would try to patrol with first and second platoons, and Hendrix would take third and fourth. They'd walk with the platoons from house to house, planning to clear every building in Adhamiya. The platoon leaders took stacks of cash and handed it out for good tips. The patrols were more about gaining intelligence than finding insurgents. If they were lucky—"lucky" for an infantryman being defined as "engaged in a firefight"—they would find weapons or bomb-making equipment.

In mid-March, Mudhafer al-Ubaidi, head of the Adhamiya District Council and a man Baka considered a friend, was killed when gunmen opened fire on his car. His predecessor had been killed four months before. A third was jailed for killing his successor. It seemed like Charlie Company could never march straight forward: Each new success brought a retreat soon after. The same week, the guys detained seventeen insurgency leaders and twenty-one operatives, found seven weapon caches, and destroyed a vehicle-borne-explosive factory.

As the mission changed, other responsibilities shifted. Because

Captain Waggoner had worked with Baka and the city administrators on reconstruction projects, he continued to play that role. Strickland stuck with planning missions because the Iraqis didn't know him, but they already trusted Waggoner.

Inevitably, the soldiers and their new commander butted heads. Strickland needed to assert control; the guys needed to push boundaries. Soon an exasperated Hendrix felt as if he were dealing with a bunch of teenagers. They were angry about the deaths, angry that Baka had left, angry that the mission had changed. One day, second platoon was working the quick reaction force, and they were supposed to take only two or three minutes' time to get loaded up after being called out. They ran late. Strickland had them run QRF drills for several days—in addition to their normal patrols.

DeNardi took offense.

"Hey, sir?" DeNardi shouted, in full battle rattle running past the command post on his way to yet another drill. "Wanna know how not to make the guys hate you?"

Strickland turned toward Hendrix, who immediately said he'd talk to the guys. "It's going to take some time, sir," Hendrix said, already striding toward the door.

Even with the difficulties and DeNardi's special "charm," Strickland admired his men. They'd already shown him they could catch high-value targets—insurgents—and work intensely even with a grueling schedule. As Strickland worked to get to know his men, he'd already learned the platoon personalities. If he wanted to find somebody, he sent third platoon. If he wanted to find something, he sent second platoon. If he wanted to "lay the smack down," he sent first platoon.

And though they were willing to speak their minds to a man, Strickland had never seen an infantry unit hold it together so well. Only two soldiers had been caught with alcohol, but there were no drug problems and no major bad behavior. There were never any negligent discharges.

That would have proved beyond embarrassing to any of his men. In fact, at Taji, they often got in trouble for not using the clearing barrels. They knew they didn't need to.

The discipline, he figured, came from the hardship, and they followed his orders to the letter.

Battalion began to send them out even more often as they gained more tips from the neighbors. They heard a funeral home hid a weapons cache, so they conducted a raid. As they broke through the gate and into the compound, first platoon, which stood guard outside, started taking fire. They shot back, figuring there must be something important inside. Hendrix went in with his men, and they started pulling aside tables and looking inside coffins. Nothing.

"No way," Hendrix told his men. "It's here somewhere."

Somebody pulled up a carpet. Underneath, they found hidden compartments filled with guns and explosives.

Another day, they found a vehicle-borne improvised explosive device—or suicide car bomb—factory in an old car shop. The most dangerous VBIEDs had been traced back to Adhamiya, and this appeared to be a major hub. Part of Charlie's mission was to find the vehicle-borne explosive device networks and snipers, while Alpha and Bravo 1-77 tried to stop the EFP networks. At the car shop, Charlie Company found welding tools and bomb-making materials: The insurgents would take the cars apart and fill them with explosives. The soldiers threw incendiary grenades through the engine blocks. "I didn't think that was good enough, so we drove the Bradleys over them," Hendrix explained to Captain Strickland, trying not to laugh.

Another time, someone called into the tip line to tell them a man kept weapons in his house. So, in the middle of the night, they rolled out, kicked in the door, and raided the house. But after questioning the owner through an interpreter, they determined he really wasn't a bad guy. Sometimes people called in tips for revenge, or simply because they didn't like somebody. Sometimes they figured if they offered a tip, even if it was false, they would appear helpful to the Americans. In this case, the man reacted calmly as one of the soldiers explained they'd pay for anything they had broken. "It's OK. It's OK," the man said. "This is what you're here to do." Then he pointed out a woodshop across the street and said bad men kept weapons there.

Hendrix and his platoons headed across the street, wary that it was another bad tip offered out of revenge. Again, they broke the lock— this time on a big metal gate—and raided the shop. They found AK-47s, detonator cord, and explosives hidden in the attic under piles of saw-dust. "Holy crap," Hendrix said to one of his platoon sergeants. "They're hiding this shit right where you'd expect them to—behind big metal gates."

The platoons started raiding any shop with a big metal gate and found cache after cache. But those shops also stored tools and equipment. If Charlie Company raided a shop, they cut the lock, leaving that equip-ment unsecured. Soon, the locals caught on, so when the Blue Spaders went to raid a shop, they'd find the owner outside with the key ready to open the gate for the Americans. Somehow, they always knew when the soldiers would be there. Hendrix figured there were narks in the Iraqi army.

They also received dozens of tips about bakeries—too many for it not to be legitimate but they never found anything.

Even with the successes, Charlie Company knew exactly where the eye of the insurgent storm sat, and yet they could do nothing. They could not go into the most-sacred Sunni site in Baghdad. The Iraqi government forbade them to raid the Abu Hanifa Mosque, apparently to avoid upset-ting the Sunnis. Having received hundreds of tips that the mosque hid a training ground for the insurgents, the soldiers again questioned their connection to the government.

As they drove past, snipers would shoot from the roof of the mosque. There were false graves in the cemetery where insurgents would hide and shoot. Tunnels ran underneath where the soldiers were sure the insurgents kept weapons and bomb-making materials. Neighbors told Charlie Company that snipers would train at the mosque by shooting at the Americans at Forward Operating Base Justice across the Tigris River.

Once, as second platoon patrolled in front of the mosque, they hit a small roadside bomb with their Humvee. It didn't damage the truck, but they figured the guy who'd pressed the button to set it off was nearby. Immediately, they started taking fire. Cardenas and DeNardi lit up the suspected triggerman with their M-4s. As they were shooting, the Humvee hit a bump. "I think I shot my mirror off!" shouted Sergeant Jose Villa. Cardenas yelled, "I think I shot my window!"

Then somebody realized the IED had set one of their prepackaged meals on fire. "Those things are flammable?" Cardenas asked, still shooting. "Hey, put that shit out, man. No! Not with the fire extinguisher!"

Private First Class Brad Rylance, who had only been kidding, put the fire extinguisher down and dumped a bottle of water on the MRE. "Mmm," he said. "Barbecue."

As they rode back into Apache, color washed through DeNardi's cheeks. "There's nothing more gangster than that," he said, laughing.

At the S-1 shop, Baka watched their antics from a distance, vowing never to interfere—to allow Strickland to do his job. But he made sure they got their awards and their pay. As he turned in recommendations for Bronze Stars, the division commander downgraded everything except awards for first sergeants and company commanders. So Baka submitted them again. And again. As they went out on patrol, he listened in on the radio, unable to turn away.

188

CHAPTER 15

Adhamiya Becomes a Gated Community

In April, the army built walls around Adhamiya, spinning it as a "gated community," as if it were a smoothly paved subdivision with homes in shades of "slate" and "bisque" and "clay," rather than motifs of "bullet-ridden" or "caved-in" or "booby-trapped."

Immediately, people protested in the streets—Sunni and Shiite alike. Shiite Prime Minister Nuri al-Maliki said he opposed the wall and ordered its construction halted. Adhamiyans said it would cut them off from other communities, creating a "ghetto" for Sunnis. Muqtada al-Sadr said it would contribute to sectarian hatred. But sectarian hatred still existed. Three Shiite garbage collectors had recently been killed in Adhamiya. And even though the Blue Spaders found fewer bodies, they still encountered electrical wires that hung loose from their posts because there was no one to fix them. Insurgents still took over the generators, forcing the locals to pay them for electricity provided by the Americans. The soldiers ran into IEDs daily and could always hear shooting in the distance.

So they argued for the walls: They would create a safe haven for the Sunnis by keeping the death squads out. And they wouldn't be permanent walls—only 1,200 ten-foot-tall concrete barriers that could be removed with heavy machinery when the tensions died down. Several such "communities" were being created throughout Baghdad.

At a press conference from the Green Zone, Iraqi Brigadier General Qassim Atta, the Iraqi army spokesman, went live over Iraqi TV stations.

189

"I would like to assert that all the security barriers which will be constructed in the areas are temporary," he said. "The main goal of these barriers is to provide security to the citizens and to save the lives of the children and the women and also to prevent the movements of the terrorists."

But anyone who had been in the Green Zone knew the blast walls, checkpoints, and barriers made the inhabitants feel like mice trapped in a maze. The barriers looked like road construction for giants—concrete slabs with numbers written in fluorescent spray paint and with bits of rebar sticking out. No one, including the Americans, would be able to get in or out of the Adhamiya neighborhood without going through two checkpoints that would cause traffic jams and provide obvious paths for insurgents to plant bombs. As the walls went up, insurgents shot at the construction companies, which worked only at night piecing the concrete slabs together like a puzzle. It took months to complete the new boundary around Adhamiya, but in the meantime they used smaller barriers and checkpoints until they finished with the larger barriers. The soldiers liked the walls. Rather than a city that bled insurgents out after an attack and allowed them to sneak in and terrorize people, there were now two checkpoints: one way in and one way out. The checkpoints were manned by the Iraqi army.

The Blue Spaders took to calling it the Great Wall of Adhamiya.

Pentagon officials said the protests were led by the insurgents themselves, and that the project, now called the "Safe Neighborhoods" program—would allow the residents of Adhamiya to live within the security of the new walls.

At about the same time, the army began building a new joint security station in downtown Adhamiya, about a kilometer away from Apache. The new JSS had been an old Iraqi police station. When the Americans and Iraqi army first took it over, the insurgents weren't happy. Every night, Charlie would create a cordon around it to keep the soldiers and police inside safe. Inside, they had to use burn shitters or makeshift toilets, and build their own cots—no comforts of home. Charlie Company created a direct line of communication with the police and the Iraqi army. Before that, the Iraqi army took hours to show up—if they bothered. And the police needed the assistance. Daily, the Iraqis tossed grenades inside the walls of the new station. One night, they attacked both Apache and the JSS. Charlie was so busy defending their own compound that they couldn't assist at the JSS, so they sent the quick reaction force over to help.

Eventually, the JSS did help, because people felt more comfortable reporting information to the Iraqis than to the Americans, but it created more work for an already-stretched company.

Then, Colonel Billy Farris, commander of the 82nd Airborne Division's 2nd Brigade, announced that he wanted Charlie Company to patrol Adhamiya on foot. At first, Hendrix and Strickland thought maybe Farris didn't understand the way the company conducted business.

"We do plenty by foot, sir," Hendrix told him, "but we get there by Bradley." Farris wanted them to ditch the vehicles completely and hump the 240s in. Nobody minded carrying weight—they were used to dirty work—but the insurgents usually stayed in the background if the Bradleys were on the scene. "We're worried that walking would start an all-out brawl, a Mogadishu situation," Hendrix said, referring to the scene in Somalia in 1993 that started with a downed Black Hawk and ended with a small number of troops being overpowered by a large number of civilians who appeared seemingly from nowhere. "They can mass large amounts of people quickly. If we encounter a VBIED and a firefight, that would be bad." But Farris wanted the insurgents to come out, and he wanted the men on the ground where people could approach them.

"You can't talk to people through the window of a Humvee," Farris said.

Hendrix and Strickland agreed with some of what Farris wanted, which is why they got out of the vehicles after they reached their destinations. But Hendrix knew they had lost the argument in part because of a cowboy way of thinking.

"I get it," Hendrix told Strickland after they lost the battle with Farris. "I was in the 82nd Airborne. There's a machismo factor: You're going to look everybody down."

They talked together at the command post, trying to figure out how to break the news to their men. Baby steps. They would start in areas that were not so bad. The quick reaction force would be at the ready. Ultimately, they would lay out what could happen if the men refused to follow an order: You could be written up. You could get extra duty, such as guarding the motor pool or scrubbing dishes. You could get an Article 15, losing rank and pay. You could be relieved of duty.

But even the battalion commander realized going out without vehicles would scare the hell out of a company that had lost so many men. So when the company walked out on the first patrol, Colonel Schacht and Sergeant Major McClaflin walked with them.

There were a couple of sporadic firefights, but things went smoothly. Strickland kept them far from Abu Hanifa Mosque, and they only walked routes that had been cleared. Still, the soldiers weren't sold on the idea.

On the day Hendrix was leaving for R&R to see his daughter graduate—May 3—Farris decided he wanted to see the new wall. He had his own men with him, but they didn't know Adhamiya, and it almost seemed as if he had thrown a dart at a map: Let's go here.

When he arrived at Apache, Hendrix and Strickland tried to reason with him. "That's a bad part of town, sir," Hendrix said. "Don't get out of the vehicle."

"Sir, don't get out and walk around," Strickland said.

"You know, I already tried that move," Schacht told the brigade commander. "I got shot. Don't get out of the vehicle."

As Farris encountered Blue Spaders throughout the compound, they all told him the same thing: "Sir, don't get out of the truck over there."

As Farris left the compound with his men, Strickland and Hendrix walked back over to the command post. "He's going to get out of that truck," Strickland said.

"Roger that, sir," Hendrix said. Both men looked grim, the corners of their mouths turning down.

They settled themselves next to the radio, after telling the medics to be prepared. Then they heard Farris tell his men to dismount. "Holy shit," Hendrix said. "He's out there walking around like General Patton with his ivory-handled pistols."

The insurgents would know who was in charge: It's always the guy doing all the pointing and talking with the 'terp. A good commander, officers learn at West Point, announces himself by the way he carries himself. Farris was no exception. Strickland and Hendrix listened to the radio traffic for a while, hoping they were wrong. And then the call came in. Farris needed to be evacuated. An insurgent had shot him in the groin and hit an artery. His medic moved in with a tourniquet before he could bleed out, and then his men rushed him back to Apache.

At the aid station, Strickland didn't say, "I told you so." He let the brigade commander know he was going to be OK, and that the medics had stabilized him and he was on his way to Baghdad. From there, Farris flew to the States. Four months later, he was back in Iraq.

CHAPTER 16
Charlie Company Beats Down Flames With Friendship

When Private Omar Avila arrived in Charlie Company, he introduced himself to his squad leader, Staff Sergeant Juan Campos, right away.

"I'm your new gunner, Sergeant," Avila said, a little intimidated by Campos's rank and serious demeanor.

"Yeah, where you from?" Campos asked, trying not to laugh at the new private's fears. The kid weighed at least 240 pounds—all muscle—and didn't look as if he should be scared of anything.

"Brownsville, Texas, Sergeant," Avila said.

"No kidding!" Campos exclaimed. "I'm from McAllen." The two had grown up ten minutes from each other. "Good to meet you, Avila."

That night, as Avila unpacked his bags in his new barracks room, Campos called. "What are you doing?" he asked. Avila didn't have much going on, so Campos said he'd be there in ten minutes. That sounded about right to Avila: He was the new guy, so he was sure he was going to end up picking up cigarette butts or cleaning equipment. Instead, Campos took him home to meet his family. His wife, Jamie Drury-Campos, cooked up Tex-Mex food while Avila played with their seven-year-old son, Andre.

From then on, Campos and Avila were inseparable, though Campos still expected Avila to follow orders at work. In Adhamiya, the friendship grew, with Campos saying often he didn't know how he could make it through the deployment without Avila to make him laugh.

If DeNardi supplied sarcasm and entertainment, Avila provided practical jokes—jokes that anywhere else in the world would have gotten his ass kicked.

Just after second platoon got dressed down for being late for quick reaction force duty, Campos tried to gather his men from third platoon to go out on patrol. "Where the hell's Avila?" he asked, angry that his friend was holding up the platoon, but worried that something had happened. Though they were fairly safe inside the confines of Apache, none of the men seemed able to shake the feeling at every second that something bad was going to happen. In this case, he was correct.

As Campos's soldiers stood outside their vehicles, geared up, waiting for the mission brief, Avila jumped out from behind a Bradley wearing a cape made of bubble wrap, a pair of children's sunglasses meant for the school kids, and big white Mickey Mouse hands someone had sent in a care package.

"Follow me!" he yelled. "I'm Captain America!"

"Avila!" Campos yelled. "Get your ass in the truck." But he laughed. The soldiers were short on entertainment.

Some of Avila's jokes proved painful.

Apache, not surprisingly, had a rat problem. They crept around the outer edges of the burn pit as trash smoldered outside the kitchen door. They slunk down by the river where garbage seemed to grow on its own. And the guys in the basement quickly learned that flooding wasn't their worst problem. They set up rattraps all over Apache.

Avila knew a good thing when he saw it.

In the middle of the night, he set up rattraps all around Campos's bunk, trying to think of where his squad leader would reach first as he got ready for an early-morning patrol. He placed traps on top of the man's pants, next to his alarm clock, in the top of his boots, and where he thought his feet might land when he placed them on the floor.

Content, Avila went to sleep.

Crack! Crack! Crack! Crack!

"God damn it, Avila!" Campos yelled, not awake enough to know what had attacked him, but understanding instantly that Avila had been involved.

Another night, after Campos made the mistake of going to sleep after a long day out on patrol, Avila handed Private First Class Joshua Reyes a video camera. "What are you going to do, man?" Reyes asked, understanding that whatever he'd been recruited into was going to get him into trouble. "Just hold the camera," Avila said. As Reyes aimed the camera at Campos, Avila hit the sleeping sergeant with a Taser. When Campos could move again, he yelled, "What in the hell are you doing?"

"Just making sure the batteries work, Sergeant," Avila said, straight-faced. He and Reyes ran out of the room in hysterics.

But Avila had to know the guys wouldn't let him get away with it for long. He'd hit everyone. The only person immune was his platoon sergeant, Sergeant First Class Widmark Quashie. Not that Avila ever got in trouble with his laughing platoon sergeant. "What would we do without you, Avila?" Quashie would ask after each of the private's antics. Campos, on the other hand, didn't let it go that easily.

One night, as Avila slept, he woke up in a cloud of smoke sure something had exploded. But the smell? It seemed oddly familiar and not like anything he'd whiffed on patrol. And then he felt it—pure pain, as if his whole body had been attacked.

It had.

First, Campos squeezed a bottle of foot powder in Avila's face, and then he hit him with the Taser.

"Payback's a bitch, bro!" Campos yelled as he ran out of the room.

When Campos wasn't messing with his young soldier, he played Fight Night on a projector with Staff Sergeant Rausch, a buddy from his neighborhood in Germany who reminded the guys of the actor Vince Vaughn. Back home, their families spent every weekend together, and the two soldiers played together on the company softball and football teams.

Campos and Rausch were close enough that they could recite the other's birthday, as well as the other's wife's birthday. In Iraq, when things got rough, they talked each other through stressful situations, as well as what was going on back home. Every day, they hit the gym, competing to see who could grow the biggest biceps.

Third platoon loved to patrol together, knowing they'd gained a reputation after capturing the insurgent leader who sprained his ankle leaping from rooftops. It was almost as if the reputation made them better at their jobs: Because they were known for being able to catch anybody—even if the 82nd Airborne or Special Forces units couldn't—they were eager to catch more, which kept them constantly alert.

They were a diverse group in backgrounds and abilities. While still in command, Captain Baka had pulled Private First Class Nicholas Hartge—redheaded and freckled and grinning—aside and asked him if he'd be interested in going to West Point to become an officer. Hartge's stepbrother had been a West Point graduate, and Baka noticed that Hartge seemed impossible to fluster. He went about each task methodically—sometimes frustrating his platoon sergeant—but whatever he worked on would always be done well. Baka had picked a soldier from each platoon, and he and Hartge had worked together on application forms and letters of recommendation, Baka hoping he could get the young soldier out of Iraq.

But in mid-May, Hartge, who had just turned twenty, found Baka in the S-1 shop.

"Sir, I know how much you worked to get me into West Point, but I don't want to abandon my platoon," Hartge said, scared that Baka would be disappointed in him and worried that he'd wasted his commander's time. "I just can't leave them now."

"There's no way I'd ever be disappointed in you," Baka said, realizing he'd just made the same speech himself to get out of going back early to teach at West Point. "I'm proud of you. We can reapply next year."

Private First Class Carlos Perez knew a different side of Hartge. At first, the pair didn't get along, especially after the night Perez and Private First Class Jorge Ramirez wrestled so hard in the middle of the night that they broke three beds.

"Shut up!" Hartge said, coming out from under his blanket as if for air. "C'mon, man. I gotta get some sleep."

"You shut up!" Perez said, then launched himself toward Hartge's bed, pinning him down and pulling his mattress to the floor.

"You asshole," said Hartge, who tended not to say such things. He was the sweet kid who had a hard time even making fun of other people. But that night, Hartge with his skinny arms, pulled himself away from Chavez and punched him in the gut—hard.

"Oof! Holy crap, man," Chavez said, when he could breathe again. "Where did that come from?" But Hartge was on him, wrestling and laughing.

At first, Perez thought Hartge was the biggest nerd, and that he talked way too much. But then Perez couldn't get his weapon zeroed. "Give it to Hartge, man," Campos said. The other soldier had his weapon straight within seconds, forcing a new respect from Perez. Eventually, that respect evolved into a strong friendship. Hartge was a little nerdy, but he was funny and good-hearted, and Perez trusted him.

But Perez still teased him. Hartge had a farm-boy gullibility that the soldiers found almost irresistible. Perez jumped into Hartge's bed one night as he gathered his stuff to go home on leave. "Hey, baby," Perez said, running his hands over Hartge's chest. "I'm gonna miss you." Hartge had been through this dance before, and eventually learned to give as much as he got—to the point that he could even make Perez uncomfortable.

"Dude, get the hell out of my bed," Hartge said, laughing.

"You better be here when I get back, baby," Perez said. But he meant it, meant that he didn't want anything to happen to his brother.

Avila went home and had a tattoo etched into his skin, one that he and Marsh had come up with while out smoking one night. Marsh and Avila had the same "Northern California" tattoo running across their bellies, and that led to a conversation about possible designs they would use if they were to lose someone. Avila never dreamed that the first name to sink into his skin would be "Marsh." Avila had an artist draw two praying hands, just as he and Marsh had planned, but instead of a rosary hanging down, he had the guy draw up dog tags: Marsh first. Then Perez's friend Private First Class Jang Kim from Headquarters Company.

The day after Perez got his tattoo, on Mother's Day, May 14, his platoon headed out on patrol. But it was another eerie day. First thing in the morning, kids should have been walking to school, cartoon-character backpacks bouncing along behind small giggly children. Men and women rushing to make it to work on time. Shop owners dusting shelves and preparing for customers.

But there was no one.

"Man, I don't know about this," Campos said. "Be alert."

Campos served as truck commander riding shotgun, Private First Class Andrew Catterton drove, Avila was the gunner, Hartge sat behind Campos, and Specialist Terry Fleming rode behind Catterton.

They had four vehicles in their convoy. As they moved toward Abu Hanifa Mosque, an IED went off right in front of the platoon leader's vehicle. No one was hurt, and there was no damage to the vehicle. They continued to patrol, hoping that IED had been the reason for the silence. Still, even Avila had stopped joking. Something just didn't feel right. But they were near the mosque, and nothing ever felt right there.

As they drove near a new U.S.-funded sewer line, someone started shooting at their patrol. The trucks in the convoy began turning off onto side roads to avoid the gunfire, leaving Campos's truck in the lead. Avila saw the group of men who were shooting at the soldiers and hit one of them with the .50 cal.

Then an IED went off right behind Hartge, hitting the fuel tank. The blast lifted the vehicle several feet off the ground. Avila had been in seven or eight IED blasts before, but this one was deafening, the loudest noise he had ever heard. All the doors blew open, and Avila felt his knees go out. He fell out of the turret and down into the truck.

As he fell, the noise and fire convinced him he would die, so he lay in the truck waiting. "Fuck it," he thought. "I'm done."

He saw blood everywhere, coming out of his legs and arms. His arms were on fire, and he tasted something unfamiliar—oil and copper and dirt and sulfur. Things no one tastes when everything's going to be fine.

All the other soldiers in the convoy could see were flames, flowing from the doors, the turret. Captain Strickland watched in horror from his vehicle behind Campos's truck as flames and soldiers moved as one. His men were on fire.

Campos whacked Avila in the head. "Get the fuck out!" he yelled, flames coming from what was left of Campos's clothing.

"No, dude," Avila replied, his mind already made up. "I'm done for."

"Get the fuck out!" Campos yelled again, time moving slowly in Avila's mind, but Campos did not have time for a long conversation.

Avila looked left and saw Catterton jump out of the truck, and stop, drop, and roll to attack the flames that consumed his clothing, his hands.

Avila looked to his right. Hartge had died in the blast.

"Wow. That's it," Avila thought, his brain still in a slow-motion film, not connected to what was happening to his body. Then he saw Fleming jump out and roll on the ground.

Avila's brain picked up on gunfire: It was an ambush! He needed to provide suppressive fire. He lifted himself back into the turret, hands on fire, and shot off three rounds before his .50 cal jammed.

"Get the fuck out of the truck," he heard someone yell. He realized he was naked. His clothing had burned off his body. His skin had burned off his hands.

Avila, still inside the truck, started hearing the rounds cooking off and suddenly remembered the extra ammo he and Campos always packed: 203 rounds. Grenades. Mark-19.

The fire would reach the ammunition, and the truck would blow up.

Avila jumped from his turret, and then rolled to the ground, trying to put out his own flames.

"Cover your eyes!" Private First Class Sean Cousino yelled, and then Avila felt the blast of a fire extinguisher. Cousino had already helped put Fleming out.

When Avila opened his eyes, the flames had died and he was lying on his side in the dirt, watching his friends writhe on the ground, in pain. He could see Staff Sergeant Octavio Nuñez shooting, taking care of the guys who had ambushed them. Doc Ray rushed from man to man, tending to anything that was bleeding or broken, but unable to do much about the burns beyond offer comfort. Sergeant Robbie Flowers, also a medic, tended to Avila.

Private First Class Jarrod Taylor and Private First Class Chad Chalfant worked to put out the fire still devouring Campos's skin. The truck continued to burn. As Taylor worked, a round cooked off and hit him in the side plate of his body armor. "We're going to get you home," he told Campos.

First Lieutenant Matt Martinez carried Fleming to his truck, Fleming's badly burned face looking like charcoal. Then he ran back to get Avila, who was sitting up near his burning truck, still perfectly calm, though it looked as though his nose had burned off and his skin was charred.

"Can you walk?" Martinez asked him, squatting down next to his friend. "Dude, can you walk?"

"I'm good, I'm good," Avila answered. Martinez wrapped an arm around him and helped him to a good Humvee. But when Martinez let go of Avila to open the door to the truck, Avila crumpled to the ground, his thigh bones tearing through the muscle and flesh of his legs. He had broken them jumping out of the turret, but hadn't noticed until the fractures broke through his skin. "My legs are broken," Avila said, still calm. Martinez sent Ray over to help.

"Where's Hartge?" Nuñez yelled. "Somebody get Hartge!"

"Hartge didn't make it," Avila said, realizing the meaning behind what he'd seen in the truck.

"Fuck!" Nuñez said. He and Chalfant ran to the Humvee to try to reach Hartge in the fire, but the flames were too high and too hot. They could see enough to know Hartge was already gone. Then Nuñez looked up the street. There were thirty to forty insurgents heading their way, and all anyone could think about was *Black Hawk Down* and getting dragged through the streets of Adhamiya.

But then two Black Hawks appeared. The pilots had seen smoke rising in a solid black plume from Avila's Humvee, and they sped in to see if anyone needed help.

"Wow, they called a medevac fast," Avila said, not understanding. Second platoon and Alpha Company also came out to help. Avila heard gunfire, and the insurgents disappeared.

Third platoon rolled back to Apache.

Avila rode again in the first vehicle, while Specialist Michael Alexander drove in a shocked daze. Alexander was new to the platoon and didn't know the area, and he had just seen four friends consumed by flames. "You gotta go straight," Avila said, directing traffic from the back. Everybody in the vehicle looked glazed over. "Left! Left!" Avila shouted. "Call the FOB to open the gate now! Tell them we need a medevac now!"

The Humvee carrying Campos stalled at the gate of Apache, and the men inside the outpost ran to carry him to the aid station. Rausch had been moved from third platoon to first platoon the previous month, so he was at Apache when his old platoon arrived. He opened the Humvee door to help his friend.

Rausch saw that Campos's clothes were burned and his body armor had pretty much disappeared. His skin was melting, his face a drawn-down mask. Rausch focused on Campos's eyes, where he could still find his friend. But within Campos's gaze, Rausch also saw pain and fear. "You're going to make it, man," Rausch said. "The docs got you."

Then Avila's Humvee appeared.

"Fuck," Rausch said when he saw Avila, shock forcing the word from his mouth.

"What? What?" Avila said.

"Nothing, nothing," Rausch said. "You're good."

Avila began trying to get up on his own.

"Stop, Avila, stop!" Rausch said. "We got you. We got you, man."

As they laid him out in the stretcher, the pain began to course through Avila's body. The adrenaline surge disappeared as he found safety with his men.

"Fucking you're gonna make it," Quashie said, fighting to stay with his soldiers into the aid station, which the medics blocked. "Go home. We'll see you in three months."

Then Quashie started yelling at Campos, "Fight, man! You're good. You're gonna make it."

But Avila wondered who his platoon sergeant was trying to convince, himself or his men.

Catterton talked into Campos's ear, ignoring his own injuries. "We got you, Sergeant. Everything's going to be OK."

But Campos didn't talk, couldn't talk. He nodded his head. He understood.

The four rode together to the Green Zone, and when they arrived, Avila had one question for the doctor, "Can I have some morphine, please?"

Again, he looked to his left. There was Campos. He tried to grab his hand, but he was too far away. "I love you, bro," he said. Campos nodded.

He looked right. Catterton. "I love you, man," he said again, feeling the pain drift away, passing the love down to Fleming, who lay near them.

"I love you, man," Catterton said.

Catterton's hands had been degloved. The others had been burned over 70 percent of their bodies. Fleming would need several surgeries to stitch internal organs back together. Avila had compound fractures in both thighs. All of them would be flown to Brooke Army Medical Center in Texas. Doctors told the families of Avila, Campos, and Fleming that their soldiers would have to fight hard—fight infection, face multiple surgeries, suffer tremendous pain—to survive.

Strickland called Hartge's father after the family had been notified, and, once again, found himself comforted by Hartge's dad even as Strickland reassured him his son had died instantly. There had been no pain, and he was surrounded by men who loved him.

One of the guys let Perez know what had happened.

Perez went in to see his tattoo artist again, adding Hartge to his praying hands, crying the whole time.

"I told you to wait for me, man," he said, sobbing as the ink penetrated his skin.

Technically, a catastrophic loss comes with the destruction of a vehicle and all of the personnel inside. But Charlie Company considered the loss of Campos's vehicle and the damage done to the men inside to be their first catastrophic loss.

Captain Baka immediately went to see Colonel Schacht.

"That's enough," he said. "Charlie's done. They've seen too much. Why are all the casualties in Charlie?"

When he realized he had Schacht's ear, Baka continued, emotion adding a pleading quality to his words, a plea that Schacht well understood.

"Let's pull Charlie Company out of Adhamiya," Baka said. "Or at least have them switch out zone 18 or 19 with Alpha Company." He pulled out another football analogy, just as he had done with Hendrix and his executive officer, Captain Brooker, and anyone else who would listen. "They've been in the game too long. Bring someone in off the bench."

Schacht shook his head, already accustomed to Baka's logic and the sketch he was drawing on a notebook to demonstrate which players could go to which parts of the field. Baka always offered explanations in doodles.

"Your men are doing an outstanding job," Schacht said. He had spent more time at Apache with Baka and his men than anywhere else in the battalion sector. He knew some of the guys almost as well as Baka did.

Charlie would remain in Adhamiya. They knew the zone. They were making progress. "We can't take them out now," Schacht said. As had been the case for generations of soldiers, the mission came first.

Charlie Company had received more bad news: Baka had left his command on the assumption that his men would only be in Adhamiya until June, when they would redeploy home.

Instead, their tour was extended another three months. They would spend fifteen months in Iraq.

Baka called Hartge's sister after the family had been notified of Hartge's death. They cried on the phone together. She told him that the day before Hartge died, he'd called home, and he talked about West Point and how relieved he was that Baka said he could stay in Adhamiya.

Hendrix was home on leave when he received news of Hartge's death. He spent the rest of the time with his family feeling miserable, aching to get back to Iraq. All he could think about was not being in the aid station when his men had arrived there, that he was not there to ease their pain and tell them he loved them and promise them he'd see them soon.

Strickland sent his men out after the person responsible for the IED—a homemade device, as it turned out—that killed Hartge. DeNardi and Staff Sergeant Vincent Clinard spotted the suspect running into a building, but as they chased him, Clinard got hung up on a fence. DeNardi jumped over and ran inside a house. He had a 9-mil gun with him, and as he headed up a set of stairs, he ran right into the target coming around a corner. DeNardi immediately stuck the barrel of the gun in the man's eye socket. He led him back to the Bradley.

In the back of the Brad, sitting with Cardenas and Ray and Montenegro and Wood, DeNardi tried to explain how that moment had felt. "I forced my gun into his eyeball," he said, not exactly bragging, his face screwed up in anger. "That's when he started crying. I wanted to kill him so bad. I pretty much crushed his eye socket."

"It's OK, man," Wood said. "You did right. We can't be like them." He didn't need to remind him about their former platoon sergeant Diaz, who now lived in a prison cell at Fort Leavenworth. After they caught DeNardi's man on May 31, they went after everyone associated with him. As they caught each man, they zip-tied him and took him back to the Green Zone for prosecution.

But the violence continued. Also on May 31, a suicide car bomb exploded at a temporary vehicle checkpoint in Adhamiya, mildly wounding six soldiers, sending another two to the hospital in stable condition, and injuring two Iraqi adults and one child.

Campos died June 1 at Brooke Army Medical Center.

Just after completing Hartge's service, Hendrix set up Campos's memorial service at Taji. He placed his soldier's boots side by side and positioned his rifle between them, barrel down. He rested Campos's helmet on top of the rifle, then draped his dog tags beneath the helmet.

After the memorial service, Hendrix remained behind long after the rest of the battalion had cleared. He sat by himself, sobbing, unable to stop, for an hour. After giving his first sergeant time to mourn by himself, Baka returned to the room. He sat beside Hendrix and wrapped his arm around him. Hendrix's tears started again.

"I wasn't there," he said. "I wasn't with him."

CHAPTER 17
Alpha Company Moves to Old MOD

On June 9, First Sergeant Jeff McKinney arrived at Old Mod to serve as Alpha Company's new top. Alpha Company patrolled two zones in Adhamiya that, so far, had remained fairly safe, but Alpha also often responded when Charlie Company needed help. They lived at the old Ministry of Defense building—hence Old Mod—on the outskirts of the city with an MiT team and half the scout platoon. It felt as if they lived in an old office building, rather than a barracks. Once again, there were rules about the bathrooms: Indoor plumbing for urinating only. Anything more substantive had to be done in the port-a-potties outside. Sometimes they had air-conditioning, but usually not, because the Iraqi soldiers in the next building over liked to splice into Alpha Company's electrical supply, leaving the flow of electricity intermittent at best.

McKinney replaced First Sergeant Marc Hickey, who left to attend the Sergeants Major Academy. Stereotypically strong-jawed, McKinney's 5'6" frame surprised people. His face looked as if it belonged to a strapping pole-vaulter, but when he smiled, it all made sense. He needed that jaw to contain a grin so big. Though he was new to the position, he'd been in the battalion long enough for most of his men to know him pretty well, and they trusted him immediately. Like Baka, he was hands-on and liked to go out on patrol with his guys. Unlike Baka, he had a tendency toward silly.

Every single damned morning on days that were already so similar that the guys said they were living in the movie *Groundhog Day*, McKinney greeted them with the same thing, "Wakey, wakey! Eggs and bakey!"

And as had been the case since they met in 2000 at Fort Polk, Louisiana, Sergeant First Class Kevin Floyd would be somewhere nearby. They'd been roommates and working at the battalion TOC together before McKinney moved to Alpha.

"Oh, shut up," Floyd would grouse, every single morning, trying to pull the covers up as McKinney darted around, singing and getting ready for his day.

"Buddy, I got things to do!" McKinney would say, whacking Floyd on the head with his soft cap.

Still, the pair was inseparable, even though McKinney's morning cheerfulness irritated the hell out of Floyd. The same age, the same tabs, the same ideals. They had fished and barbecued together at home, and in Iraq, they both had reputations as go-to NCOs whenever someone had a problem. All throughout the battalion, soldiers knew them: McKinney had been a platoon sergeant in Bravo Company, and Floyd had been in charge of Charlie's second platoon. They competed for everything—sending soldiers up for Soldier of the Year boards, using Q-tips to disturb dirt before inspections, and racing through land-navigation courses specifically to beat each other. Then they'd go home, gather their families, and light up the barbecue together.

At Old Mod, McKinney found he had a new sort of competition: female MPs. When he called Floyd back at battalion to ask for advice, Floyd laughed his ass off. Infantry battalions don't have women. Infantry troops start out in all-male units in basic training, and they stay in all-male units until retirement.

"Good luck," Floyd said, snickering. "Your boys haven't seen women for months."

In general, there weren't many problems. The female MPs had dealt with circumstances similar to what the Blue Spaders had, and most of them were badass, enough so that some field-grade officers had called for allowing women into infantry-specialty positions, even if it was only to increase the number of minorities and women making general-officer rank. There were more general-officer positions given to soldiers who had served in the infantry. Women had already proven themselves in the air, and anyone fighting in Iraq knew the women faced the same dangers as the men, and had earned the same medals for shooting off suppressive fire while in danger, throwing their bodies down as shields to protect fellow soldiers, and providing medical aid when they should have been jumping behind barriers.

The guys, with all their bravado, weren't that upset about having women around.

Half of the scout platoon, which had been living at Apache, also moved to Old Mod in June to patrol with the battalion MiT team, while the other half of the scouts remained at Apache to patrol with the MiT team there. Sergeant Keegan Swope of the scout platoon suddenly found himself living in the same building with a bunch of female soldiers.

"Holy crap," he said to a pal when he arrived. "I'm not used to being around girls at all. Not that I'm complaining."

Even with spotty air-conditioning, designated latrines, and cramped conditions, Swope didn't complain, not even when one of the "girls" made fun of him.

Soon after he arrived, he tossed a football back and forth with some buddies in the sand lot behind the building. Corporal Kristine Harlan and some girlfriends sat outside on a balcony smoking, mostly because they were too lazy to go all the way downstairs every time they wanted a cigarette. It wouldn't have allowed time for much else. "Hey," she yelled down to the guys after watching Swope toss the ball. "You throw like a girl!"

Swope insisted that he did not, in fact, throw like a girl, but the insult hit like cupid's arrow. After that, he spent an awful lot of time with the MPs. The two units had come in contact before, in worse circumstances. Charlie Company had responded in March when the MPs had encountered an IED.

But now, at Old Mod, the scouts got to know the MPs, both male and female, as they hung out in the hallway playing cards between patrols. Harlan always could be found with specialist Karen Clifton, a bitty thing at about 5'4" and 120 pounds. She made up for her size with noise—lots of it. Loud, a little crass, and not even sort of girly, she'd spent her time in Stuttgart being coached by Harlan and her girlfriends on how to properly wear clothing and makeup. Harlan teased her nonstop, "Dude, you are not girly whatsoever." And dance? Not to save her life, but Clifton danced anyway.

Harlan, on the other hand, emanated an earthy girliness that involved painted nails, low-cut blouses, and big blue eyes. But without the trappings of fashion—or even daily showers—Harlan and Clifton grew close at Old Mod. Clifton, as it turned out, was a sweetie who cared about her family and kept a picture of her stepsister in her truck. For Harlan's birthday, she brought back Cinnabons, a huge treat for an FOB with no more than an Iraqi stand with stale candy bars. And Harlan, for all her girliness, did her best to keep up with Clifton's practical jokes. On one occasion, Clifton returned to her room to find tampons fresh from the platoon medic hanging from the ceiling and maxi pads stuck all over her bed—and all over Harlan and a partner. "Fuck you guys," Clifton said, but then it struck her as just as ridiculous as living ten to a room in an office building in Iraq, and the stress of it all caused them each to giggle until they ended up in a puddle on the floor laughing until they couldn't breathe.

Clifton had caught the eye of her battalion officers, too. Major Eric Tangeman had been with Clifton's company, the 554th, and then attached to the 630th Military Police a month before they deployed. Tangeman met her when she was a brand-new private and immediately thought, "This is a very quiet, prim, proper-type soldier."

Like the rest of her company, he learned quickly. Clifton gave everything she had. On a company run, she couldn't always keep up, but anyone glancing backward would see her trailing behind, still pushing.

And she wouldn't back down from anyone. One day, looking at a duty roster, she said, "This doesn't make any sense. Why do you have the new private on CQ every Saturday for three weeks? You hoping that when you send him to Iraq, he'll think it's better to be deployed?"

Clifton always voiced her opinion, but always with a joke, and always in a way that made her superiors think about rethinking what they'd done. That didn't necessarily make her popular, but the people who respected her willingness to speak her mind liked her a lot.

Her platoon, coming from a different battalion, had also earned the title of "bastard platoon," but they wore it with a kind of swagger. Back home in Stuttgart, Germany, the whole platoon went out drinking together after long days preparing for Iraq, causing them to develop bonds that went beyond professional.

But that's what McKinney saw—professionalism—even as the female soldiers gathered in the hallways to play cards with his men, asked if they might have shower hours that differed from the men's, and complained—just a little—about the porn that graced some of the rooms.

In fact, he found he kind of enjoyed the new dynamic. He missed his own family.

McKinney had just returned from leave, where he'd met his brand-new son, Jeremy. He'd just married his wife, Chrissi—Floyd had been at the wedding—and while home, they made plans for his retirement. They would build a house on her father's property in Germany, but they'd spend some time back home in Texas so McKinney's parents could get to know the baby. McKinney also had an eighteen-year-old son, James, and he'd spent part of his time at home talking with him about where he would go to school. In Iraq, he showed Floyd a video of the new baby. McKinney bathed Jeremy in the sink while Chrissi videotaped the moment. He sang to his son, and then teased him. "Someday, we'll show this to your first girlfriend," McKinney said, grinning as he gently sponged water over the baby. "Cuz that's how our folks done us." McKinney showed the video to anyone who would watch and sent copies of it to his parents.

Of course, Floyd took advantage of the situation.

Shortly after McKinney's son was born, Floyd gave an important death-by-PowerPoint presentation to the chain of command. McKinney nodded off a bit in the back of the stifling room, but he woke up when everyone—from the company commander to Sergeant Major McClaflin—started laughing. Floyd had pasted McKinney's head to the body of a baby, and included it in his slide show. For the rest of the day, people asked if McKinney needed his diaper changed. But Floyd would never have done it to anyone but his best friend, and McKinney laughed just as much as everybody else did.

Their styles were completely different. If someone had asked Floyd to set up the TOC, he would have broken out a folding table and said, "Here you go."

Not McKinney. McKinney got the civilian contractors to build furniture. He wanted everything up on the walls so the officers could see each piece of information at once. So he had the contractors build a U-shaped desk, and had them make it pretty.

"What do you think?" McKinney asked Floyd when he was finished, obviously pleased with his work.

"About what?" Floyd said, and then ducked as McKinney's hat whipped toward Floyd's head.

As a child, McKinney's eccentricities made him seem a little odd. He was the shortest boy in his high school at age fifteen, but he decided he was going out for the football team. "Jeff, you're too little," his father told him. "You're not going to make the team."

But he did.

And no kid was that ridiculously neat. Even when he was playing, McKinney was orderly. He and Floyd had a SpongeBob SquarePants competition going on. All their towels and sheets and pillowcases had goofy cartoons on them. But McKinney made his bed quarter-bounce tight with those sheets, and he hung his towels dead center on the headboard of his bunk. He collected thousands of the tiny toys from inside

Kinder Eggs. These were German chocolate children's treats that featured little plastic puzzles that formed into robots and trucks and dragons. Not only were McKinney's Kinder Egg toys lined up neatly; they were dusted. As a first sergeant, that sense of order provided a sea of calm in the chaos his men faced every day. With McKinney, there was no gray matter. It was all by the book. But that perfectionist streak could also cause him some grief.

"Trees that don't bend, they'll break," his family liked to tease him. But he always teased back, and, for his men, that made his rigid moral compass seem like a good thing to emulate. And he wanted everyone around him to shine. He wanted his troops to be proud of him; he wanted to be proud of them, too.

His driver, Specialist Anthony Seashore, adored him, and they'd sit for hours shooting the shit, talking about family or the future or how bad the chow was. McKinney teased the rest of his men until they felt like family. He knew exactly what all 140 of them did within the company—who was armorer, who drove, who was a gunner.

He knew how to make a day that had started, once again, with "Wakey! Wakey! Eggs and bakey!" not seem so bad after all.

Locked and loaded and heading out into the streets of Adhamiya, McKinney would break into song—and force his guys to sing along with him. He had an affinity for show tunes: *Sesame Street* and *Mister Roger's Neighborhood* being the shows.

"Somebody come and play," he sang, scanning his sector for snipers and IEDS. "Somebody come and play today . . ."

Usually the insurgents were more than willing to meet his challenge, but the song still made his men laugh and somehow feel safer. It wasn't just the singing.

As soon as he showed up, he started looking out for them. They'd just gotten a new commander, too—Captain Jesse Greaves—and McKinney had to provide some stability and sense that someone cared about Alpha Company before he could do anything else. At Old Mod,

213

Alpha Company was forced to share a building with two other companies. They had ten guys to a room with bunk beds. They sweltered because of the stolen electricity, and in June the temperatures were heading north of 100 degrees Fahrenheit. For whatever reason, McKinney's room never had issues, but he refused to turn on his air-conditioning if his men didn't have it. He got the air for the whole building fixed. He wanted his guys as together as possible for the tough job they did each day. McKinney wasn't afraid to ask for help, and often asked First Sergeant Hendrix for advice about how to acquire supplies or how to handle soldiers behaving badly.

There were some issues with the new company, as there are with any new group, and McKinney immediately went to work moving folks around until the dynamic changed. Sometimes, a soldier with a strong personality just needed a platoon sergeant to match. And he worked with Greaves, too. Greaves quickly earned a reputation as a gung ho, high-speed officer, and McKinney encouraged him to engage in tactical patience. Rather than jumping in at the first sign of badness, McKinney would say, "Hey, sir, we need to slow this down." Wait for backup. Wait for darkness. Wait for intelligence.

Even as Hendrix advised McKinney, Greaves asked Baka a million questions. Greaves was eager; he always wanted to move. Sometimes that could be fun for his guys. But one night, they complained fiercely to their first sergeant after they said Greaves called in air support to hit a weapons factory where his men had found no proof of a weapons factory.

But they were all learning their new positions, and McKinney found he needed plenty of patience himself.

"Seems like a pretty good company on the surface, but there are a lot of issues which have come out recently, which would make you think otherwise," McKinney wrote to his dad, Charles McKinney, whose marine utilities Jeff McKinney wore proudly, though swimmingly, as a little boy. "I've got guys getting drunk in sector, dudes taking drugs, huffing inhalants, stealing, and one who will probably get court-martialed."

McKinney immediately moved the troublemakers around and made the company stronger. Part of the problem was morale from living in miserable conditions. By the end of the month, he had the electricity going and a dining area.

Even with the problems, he was proud of his guys and bragged about them to his buddy Floyd. He understood what they faced. Every loss in the battalion felt personal. So many people had been there for several years, and everybody knew everybody. The last hit—Hartge and Campos and Catterton and Avila—had been the worst yet.

"Charlie Company has been hit pretty hard down here," he wrote to his dad. "This last one was pretty bad, and a few of the guys have a fifty-fifty chance of pulling through."

Like most of the men, each event made him think about going home and seeing his family. "Summer is here, and the days are long and brutally hot," McKinney wrote his father. "I've been thinking about the family a lot lately and am really looking forward to seeing everyone again. I can't tell you how ready I am to retire and finally settle down and have a home of my own, and to be able to come home each day at a normal time without having to worry about what some knucklehead did today or last night."

Still, he loved those knuckleheads.

He'd served with them before, in Samarra when 1-26 had gone to Iraq the first time. There he'd earned the Bronze Star. But during that tour, he'd patrolled a neighborhood with a squad when they started taking automatic fire from a school. The insurgents got away, but children died in the crossfire.

The cries of the mothers stayed with him. A year and a half later, he talked about it with his father, trying to reason out the why. "After Samarra," he said to his father, "I'll never be the same."

He talked it out with his dad because he felt he couldn't go to counseling. He feared the stigma of post-traumatic stress disorder would ruin his career, or at least his reputation as a hard-ass who could handle anything.

But something else stood out for Charles McKinney after his son's first trip to Iraq: While Jeff McKinney was stationed at Fort Polk, Louisiana, Charles had bought his son a deer rifle for Christmas. Jeff grew up shooting skeet and hunting. He asked his dad to store the gun for him while he was stationed in Germany.

But Jeff McKinney said that, after his first tour in Iraq, he didn't like guns anymore, and he asked his father to keep it.

CHAPTER 18

Charlie Company Senses a Storm and Tries to Remain Calm

Just after Memorial Day, First Sergeant Hendrix, Sergeant Derrick Jorcke, and Sergeant Alphonso Montenegro flew to the American Embassy to receive an award from a Special Forces unit they'd helped on a mission. All three were excited to leave Apache, but receiving the plaque was bittersweet: They'd lost Hill the day of the mission, and Grose had been badly wounded.

On that day, second platoon had formed a cordon around an area while the Special Forces troops went in after insurgent cell leaders. That wasn't unusual. Often Charlie Company headed into Sadr City and other hellholes to provide similar services. When the Special Forces unit learned Hill had been killed on one of their missions, they had his name emblazoned on a plaque. The guys loved that Hill had been honored in that way, but they also enjoyed their time away from Apache. None of them had spent much time in the Green Zone, and certainly not at the embassy, which was situated inside another of Saddam's palaces. Murals covered the ceilings, every fixture was gilded, and marble floors ran underfoot. Each of the offices contained antiques and Persian carpets and, as usual, vases filled with plastic flowers.

Because Hendrix and his soldiers had arrived in the middle of the night, their hosts took them down to the kitchen and unlocked it. "Take whatever you need," the soldier told them, grinning, and then left them on their own. There were shelves and shelves of food. "Hey," Hendrix said. "Fill your pockets. Let's take some back for the guys." Laughing like teenagers, they pocketed M&Ms, granola bars, and glass bottles of Coke, making sure to take enough for their own late-night feast.

The next morning, they awoke with big plans: breakfast, swimming pool, shopping.

But they were again stunned by the dining facility, where they found Belgian waffles with any kind of topping. They could order scrambled eggs or poached eggs or fried eggs or omelets—or all of it. They had a choice of bacon, sausage, hash, or ham; pancakes, French toast, or biscuits; oatmeal, grits, or cereal. "Fill your pockets," Hendrix reminded his guys when he spotted packets of peanut butter and Gatorade mix.

They wandered back to their hooches. Hendrix had a trailer all to himself and Jorcke and Montenegro roomed together—a fine change from Apache. But instead of going shopping, all three fell into a food-induced coma. They hadn't had a nap free of explosions, yelling roommates, or practical jokes in months.

It was the most time Hendrix had spent with Montenegro. Jorcke had worked with Hendrix in headquarters platoon before switching to second, and they had their own bit of history. Osterman and Jorcke kept tab on the command post and usually pulled twelve-hour shifts. But both of them—and Sergeant Edward Pelle—would sneak out on patrol with the platoons, all of them certain they'd eventually end up replacing someone. It turned out to be prescient, but it pissed Hendrix off.

"One of you guys is gonna get shot," he told them one day at the command post, glaring, but silently proud of their initiative.

"But, Top, if I don't go out now, I'm not going to know the sector when I need it," Jorcke explained. "Then I'll end up getting someone killed." The three sergeants continued to head out on patrol after their shifts in headquarters platoon, until Pelle was, in fact, shot and sent back to recover in Germany.

Soon after, Jorcke moved to second platoon, and the men who worked for him appreciated not only that he knew the area, but also that he hadn't used his position at headquarters as an "excuse" not to go out.

Even though Hendrix and Jorcke had worked side by side for several months, Hendrix still learned a lot at the embassy. Jorcke had been a contractor who later joined the military. Usually, soldiers leave the military to become a contractor because the pay is much better. But the rest of Jorcke's history wasn't typical, either: The year he spent working on a ship as a "pirate" to entertain people didn't seem as if it would point toward a career as an infantryman, though he did both jobs well. Hendrix already knew Jorcke would push to learn all he could, especially if it meant helping his men.

Hendrix had to work harder to learn about Montenegro, who was soft-spoken and tended to keep quiet until he felt his opinion was needed. Still, there was a hardness about him—and a wild side. As soon as a new regulation came out stating that soldiers could have tattoos on their necks, Montenegro and Sergeant Wood, who were close friends, rushed out and got them. Unfortunately, they didn't read the part of the reg stating the tattoos had to be small and couldn't be in front of a soldier's ears. Monte and Wood went for large and too far forward. In every battalion formation, Wood and Monte slumped down in their collars to try to hide their tattoos.

Hendrix figured the body art wouldn't affect his soldiers' performance in Iraq, so he let it slide. But in the Green Zone, Hendrix learned that Monte's brother was also a soldier and that Monte wanted to be a music producer when he got out of the army. Both Monte and Jorcke were Native American, and a tradition of joining the infantry had passed down through their families. Sizemore had been Monte's squad leader, and Mock a close friend. He had been scheduled to finish his time in the army in June 2006, but he had been stop-lossed to go to Adhamiya with Charlie Company. At age twenty-one, this was his second tour in Iraq.

At lunch, the three decided to get out of bed long enough to eat, and they found ice cream and steaks and a dessert case. Then they went back to their rooms, pockets stuffed full of treats for their friends back at Apache.

That evening, after another huge meal, Hendrix peeked into the mini-fridge in his trailer. Inside he saw a six-pack. He walked over to see Jorcke and Montenegro.

"Did you look in your fridge?" he asked.

"Uh, yes, First Sergeant?" they answered, mumbling a bit, as if they might be in trouble.

"What was in there?" he asked.

"Beer, First Sergeant?" they answered, both looking at their boots.

The Special Forces troops had hooked them up.

The three of them shared two six-packs of what must have been near beer, because real beer would have violated General Order No. 1, which states that no U.S. service member in Iraq may drink alcohol. It didn't matter. It could have been water. They sat together for a few hours, Jorcke excited about his wife and the baby due soon; Hendrix bragging on his three daughters, one of whom could take him down wrestling; and Monte fixated on his mother's cooking and how hard it was to hang up the phone after he called home. The evening would become one of Hendrix's favorite memories.

On the battlefield, things continued to get worse. The death rate for Americans in Iraq had gone up significantly: 192 troops had died in 2007. In January and February, 40 percent of those deaths had been by IED. By March, the number had risen to 70 percent. In Adhamiya, the insurgents understood that Charlie Company was after them, and Captain Strickland could see the response: If, at night, he sat at the intersection of Remy and Route Absolut, he could watch an IED go off every day.

In June, the company was tasked to remove burned-out and broken-down vehicles. They had a $10,000 contract and worked with the Adhamiya District Advisory Council: Charlie Company would call in the coordinates, and twenty local workers hired just for that purpose would remove the cars. They hadn't been able to remove the cars before the

Great Wall of Adhamiya went up because the neighborhoods had used the cars as barriers to keep people out. But the improvised barriers also meant that the insurgents always knew where to plant a bomb.

The civilian death rate plummeted 61 percent from April until the end of May.

Charlie kept going out, combating the fear with yet more joking. As Hendrix rounded a corner in the motor pool one day, he saw Private First Class Anthony Hebert, a nineteen-year-old who had joined the army immediately after graduation, sprawled out on the hood of a Humvee. Hebert, normally a blond, flirtily flipped the hair from a purple wig out of his eyes, showing off his stomach from beneath a T-shirt tied up like Daisy Duke. One of the soldiers took pictures as Hebert posed. Hendrix shook his head and kept walking. Sometimes it was better not to know. Hebert wore the wig all day, even out on patrol.

The more experienced soldiers pulled the younger guys, including Hebert, under their wings as if the privates were ducklings, Johnson and Agami passing off the last of the energy drinks to DeNardi and Cardenas, or reminding them to sleep rather than stay up playing video games. They looked for signs of anger and talked the privates down. They made sure the guys called their mothers. They acted as surrogate big brothers.

All of the soldiers understood that some of the things they did in Adhamiya made the situation worse. None of the neighbors were impressed when the troops chased down a guy on a moped with a Bradley. If the soldiers accidently bumped a car going through one of the skinny streets, the Adhamiyans became as upset as any New Yorker might. And the Bradleys tore up the roads, leaving behind even more ruts and potholes.

Most of the violence—that not aimed at Charlie—became Sunni on Sunni, and seemed to be part of an internal struggle for power. Charlie Company had heard the pep speeches from their own leaders: Get the Iraqis to reject the violence. Ask the "fence sitters" who haven't allied themselves with anyone to become interpreters, police officers, and soldiers. But as the guys tried to work with the fence sitters, they had to watch out for bullets.

Every day, the Blue Spaders would gather in the hallway to make their phone calls and send their e-mails, and every day, faced down by the soldiers' photos on the memorial wall, they talked about whether they were making progress and if it were worth it.

"I believe in the mission, but the Iraqis have to want it," Osterman said, sitting against a wall waiting for a computer.

"The surge isn't working because it's us," DeNardi said, leaning back in his computer chair to join in. "The Iraqis have to make it work."

But they also believed they hadn't gotten to the point where they could make a difference. If the insurgents were still blowing things up, what was the point of rebuilding?

"You can't reconstruct without finishing the war part," Osterman argued. "The Iraqis have all given up. I don't think things are getting better."

After they lost Hartge and Campos, the soldiers had lots of ideas about using their infantry skills.

"We got hit on Route Johnny Walker, so we should have blown up the whole street," DeNardi said, starting to talk fast, his knee bouncing up and down. "But then they said we couldn't do that anymore. So the Iraqis have fear on their side. I don't see anything that shows progress. We caught a lot of HVTs, but that's just a speed bump. We can't really do anything because of politics. We can't even go into the Aba Hanifa Mosque even if we can see them shooting at us. We shouldn't have to have your permission to raid a place you know is bad. It's like, 'We have this guy locked in.' 'No, you can't go in.'"

And they were angered by what they saw as the lack of reaction in the United States. Wood raged that more people had watched videos of Britney Spears shaving her head and not wearing underpants than knew how many soldiers had died. He read out from an essay he had posted online: "This little piece of truly heart-breaking news captured headlines and apparently American imaginations as Fox news did a two-hour, truly enlightening piece of breaking-news history," he said, reading as if he were Morley Safer on *60 Minutes*. "American viewers watched intently and impatiently as the pretty colors flashed and the media exposed the inner workings of Britney's obviously deep character."

Johnson, the scout platoon sergeant from South Boston, nodded his head. "I can't stand to see the media reports when our guys die," he said. "It's just a number. Nobody knows who they were or how they lived their lives. Nobody cares."

"Exactly," Wood said. "Listen to this," and he kept reading. "It's almost to the point where, from a real soldier's standpoint, I wonder on a constant basis what the hell I am fighting for," he said. "I mean really, we lose an average of four soldiers daily in some of the most grotesque and gruesome attacks imaginable—something I've seen firsthand on more than one occasion—and this is the best piece of news I get to chew on?"

"Hell yeah," DeNardi said.

Wood continued, voicing a complaint many of them had: They desperately wanted people to know about the friends they'd lost, but even if they had their own ideas about whether the United States should be in Iraq, they didn't want to see Ross McGinnis or Ryan Hill or Garth Sizemore used to express an agenda.

"You do a piss-poor job of relaying any piece of any story from Iraq without a media spin," Wood continued, anger seeping through his voice, Morley Safer lost. "Congratulations, you keep the masses ignorant and uninformed. You are truly a system that is a product of social conditions."

"You going to post that?" Johnson asked.

"It's already up," Wood said, and then went back to typing. He had a promise to make to his family and his girlfriend. "My enemies are determined to take me, but the survivors of any battle will tell you, 'The ones who live were more determined to live,'" he wrote. "And no enemy of mine will waiver that determination, nor stop my will to live. No enemy of mine is that powerful.

"I'm coming home."

On June 16, Charlie Company conducted a raid with the Iraqi army. As usual they were trying to catch the guys making the bombs.

Osterman was in the last truck. First platoon was driving through zones 18 and 19 when the front and rear trucks started catching small-arms fire from men in ski masks. Osterman and the other gunners had .50 caliber machine guns. The insurgents had a PKC and AK-47s. The Americans chased after the insurgents, but when the guys turned a corner, they found a larger group of insurgents. The Americans began firing again, and the insurgents ran into a courtyard.

The company standard was not to kick in doors after the soldiers had been shot at and then saw an insurgent enter a house. That was an invitation to lose soldiers. Instead, they'd shoot at the house with Bradley guns, toss a grenade inside the open door, and then go inside.

So Private First Class Ismel Sanchez threw a grenade into the courtyard, and the insurgents stopped shooting.

Osterman's crew drove back around the block to make sure it was secure as the rest of the platoon went after the men in the courtyard. As the crew drove, an Iraqi man in a car began firing at the first Humvee. All the American gunners fired back, but then it turned into a high-speed chase with the Humvees running after the car. Then, as the soldiers realized the guy in the car wasn't the only gunner, the Americans started jumping out of Humvees to continue the chase on foot.

Osterman stepped out of his Humvee and returned fire at more guys in ski masks shooting rocket-propelled grenades at the end of the street. By his side was Staff Sergeant Michael Mullahy, who had been itching to shoot a rocket. Ever since the man had gotten to Iraq, he seemed like a magnet for rocket-propelled grenades. One flew past his bumper, another right past his face. Every time he went out, it seemed as if he had a near miss. Each time it happened, it shook Mullahy a little bit more. No one has that many near misses. After his last close encounter, he made a promise. "Next time I get shot at with a rocket, I'm gonna shoot back with a rocket," he swore to Osterman.

So now, with the men at the end of the street shooting RPGs at him, Mullahy had only one request.

"Man, I wish I had a rocket," he said.

Sergeant Richardson wasn't about to wait for a particular type of weapon. He started shooting back immediately with his M-203, aiming slightly upward. Fop! Fop! The grenades angled up into the air and then back down toward the target. The insurgents disappeared into an alley, but the soldiers weren't going to expose themselves by running down the street after them.

"Man, I need a rocket," Mullahy muttered again, shooting off his M-4.

Osterman ran to the truck to get more ammo, and while he was there, he picked up an AT-4, a portable antitank weapon. "Here you go, man," Osterman said, handing it to Mullahy, whose face immediately lit up. "Yes!" he said.

Then the Iraqi with the rocket-propelled grenades appeared again at the end of the street, standing like a bull rider in the middle of the road and getting ready to launch another rocket. With the khaki-colored landscape and bright sunshine, the scene felt like something straight out of a Western. Mullahy jumped out with the AT-4. The Iraqi shot off two grenades just to the right of Mullahy.

And Mullahy misfired.

"Fuck!" he said.

"C'mon, man!" Osterman yelled from the side of the Bradley. "What are you doing? Get over here!"

But Mullahy stood his ground, fiddling with the AT-4. He would have his chance with the rocket launcher.

Another Iraqi guy came running out with a grenade launcher at the other end of the street, but he slipped on some gravel, his legs twirling and kicking up rocks like the Roadrunner. Even as he fell, he shot off another grenade.

He missed.

Mullahy stayed put in the middle of the road.

He fired off the AT-4.

Misfire.

"Dude! Get out of the street!" Osterman yelled, laughing with relief every time his friend lived through another brush with a grenade. "You look like a fucking cartoon!"

The weapon had been bouncing around in the back of a Humvee for months, and the firing order was easy to mess up—especially if the shooter was stressed or excited. But Mullahy was determined to make it fire, if only by pure force of will.

A third Iraqi ran into the street with an RPG.

Methodically cool, Mullahy fired.

And hit his target.

"Yes! Yes!" Osterman yelled, bouncing up and down on his toes. "Now get the fuck out of the street!"

They jumped back into the Bradley and chased after a car with more insurgents inside. The car crashed, and the six men inside ran away. The soldiers found empty rocket-propelled grenade launchers in the car, which confirmed their suspicion that they were chasing some of the men who had been shooting at them. Osterman and his squad chased them on foot, throwing grenades and then launching themselves over a wall as the insurgents disappeared into a courtyard.

Inside the house, Osterman, Richardson, and Mullahy found a completely wet Iraqi man. He had jumped into the shower to clean off and change, but he was soaked. He'd jumped in fully dressed.

Then the soldiers found three more Iraqis in the yard: Whiney guy, dead guy, and not-dead guy, the soldiers dubbed them. Whiney guy talked incessantly, but didn't have a scratch on him. Dead guy turned out to be just playing possum, but he was lying on top of another guy who was in trouble. Doc Lawson performed first aid. The man had multiple sucking chest wounds and was bleeding from the femoral artery. Osterman didn't interrupt Lawson's work, but figured he didn't have long for questioning. But when he started making inquiries, with the help of an interpreter, all three Iraqis acted as if they'd never seen each other before.

Osterman found the PKC gun nearby, so he asked the insurgents some more questions. The two living Iraqis both pointed at the dying guy, saying they didn't know him, but he must have been the one causing trouble. But when the man died, despite the ministrations of Lawson, the other two men began crying as if he'd been their brother.

"You guys do this shit and now he's dead," one of them accused the Americans, crying.

When the soldiers searched the dead man, they found the other two Iraqis' passports in his pocket. The men continued to say they didn't know each other.

The Americans zip-tied the men and took them to the joint security station. First platoon laid the dead man Mullahy had shot out on the hood of the Humvee—like a deer—because they didn't have anywhere else to put him. When they pulled in the gate of Apache, Charlie Company cheered. Finally, an enemy who hadn't flipped a switch and then slunk off down an alley.

Ultimately, though, the incident would cause them grief. Army combat cameraman Sergeant Mike Pryor went out with Charlie Company that day, anxious to catch the "hardest-hit unit in Iraq" in action, and was thrilled with the series of photos of Richardson, Osterman, and Mullahy as they worked the rocket. But none of them was in proper uniform, and Mullahy's sleeves were rolled up. He wasn't wearing gloves, as was the brigade standard operating procedure. The photos ended up in the brigade magazine, and instead of receiving praise for that day's mission, all the guys heard about were Mullahy's sleeves.

"You gotta be kidding me," Osterman groused upon hearing the news. "Who had time for gloves?"

But they made the Multi-National Corps-Iraq newsletter just days later. On June 14, while out on patrol, one of their Bradleys hit yet another roadside bomb. The blast did not injure any soldiers, but they had been traveling through a market area, and shrapnel from the blast struck and injured seven civilians who stood nearby on a sidewalk. The guys rushed out of the Bradley to help.

Staff Sergeant James Lesco immediately realized the injured needed shelter so his medic could administer first aid. Lesco kicked in the door of a nearby building, and Doc Hewett bandaged them up. As Hewett checked out one victim, he realized the elderly man's heart had stopped beating and he needed a doctor immediately. "Sir, he's going to die right here on the floor," Hewett called out to Captain Strickland. Strickland radioed for an ambulance.

Everybody knew the ambulance would take its time, if it arrived at all, so Lesco and his men loaded the wounded into their vehicles and rushed them to Adhamiya's Al Numan Hospital. Doctors there resuscitated the old man.

A couple of days later, the soldiers made the "Good Samaritan" section of the brigade newsletter when they were out on patrol again. The soldiers saw an Iraqi man wreck his motorcycle, so Doc Lawson, Staff Sergeant Rick Hamblin and Private First Class Michael Blair rushed over to help. The accident had knocked the man unconscious, so Hamblin and Lawson bandaged his head and then they took the man to the local hospital. Usually, the soldiers worried about men on motorcycles because they could toss a grenade and make a quick getaway, but the men had also learned that "usually" didn't mean a lot in Adhamiya.

The same week, after catching five men with car-bomb-making materials; assisting after an IED in front of the mosque had killed civilians—the soldiers were pretty sure it had been meant for the Americans—and responding to a shooting of a minibus full of civilian government employees, second platoon prepared again to go out on patrol. At this point, no one made fun of the guys who said the same prayer or filled their pockets with the same charms before each patrol, and they all put more faith in making sure they were kind to each other. No one ever let a friend go in his place, and even the guys who were supposed to have the day off would go out. How could they live with themselves if someone got hit? What if they'd been able to help? All of them had problems sleeping, exhausted as they were, because the scenarios replayed through their minds. How would they react? Doc Ray tried to figure out where he could find cover if something happened to a Humvee and he needed to work on a friend. DeNardi and Cardenas rehearsed daredevil moves, always managing to get the bad guy at the last moment. Wood went over what he could tell his men to keep them safe.

On June 20, just after lunch, when the temperatures had bounced up from 60 in the night to more than 100 degrees in the afternoon, they gathered outside the Bradleys.

"Second platoon!" Ybay yelled, a grin on his face. "Somewhere on that street, there's an IED."

"I'll find it!" Martin yelled, widest smile ever on his silly, handsome face. They all laughed, always laughing because laughter fought off fear. Agami grabbed Martin's head, pushing his face down to his chest.

Grinning still, Martin caught sight of Cardenas walking toward the Bradleys. "Hey!" he yelled. "Gordito!"

"Hey, man," Cardenas said, laughing at being called the "fat kid." There wasn't an ounce extra on his stout frame. "Only my father calls me that."

In a quiet moment with DeNardi, Cardenas had talked about his fears, feeling that the next IED was not a matter of *if* but *when*. Every single day they saw IEDs. But they trusted their Bradleys, and would enter them almost triumphantly, expecting no more than a headache and sore ears. But what if the bombs got bigger? Bigger than the one that had killed Hartge and Campos? Cardenas wouldn't think about it now.

Monte spotted Wood.

"Hey, man," Monte called out. "You get the first truck. You talked to your mother today."

Woody just smiled, dark eyelashes framing big blue eyes. He had, in fact, stayed up late talking to his mom online. Talking religion, again. He told her he wasn't sure he could believe in God anymore. "Just wait, sweetie," his mom wrote. "Something big will happen and you'll know." But that morning, Woody grinned because, more important than the answer at that moment, he had just talked to someone who loved him.

Ybay always said a prayer before he went out, always riding in a Humvee so there would be a safer seat available for one of his guys in the Bradley. "Be careful," he said, more to himself than to anybody. He had promised to take them home.

They rolled out with the explosive ordnance disposal team, five or six guys enclosed in the back of each Bradley. Almost immediately, Martin's Bradley stopped. They'd found one. Wood's voice came in over the radio, "You'll feel a little charge," he said, just before the EOD team shot the device with a stream of water, "So don't shit your pants, Cieslak!" Cieslak laughed and nodded his head. He was one of the biggest guys in the company, width-wise, and had obviously spent his time lifting weights. It just figured that Wood, one of the littlest guys, would pick him out for an insult.

"*Boof*!" went the charge, and no one even twitched. They blew one or two a day.

On cue, the guys start bragging about how many times they had each been "blown up"—or inside a vehicle that had hit an IED. Hebert said he'd been blown up about thirteen times. So had Montenegro. So had Leemhuis. They figured with that many explosions, they were probably golden—unstoppable. Or at least were on the winning end of the numbers' game.

The guys passed around one cigarette because they worried about air quality in the back of the stifling Bradley. Dust stuck to the sweat on their faces, creating streaming rivulets of mud leading down their necks and into their T-shirts. Doc Ray asked the Iraqi interpreter, who shared the cigarette, if he had a girlfriend. He told them he did, and the boys dug in. "What does she look like? Have you, you know? Have you?" The interpreter looked just like a thirteen-year-old who knows he's supposed to say yes, but hasn't really, so he giggled. "Wait," Martin yelled from the driver's seat, "do you have a boyfriend?" "Noooo!" the interpreter moaned and giggled some more, knowing they were just teasing him. He looked like he adored the American soldiers, but he risked a lot to be with them. When they left the Bradley, unlike Santana, he covered his face with a scarf. He knew that if the locals found out who he was, his family would be at risk. And when the war ended, if it ended, he could be killed for working with the Americans.

The ordnance team found another explosive device. "It's a rocket," Wood yelled. "They're gonna blow it. We're gonna have a little bit bigger charge."

Boof.

Letdown.

"Pussy-ass 'bomb,' " Cieslak muttered.

They stayed out for another hour, sure there was a bigger bomb waiting for them. The ones they'd found were just teasers, enough to blow out tires. Enough to divert their attention. There had to be another.

But not that day.

They drove back to Apache, took care of their vehicles, and then tumbled like puppies through the door leading to the basement, pulling off gear and deciding what to do next: nap, eat, Internet. The cooks served up something resembling boiled steak, but afterward a German contractor there to help renovate the building made Black Forest cake. Doc Ray ate the cake as if it would disappear—or he might be called back out on patrol—and the bags under his eyes seemed to deepen. They had gone out three times that day, and he hadn't been needed. A good day. He would go back out again at 6:00 A.M. the next day, June 21, 2007.

CHAPTER 19
Charlie Company Faces Its Worst Day

At six the next morning, the guys stumbled out of their basement in full gear, already sweating in the heat. Ybay gave them another pep talk and told them to watch for bombs, as if they had ever stopped watching for bombs. But if they sat inside the guts of a Bradley, they couldn't watch for an IED, only wait for it.

By 6:30 A.M., they were waking up the neighbors and conducting searches. No one looked happy: Babies cried, mothers sullenly opened their homes to the strangers with the guns, and young men disappeared out back doors.

Second platoon did their best to seem friendly and helpful, but they also made sure they didn't stand in open doorways. They entered every room with their M-4s up and ready. In one home, a civil affairs team of soldier and interpreter sat down with an older woman. Nearby lay a sick old man, and a boy and girl, about seven and nine, hid behind the adults. Soldiers passed out chem lights to the children, and the little girl sat in a pink sweatsuit twirling the light stick back and forth to watch the fluorescent fluid ooze.

They always brought chem lights and candy. When they walked into the houses, they'd immediately try to calm the children. If the children were calm, the adults tended to follow suit. The soldiers had learned they could even take away the men in the family, as long as they left the children and the money.

232

A soldier asked the woman what the family needed.

"Everything!" she wailed, and the interpreter struggled to keep up with her tirade. Her son had died from a kidney problem. Her husband needed to go to the hospital, but traveling to Shiite central Baghdad from the Sunni neighborhood put him at as much risk as his illness. The soldiers offered up food and water, but the woman said their needs weren't that basic. She wanted jobs, electricity, and a future for her family.

They offered what they could, and then asked if she had anything to share—information about IEDs or unusual activity or people being threatened or kidnapped.

Nothing.

Each group of soldiers hit a different house and asked the same questions. They played with the children and asked what people needed. They passed out soccer balls and Girl Scout cookies. Any unusual activity?

Nothing.

They went back to Apache just long enough to toss back an energy drink and write an e-mail or two. They rolled out again, Ybay making his daily promise to himself that he'd bring them all back; Doc Ray thinking about all the things that could go wrong and how he could fix them.

From his turret, coming back in the gate from patrolling with first platoon, Chagoya nodded across to Agami, who was on his way out of the gate with second platoon. "What's up?" Chagoya said. Agami nodded back at him, "What's up."

Half an hour later, the scouts were working out with the gym equipment next to the patio, where the aid station medics sat at a picnic table for a break. Everybody heard the explosion.

Silence. The whole base immediately stopped. The blast had been close—and loud. Way too loud.

Then they heard gunfire. AK-47s. Then RPGs. People started moving out, the medics rushing for the aid station, the scouts to the radios. DeNardi, who had the day off, ran to the front gate where the guards sat with radios. He would be able to hear what had happened. DeNardi usually served as a gunner for second platoon.

Soldiers ran to the remaining Humvees, snapping chinstraps as they jumped inside the vehicles. Pieces of conversation rang out.

"A bomb."

"They drove over it."

"Flipped over—burning."

"Trapped inside."

The image leaped instantly into everyone's minds. Were they trying to get out? Had they lived through it? Could they breathe? Were they suffering?

No one could shake the memory of Campos and Avila and Catterton and Fleming leaping from their Humvee in flames, and it came again now in a flash.

The explosion came from the same place as the IED that had destroyed the MP vehicle in March. Many Charlie Company soldiers had responded and helped to retrieve the bodies of the three soldiers who had died that day. It had been horrific, and now they stood terrified, waiting to hear the fate of their friends.

Around the corner from the aid station, half a dozen soldiers holding their heads stood around a Humvee with a radio. The gunshots continued. A soldier fell to his knees, helpless inside the compound.

"They can't get them out."

"This is taking way too long."

"They should have been here by now."

Others continued preparing the aid station. They couldn't help outside, but they had to do something—anything. They set up litters, provided more shade with tarps spread above tent poles. Readied IVs. Handed out body bags.

Second platoon wouldn't be allowed to help with their own men. The Special Forces unit on the other side of the base stood guard at the gates, just as much to keep guys out as to keep guys in. DeNardi realized no one had actually left the compound. He knew it was Wood's Bradley—Woody who kept the words to "Adhamiya Blues" in his pocket and who wanted to marry his girlfriend and go to art school.

The scouts had been told the quick reaction force had already gone out, but there had been a breakdown in communications. DeNardi yelled at a cook, "Where the fuck's the QRF?' "

"I don't know," the man replied. "Go find it."

DeNardi chucked his Kevlar helmet at the cook and then took off across the compound, trying to find Johnson. Johnson would know what to do.

"There's no QRF!" DeNardi yelled at Johnson. Johnson, already geared up, grabbed a bunch of Humvees and filled them with scouts. He told DeNardi to stay back when he tried to climb in.

"No way, brother," Johnson said, hand on DeNardi's shoulder. "I can't let you see this."

Only two Bradleys had gone out on patrol, but no one at Apache knew who was in the Bradley that had been hit. Cardenas was out. Doc Ray. Leemhuis with his purple wig. Cieslak. Ybay. They were all out on patrol.

An hour passed. No word.

More shooting. More explosions.

"Fuck!" DeNardi screamed.

He stood at the gate yelling at the Special Forces men to let him out. "Open the door!" he yelled. "I can run it!" The guards pulled DeNardi back after he fired a couple of rounds out of the gate. The guards had a radio. Everyone in a twelve-mile radius tuned in when something was going down. DeNardi stopped long enough to listen to a casualty report come in.

The first Bradley had rolled over a deep-buried IED so big that it left a hole the size of a Humvee in the ground. The Bradley flipped, landing in a swamp of gasoline as the tank emptied itself, adding fuel to the fire.

KELLY KENNEDY

Doc Ray rode in the second Bradley, something the guys all hoped fervently for as they waited for word of who was inside the first Bradley. They always wanted the medic to be OK. As soon as he heard the explosion, Ray jumped out and ran, not even registering the rounds that flew around him. But the flames were too high. As the fire died down, and as hope began to dwindle, he worked in the mud around the fighting vehicle, but he couldn't get to his friends quickly enough. Probably, he reasoned, they died quickly.

All but one.

As soon as they arrived on scene, Johnson started yelling commands at the guys. They had all jumped out with Ray to help, but Johnson decided they didn't need to see any more than they already had. He pointed toward the second intact fighting vehicle and steered each soldier back into it. "Go get in the Bradley, man," he shouted. "I got this." His reasoning was simple: "Let's take over so they can get that image out of their head." But it was Agami. Agami who had helped him make it through when Mock died. Johnson wouldn't let himself think about that. Not yet.

Hendrix arrived, and the scene changed again. He told the platoons to face the Bradleys outward to guard the perimeter, but also so they would not see the destruction. Alpha Company had already arrived on the scene to help. First Sergeant McKinney, the man who sang *Sesame Street* songs on patrol, was at Hendrix's side. Hendrix's medic, Sergeant Guenther, tried to prepare for the worst. They needed to recover their soldiers.

A couple of Iraqis had been killed in the blast. They'd been walking down the street during the explosion. A couple of women stood on the street crying, but no Iraqis tried to help. The carnage spread for at least three blocks. Wood and Leemhuis were in the turret. The explosion blew the turret off and it landed on them, killing them instantly. Montenegro and Hebert were in the back, but they were blown out by the explosion, as was their Iraqi interpreter. Guenther and Monte had been tight, and

236

Guenther was with Hendrix when they found his body. Agami was the only one still in the Bradley.

Hendrix and McKinney could see Agami hadn't died instantly. He'd put up a struggle, trying to escape the flames. Rylance and Doc Ray had watched helplessly as Agami tried to get out of the hatch, but they couldn't get close because of the heat. It wouldn't have mattered. They couldn't have lifted the front of the upside-down Bradley to help their friend escape.

The explosion had blown a water main, flooding the hole left by the explosion and making it particularly difficult to recover the bodies. The explosion also made them difficult to identify.

Hendrix knew Montenegro and Wood by the neck tattoos they'd gotten together just before heading to Iraq.

At Apache, DeNardi rushed past the aid station; pure agony flushed his face bright red.

"They're all gone!" he yelled, and slammed a magazine into a wall. He went inside and punched a hole in the wall. He had heard the news over the radio. But the others continued to wait for word, hoping DeNardi was wrong.

The medics showed no emotion at all, game faces on as they calmly set up shade stations. If they thought too much, they wouldn't be able to help their friends. Men they dreamed with. Men they fought with. Men they loved.

The gunshots continued, and then another explosion.

The soldiers gripped each other, crying with faces buried in shoulders. Jorcke, who had been with Hendrix and Montenegro for that last beer in the Green Zone, sat lonely with a cigarette, his head hung low while he waited. Someone threw a water bottle and stormed away.

The MPs based with Alpha Company at Old Mod were out in Adhamiya that day with the major crimes unit, set up at a small Iraqi prison across from Apache. Major Eric Tangeman, the commander of the 630th Military Police Company, was talking with Major John Meyer, of the

Blue Spaders' Headquarters Company, at the prison. In the background, the radio suddenly woke up. The men didn't hear the explosion, but they heard the noise from a .50 cal.

Outside, Corporal Kristine Harlan pulled radio watch in a Humvee. She got a call. They needed to grab the fire trucks and head over to help Charlie Company. She ran inside the prison, looking for Tangeman. "We got to go!" she yelled.

But the trucks weren't close, and traffic seemed endless. At an Iraqi army checkpoint at Antar Square, Harlan lost it when she saw the line of cars. She jumped out of her truck and yelled at the Iraqi troops. "Move this fucking traffic!" The Iraqi fire station was just northeast of Antar Square, but it took too long to get the trucks. The Iraqi firefighters didn't seem to think there was any particular hurry. Finally they got the trucks, the MPs ready to scream with impatience.

Driving in, they knew the Bradley had flipped not far from where they'd lost their three MPs in March, and everybody felt nervous driving into the area. Already, the sounds were the same: gunfire and helicopters and explosions. Harlan could feel her stomach dropping out as she worked to remain vigilant. When the MPs finally reached their devastated friends, Hendrix asked them to provide an outer ring of security.

Tangeman had his company set up a cordon at Remy and Absolut, just southwest of the blast site. By that time, the mission was purely recovery.

As Harlan sat pulling guard, making sure Hendrix and McKinney and Guenther could work without any more grief from the insurgents, she could see bullet holes in the walls. Just in front of her truck sat an old car that had been used as a vehicle-borne explosive, seats shredded and windows blown out. Usually, with the helicopters and the cordon already deployed, the insurgents slunk back into their alleys. But Harlan expected action at any moment. June 21 was different. June 21 was coordinated.

Already nervous, Harlan jumped when she heard an explosion. She looked toward Clifton's Humvee sitting nearby. Clifton was the vehicle's driver.

She saw a poof of white dust coming from her friend's side of the Humvee—as if someone were spraying a fire extinguisher. Harlan radioed over, desperate to hear Clifton's voice. No one responded.

A rocket-propelled grenade had entered the truck through Clifton's side window and exited through the windshield, leaving two perfect softball-sized holes. Clifton had leaned forward at just the wrong moment, maybe to respond to a question or because she saw someone peek out from around the corner, and the grenade instantly decapitated her. Harlan, debating what she should do next, watched as the passenger's side door of the Humvee opened and Sergeant Douglas Quick got out of the truck, looking dazed. Shrapnel had hit him in the left side of the face. Immediately, he started taking fire.

Specialist John DeWeese felt a large chunk of shrapnel sear his right thigh while he sat in his gunner's harness in Clifton's Humvee. Out of the corner of his eye, he'd seen the rocket launch, and then he saw movement coming from the same area after they'd been hit. DeWeese let loose with his gun, going through a box of .50-cal ammunition. As the other MPs worked to evacuate First Lieutenant Ari Fisher, who had inhaled fumes from the fire-oppression system—the cloud of white Harlan had seen—DeWeese grabbed his M-249 light machine gun to cover them.

As Tangeman listened to the radio, he heard Staff Sergeant Joshua Manuel's voice come through, "Clifton's dead! Clifton's dead! We're evacking out!" Tangeman could hear gunfire in the background over the radio. Charlie and Alpha companies had sent trucks down to help, and Alpha Company commander Captain Jesse Greaves gathered his men to help the MPs move their wounded to Apache.

Because of the state of Clifton's body and because her door was jammed, Manuel decided to leave the truck there. He didn't want his soldiers exposed to that image for any longer than necessary.

Tangeman pulled up to the square to recover Clifton's truck. He ran to her door, taking intermittent potshots, and realized the door was jammed. Then he realized she was still inside. He decided to hook her truck up to another Humvee and tow it back to Apache without removing the body first.

As they worked to get the truck hooked up, Staff Sergeant Jonathan Mann and Chaplain Choi were on their way out to help. As they drove just east of Clifton's Humvee, an IED hit the right front of the chaplain's truck. The truck absorbed the blast, but the armor collapsed on Mann's leg, shattering it. Specialist Ranessa Gearhart, the truck's gunner, slammed her head. Chaplain Choi had massive contusions on both legs.

Tangeman could hear the attack over the radio. He needed to get Clifton's body back to Apache. As Alpha worked to evacuate Choi and his group, Tangeman turned his squad around and drove down Absolut. Not a soul walked down that road, or stood in front of a house, or looked out a window. As soon as the squad reached Antar Square, traffic rolled as if nothing had happened just yards away—and as if everyone had been warned not to be on Absolut.

No one had warned Charlie Company. Not on patrol that morning. Not as the MPs chatted with their Iraqi counterparts. Not through the anonymous tip line.

Back at Apache, the guys could see Apache helicopters popping out flares as they took rounds and rained down hell.

As the helicopters came closer, a soldier yelled, "Someone's coming in! They're hurt!"

Four military police soldiers rolled in, and the medics brought them in to the aid station, treating them for smoke inhalation. Mann, with his shattered leg, sat up on a stretcher outside the station, trying to help a medic with his leg. Blood and bone glittered in the sun. "You got to lay down, man," Specialist Tyler Holladay, a medic, told him. "We got you."

Osterman quietly worked on the details. He sprinkled water over the sand-covered road in front of the aid station to keep down dust. He handed out bottles of water to the men who had forgotten that it was 111 degrees. He gathered scouring pads from the cooks to wipe the blood from the inside of the vehicles.

Tangeman had all his soldiers inside the wire, and most of second platoon had come back, the scouts and Alpha Company taking over the recovery efforts.

Tangeman had his team put Clifton's truck in a corner of the compound away from everybody else. Colonel Schacht and Major Meyer came over to help deliver her body into a body bag, and then they carried her over to the aid station. "She must have been sitting forward," Tangeman said to the other two officers. The grenade went out through the windshield without ever exploding, leaving Clifton's body untouched from the neck down. The picture of her family remained taped to the dash of her truck.

Osterman came over to wash out the Humvee.

"I can't let you do that," Tangeman said. He would do it himself, wondering at the strength of soldiers who had lost so much but continued to offer up more, treating the MPs as if they were part of their family.

As the trucks began coming in with the remains of second platoon's men, officers started shooing the guys inside as the medics passed out body bags.

"Top said everyone, Osterman," DeNardi yelled as he stalked toward the building. Osterman nodded his head and stood fast. As the trucks rolled in with the injured and the dead, he would clear everyone away from the vehicles so he could clean them.

He drove the first Bradley to the hose. One of the cooks, Sergeant William Redding—the one who always volunteered for patrol when Hendrix needed headquarters platoon—appeared with scrubbies and bleach. "Are you OK?" he asked Osterman.

"I can handle it," Osterman said, as a grimace spread across his face that belied the numbness he tried to maintain. "I mean I can't. But I will."

Doc Ray walked toward the aid station, and his face looked as if it had aged twenty years, the lines usually reserved for laughter instead gathering dust and sweat and pain. His pants were wet to the waist from trying to get to Agami in the Bradley. "This is the hardest part," he murmured as he walked by, trying to accept that his friends were gone.

Inside the aid station, the chaplain bawled loudly. Choi should have been dead. Normally, he sat in the seat behind the truck commander, but for whatever reason, he tossed his bag in that seat and sat somewhere else. The blast hit directly beneath his bag. Everyone in his vehicle survived, but it wasn't the right day to praise his God because no chaplains had been killed in Iraq.

Choi had deep bruises to his leg and knee. But that wasn't why he cried. He had just performed last rites on ten people, including the civilians. He hadn't been able to tell who was Iraqi and who was American. Choi knew he had to explain to the men why God had let this happen. He knew he had to enable them to face the next day in Adhamiya.

"Jeez, chaps," Doc Holladay said, trying to face off desperation with a joke, and wanting more than anything not to see his chaplain cry. "I think your worst injury is the IV."

But Holladay knew the worst was still coming. He and Guenther and Whelchel and Hendrix and the other medics would identify the dead and fill out the paperwork. Holladay would look into the faces of his friends, and those faces would remain forever a snapshot in his memory. He would smell burned flesh.

But he wouldn't share those memories with his friends. He would build a fortress around them; he would remind himself that it was a privilege to spend that last bit of time with his friends; he would talk to the other medics about what they'd seen and what they'd felt.

Everybody else? They would hear that their friends had died quickly. That they had probably been gone on impact. Holladay would take comfort from his friends' ability to celebrate life rather than mourn death, even when the misery seemed insurmountable.

The quick reaction force soldiers began carrying in the body bags.

Some of the bags hung loosely, not possibly holding the strong men who had gone out.

Baka walked into his office at the S-1 shop. He looked at the noncommissioned officer in charge and immediately knew that Charlie had been hit. When he heard Sergeant Wood's name, he whipped his hat against the wall. His ballistic eye goggles were inside the hat. They shattered. "This is one horrible dream," he thought. His NCO told him there were four other soldiers inside.

Agami.

Leemhuis.

Montenegro.

Hebert.

And their Iraqi interpreter.

Baka had been scheduled to head to Apache that day for a battalion mission, but the news of his soldiers came in before he was due to leave Taji. Several of the men had talked to Baka about leaving the military after serving previous tours in Iraq, and their commander had worked with them to find good options. But Wood and Montenegro had both been stop-lossed. Baka had talked Agami into reenlisting so he could go to Fort Benning after Adhamiya, rather than facing stop-loss and another tour in Iraq.

Impossibly, June 21 grew worse. Every day, as part of his job, Baka looked through the list of people who had died in theater. A close friend, Major Sid Brookshire, was on that day's list. Baka and Brookshire had served together in the 101st Airborne where Brookshire had been a company commander and Baka had been a company executive officer. In Tennessee, the officers had lived two houses from each other on a neighborhood block. Brookshire had died June 20 when an IED went off under his vehicle in West Baghdad.

When everyone was back at Apache and dusk had fallen, Chaplain Choi gathered them inside the dining area. The guys weren't all ready to hear what he had to say. God had let them down. They wrapped tightly into themselves, unable to think about anything but how much it hurt.

Soon, though, the pain became about everybody else. The brothers looked around, their courage and pain mixed inseparably, and tried to comfort each other. One would break down, and another would speak up.

I love you, man.

We're going to be OK.

They're watching over us now.

Ybay wandered around, trying to offer kind words, but he couldn't force them through his own hurt. He could offer nothing but tears.

Tangeman and his soldiers remained until nightfall, when Tangeman witnessed an odd conversation. Sergeant Major McClaflin told Colonel Schacht he would be returning that evening to Taji to meet with the brigade commander.

"Why do you want to send me back to Taji?" Schacht said, obviously angered at the thought. "I need to be here. I need to be with my men."

McClaflin insisted.

Baka and Strickland thought the brigade commander's insistence on seeing Schacht meant they were going to be pulled out of Adhamiya, that the company had finally seen enough. Back at Taji, Baka called Cathy, "I think they're going to pull us out."

But in Germany, Cathy soon learned the day would only bring more misery.

Justin Schacht, the battalion commander's fifteen-year-old son, had just returned from a youth group trip to Italy. While his dad was deployed, Justin had let his hair grow into long curls, and his dad liked to tease him about it. But Justin was a confident kid whom everybody liked. The girls loved him because he was cute; his family loved him because he had stepped in to take care of his mom and his little brother, Brian, while his dad was away.

"I've got it, dad," Justin told his father as Schacht prepared to load on the plane for Iraq. "I can take care of this."

On June 21, after returning from Italy, Justin told the family he had been staying with that he wanted to go home and do some laundry and finish up some other chores. "OK," his friend's mother told him. "Just be home in time for dinner."

But he didn't come back. Justin's friends went to his house to check on him, and then the rear-detachment command staff broke into the house. They found Justin inside, unresponsive, and tried to resuscitate him. It was too late. Justin had an undiagnosed heart condition, and he died that day.

As the Schweinfurt community mourned the loss of five soldiers, they would also weep for Justin. Several of the men had teenagers who were also friends with the battalion commander's son.

Schacht immediately boarded a plane back to Germany, not even stopping long enough for an overnight bag. As he traveled, he carried the Blue Spaders' pain with his own.

At Apache, the medics carried their fallen brothers out to the helipad at nightfall for the Honor Flight back to the Green Zone. They laid each person out, with Karen Clifton and their interpreter side-by-side with second platoon. The medics identified the person inside each black bag.

The air grew quiet, as if Apache itself respected their loss.

Some soldiers talked, saying, "I love you," one last time.

Some laid their hands on the bags, needing one last touch.

Some cried.

They loaded their dead into the helicopter in the growing darkness, and then the soldiers wrapped their arms around each other as they watched the bird lift off, carrying their friends into the sky.

CHAPTER 20
Charlie Company Pulls Back, but Seethes

The men couldn't go back out—not yet. And probably not in Adhamiya. Not only were the lower-enlisted soldiers hurting, their bosses mourned from the same soul-crushing place.

"I've lost nine men," Ybay told Hendrix. "These are my guys, the best guys ever."

Hendrix felt the losses just as deeply, treasuring the time he'd spent with Monte and Jorcke in the Green Zone. He didn't know what to tell his platoon sergeant or his men. It wasn't just the platoon, it was the whole company. The losses created large holes: Someone would be missing on every patrol. Five empty beds made whole rooms feel like hallowed ground. Martin had lost his entire squad, the men he had turned to for comfort. At the last minute, Martin had been switched to a different Brad because they were short a driver. Hendrix didn't know where to begin. His men had bonded over too many losses.

And they'd lost their safety net. The Bradley had been their fortress. Inside its walls, they felt fearless. Now, no matter what they did, they would not feel safe. The bombs lay in wait for them.

None of the men could sleep. They took as many as ten Ambiens a day trying to find some time without nightmares, but the dreams never stopped. All of the men thought they should have been in that lead Bradley. Again, they replayed what they could have done to save their friends, Johnson unable to forget the sight of Agami. They wondered who would be next, because how could there be a future in Adhamiya that didn't include more death? They gathered and talked, but the same words came out every day without any resolution, no way to move forward.

On June 22, the day after their friends' deaths, they watched the news on the Armed Forces Network, numb and quiet and unable to do much more than sink down into themselves. General Petraeus came on the air and said Baghdad was getting better.

"You know what?" Johnson burst out. "Adhamiya's getting worse."

They railed, all of them, wondering how they could ever patrol again.

"How could you ask us to give out toys after something like that?" Johnson said, a muscle twitching in his cheek as he talked with his friends. "The guys—that's all you got. Anger. It just kind of becomes everything you are. You become pissed off at everything. You're pissed at the gate guards at Taji because they don't go outside the wire. You're pissed because you don't know why you're there in the first place. Why are we fighting with rules when they're not?"

Cardenas looked down at his boots from his seat on the couch as he talked about his loss of compassion—his loss of the piece of him that made his mother, and himself, most proud. "When they told us a couple of kids died in the explosion?" he said. "I was like, 'I don't care.' They knew the bomb was there. I cared for the first few months, but then the enemy started planting IEDs, and no one tells us. I stopped caring."

Johnson nodded his head, hands opening and closing into fists as he watched Cardenas's pained face.

"Man, I want to destroy everything in my path," Johnson said. "But we're not allowed to do that. We just keep building sewer systems and handing out teddy bears."

Their attitude toward the people who had sent them to Iraq—the American voters—plummeted to nothing. As Americans continued to obsess about Britney Spears's bald head—despite Woody's treatise— and Lindsay Lohan's drug problems, the Blue Spaders wondered if people ever heard stories about the troops. The Blue Spaders wanted people to know who had died: That Campos had a son who would grow up without a father. That Agami would give up the shirt from his own back to make sure Johnson had clothing after his laundry had been stolen. That McGinnis would throw himself on a grenade. That Hartge always had a grin, even on the worst days. The men who died had stories.

"Americans?" Johnson said, talking at the TV. "You don't support us. You don't know. You don't have a clue. Shake our hands. Say thanks and walk away. Leave us alone. We don't want to talk about it. If you want to know, sign up and find out. Other than that, live in your happy fairytale world."

Bitterness crept into a company that prided itself on catching insurgents. If the folks back home didn't care—didn't care about the deaths of their brothers—then what was the point? Even their accomplishments started feeling short-lived. It became hard to believe in their war.

"I don't think it's ever going to end," Johnson said. "For every one we kill, three more are going to pop up. We can defeat each network, but they'll just go everywhere else. We used to make fun of the people in Baghdad when we were in Fallujah and Samarra. Then it was Ramadi that was bad. Now it's Baghdad. It's almost like we're chasing our tails. For a time we'll make it better, but the Iraqi people don't keep it better."

Jorcke, who had been with Monte for his friend's last beer, said they should be able to "pull a Fallujah"—give the neighbors time to abandon their homes, and then clear the neighborhood knowing that everyone who remained was a bad guy. "Why can't we give them seventy-two hours' notice and just go through the neighborhood?" he said. But then he remembered the surge and the counterinsurgency and how well things were going in Baghdad, as Petraeus had just pointed out. "It's politics, man. Everything's going perfectly, and we're right across the river from the Green Zone. If we light everything up, people back home are going to hear about it. That's not going to happen, not while they're talking about how well everything's going."

"They don't let us take care of the people responsible," Cardenas said, baffled. "They tell us, 'It's too late in the game. We've already made so much progress.' In the past—like World War II—they kept pushing forward. That's what people don't understand about this: There's nowhere to push. So they just let us die."

On June 24, Charlie Company captured two insurgents, one of whom may have been involved on June 21. On July 2, they caught three more known insurgents and nine associates in Adhamiya. But the violence continued. On July 1, an IED killed Iraqi citizens near the Abu Hanifa Mosque. Charlie Company saw the insurgents run into an abandoned building and engaged them in a battle, killing them. Charlie Company figured the IED that exploded was a mistake, that it had been meant for the soldiers. Instead, it went off around a bunch of civilians and killed them. Usually, the people had been warned to desert the streets, otherwise the populace might turn on the insurgents. Ironically, third platoon secured the site and called an ambulance, providing just the assistance the insurgents would rather not see. Charlie Company brought out the explosive ordnance team to check for more explosives and found a second IED.

To save face, the insurgents found a local man and said the explosion was his fault. In the street outside the mosque, in front of a large crowd, the insurgents cut off the man's head, placed it in his lap, and set him on fire. Then they issued an announcement explaining that the insurgents had once again helped the citizens of Adhamiya.

Strickland and Hendrix sent second platoon to Taji to recover, figuring time in a safe zone with plenty of phones and e-mail access and Burger King and sleep would be the best treatment for the moment.

A few days later and a seeming world away, Major Patrick Brady, the brigade psychologist for 4th Brigade, 2nd Infantry, to which 1-26 was attached, started seeing men from Apache in his office at Taji. Two groups came in for debriefings to talk as a squad or a platoon about what they had seen. Sometimes, letting everyone talk about what he had seen cleared up some misconceptions. A soldier might say, "If only I'd gotten to Agami faster," and played ways over and over in his mind about how to do that. But another soldier could say, "I was there, man. It was way too hot. You would have burned up before you got there."

With Brady, they could talk about the problems they were having sleeping, or how scared they were to go back out again, or how they were so angry that they no longer wanted to help the Iraqis.

His office was situated far from everything, and soldiers could go there without being seen by their friends. In the sitting room, they could watch movies, drink Cokes, and sag into deep couches as if just that little bit of time away from the unit with no one judging them caused instant relaxation. Brady could talk to the men, but he knew he'd have to send them right back out into the same situation that had caused their mental duress in the first place. He might be able to get them a job at battalion, since most commanders were open to that idea if someone was suffering. But the commanders who were not? Their men weren't making it over to see Brady in the first place. He'd had that problem before, especially with infantry leaders. Their men weren't allowed to seek help.

But 1-26 seemed to get it, for the most part. It was more than Brady expected, considering Iraq was the first time the option had even been available. Brady had discovered that some platoon leaders were even aggressive about mental health, and had no problems marching their men in for help, possibly because they grew up in a generation of learning disorders and Ritalin, as well as surrounded by adults taking medication for depression. Other leaders still played General Patton, demanding that soldiers perform unnecessary tasks so they wouldn't think about the problems, when what they really needed was downtime and time to sleep.

A few men came back to Brady for one-on-one services. Three Charlie Company soldiers had been coming in regularly since early in the deployment. The commander of another company had just brought all of his men in so they would know the commander was open to their receiving care. Brady called that progress. He hadn't been anywhere else where platoon leaders came in after a traumatic incident.

But second platoon seemed to have reached a turning point from which they couldn't return. They wanted revenge. Brady made some phone calls: Maybe it was time to pull Charlie Company out of Adhamiya.

Baka worked the same request from the S-1 shop.

A week later, after the memorial service for the men they lost June 21, Strickland asked if the men were ready to go out again. Hendrix checked in with his soldiers, and they returned a couple of days later.

But two weeks later, Charlie Company, with the exception of first platoon, moved to Old Mod with the MPs and First Sergeant McKinney's Alpha Company.

Ybay told Hendrix he didn't think his men would be able to accomplish the mission any longer and that he couldn't handle losing any more men. He couldn't handle any more memorial services. He told his men he would keep them out of Adhamiya.

Strickland saw it in a more practical sense: He wanted to complete the mission in Adhamiya, to finish what they had started. But battalion had sent down word: You're pulling out. Strickland agreed that his men needed a break. He was afraid that one of his soldiers would get in trouble because of the extreme emotional state they were in.

"If they stay here, they're going to take the gloves off," he told Hendrix one evening. "That can't happen."

The 3rd Battalion of 7th Cavalry moved in to Adhamiya. They had more people, and they had just started their rotation in Iraq, so they had longevity. First platoon remained behind to show the new battalion around.

The battalion moved Charlie Company to Kadhimiya, a calmer neighborhood adjacent to Adhamiya.

Strickland saw zone 17 as the perfect spot for his men. It was a nonlethal fight—no explosions, no guns, no insurgents. They began working with the neighborhood advisory council and focusing on the "hearts and minds" end of the mission: schools, security, and diplomacy.

But Charlie Company's soldiers still saw grenades behind every wall and deep-buried IEDs at every corner. They were aggressive. They were used to thinking every child asking for toys served as a trap to get them killed. And first platoon remained at Apache. As time went on, Charlie Company realized they weren't going to get them back.

And the battalion still owned Adhamiya.

CHAPTER 21
A First Sergeant Breaks Down

As Charlie Company tried to recover, Alpha Company took over their patrols. Alpha, comparatively speaking, had had it easy to that point. The outer streets of Adhamiya featured mostly calm neighborhoods. In fact, their hardest days had come with assisting Charlie Company. But on those days, nothing could hold them back.

As Charlie Company moved into Old Mod from Apache, Hendrix began spending more time with First Sergeant McKinney, who had helped him recover his soldiers' remains June 21. Because McKinney was new to the position, he often went to Hendrix for advice. If anyone in the battalion could help get the building in shape, it was Hendrix.

But McKinney hadn't been acting quite right since June 21, and no one knew what to think of his newfound need to take care of his men to the detriment of himself. He seemed almost obsessed. Not only would he make sure his men got their proper nutrition, he wouldn't eat himself. Not enough water? Top wouldn't drink any, not even a sip. For days.

And no one had time to question it. The operations tempo had increased to the point that everyone was exhausted. Both first sergeants continued to go out with their men to try to improve morale, but then they both spent hours in the TOC helping with plans.

On June 24, a second IED exploded two feet in front of McKinney's vehicle, and the way he'd been acting triggered rumors that a traumatic brain injury may have been the cause of some of the changes his guys saw. But often, with TBI, the contusion affects the frontal lobe, and the damage causes anger-management issues—yelling and arguing. McKinney seemed to be looking inward—he was not yelling at his men—and the problems had begun before the explosion.

His medic, Sergeant Gary Pritchett, had a different theory: If the bomb had exploded underneath the vehicle, they all would have died. Each event McKinney encountered spoke to him of death.

Two days later, one of McKinney's men, Private First Class Jay Fain, lost his leg at the hip to an explosively formed projectile as he was leaving Old Mod to go on leave. McKinney was distraught, and he flew with his driver, Specialist Anthony Seashore, to the Green Zone to visit Fain in the hospital. Usually, the news of an injured soldier travels home by phone call, and families don't see their wounded sons until they arrive home. But Fain's father worked as a contractor in Iraq, so he also rushed to the hospital to see his son.

McKinney and Fain's father met in the Combat Support Hospital in Baghdad. More than anything, McKinney wanted to offer an explanation, but words about the importance of the mission felt inadequate. Instead, he broke down.

"I'm so sorry," McKinney said, crying. "I should have kept him safe. Please forgive me."

He repeated the words over and over, leaving Seashore shocked and Fain's father trying to comfort his son's first sergeant.

"This was not your fault," he said. "My son says nothing but the best about you."

When Fain was stable, he and his father flew back to Brooke Army Medical Center.

But McKinney would return to Old Mod, where his behavior would grow even more erratic. McKinney didn't sleep or eat for days, convinced he was taking away from his soldiers. Pritchett grew so concerned that he went to Captain David Escobedo, the battalion surgeon. McKinney himself told his company commander, Captain Greaves, that he had not been sleeping. After talking to Escobedo, Pritchett gave McKinney Ambien to help him sleep. But Pritchett later found McKinney sitting on a bunk in the aid station, where he had been for two and a half hours, just looking for some quiet. "Top," Pritchett said, "you need to go see Doc Escobedo yourself. This isn't right."

"I know," his first sergeant said. "I don't feel right. It feels like something bad's going to happen."

But over the next week, he didn't go see Escobedo. He continued to patrol, not sleeping and not eating. Seashore watched McKinney move as if he were in a trance. McKinney took the sleeping pills Pritchett gave him, but still didn't seem able to sleep. This was a man who normally refused to take aspirin for a headache, and yet the medication seemed to have no effect.

McKinney's cheekbones began to angle out from his face, and dark circles stretched beneath his eyes. Though he'd never been overweight, he kept a solid 185 to 200 pounds on his 5'8" frame. At Old Mod, that dropped to 170. He repeated the same thing over and over to Seashore and Pritchett: "I'm failing," McKinney said. "I'm not doing enough for my men."

Still, McKinney insisted on going on patrol. He wanted to be with his men and believed they were better off seeing him going out, even when he was just as scared as they were, than seeing him safe and waiting for them back at Old Mod, as is traditionally the case. Even while he seemed stressed out, he loved passing out the toys and toothbrushes and clothes his parents sent him to give to the kids. He liked seeing the reactions of little girls who acted as if they'd never before received a present. The children seemed especially excited by the toothbrushes, which was only surprising until McKinney learned most of the children had never seen a dentist and many of them were in pain.

He kept himself going by thinking of his family, ordering a fancy new computer, making plans for a new house with his wife, telling his nephew they'd get a beer as soon as he returned home.

On a Sunday night, McKinney called his wife Chrissi, who told him how his sons were doing. Jeremy was already a duplicate of and just as friendly as his dad, Chrissi told her husband. McKinney could hear the baby "talking" in the background. They had almost decided not to have the boy because they knew McKinney would deploy again soon. "I don't want to wait two years," Chrissi had said, as they made the decision to try. "I just have to have something of you if something happens."

On the phone, she instantly realized that the man she married because he made her feel safe even as he made her laugh was not safe himself.

"What's wrong?" Chrissi asked.

"I don't want to tell you," he said.

"Please tell me," she said. "What's wrong?"

It came out in a slur of quick sentences, like a rhyme.

"I feel really weird," he said. "I can't think straight. I'm not doing a good job."

He talked about the alcohol and drug abuse of some of his new soldiers, and said he was the third or fourth first sergeant the group had had in a year and a half. They were good men and he loved them and he didn't think he could give them everything they needed. He told Chrissi he wasn't sure he could make it through.

"We need you here," she said.

"I can't sleep," he said.

"Close your eyes and think of me and Jeremy and James," she said. He laughed and said, "OK. I'll do that."

But he'd fallen asleep on her as they talked, and she told him he needed to see a doctor so he could rest. He said he would do it on Monday. She believed him.

At the memorial service for the second platoon men who had died June 21, McKinney pulled his best friend, Sergeant First Class Floyd, aside. "I need to talk to you about something," he said.

But they never got a chance to talk.

(From left to right) Sergeant Derrick Jorcke, Private First Class Gerry DeNardi and Private First Class Armando Cardenas drink strong, sweet tea with an Iraqi family while out on patrol.

(Photo courtesy of Armando Cardenas)

Members of Second Platoon jump out of the back of a thirty-ton Bradley to patrol a street in Adhamiya.

(Photo courtesy of Gerry DeNardi)

The basement room at Apache where several members of Charlie Company slept.
(Photo courtesy of Armando Cardenas)

A Bradley rolls through a main street in Adhamiya. Insurgents often hid explosive devices in the trash that lined the streets.
(Photo courtesy of Armando Cardenas)

Abu Hanifa Mosque, where many of Charlie Company's battles took place.

(Photo courtesy of Mike Baka)

Sergeant Shawn Ladue received three purple hearts before returning home to Schweinfurt, Germany, where Charlie Company is based.

*(Photo courtesy of James J. Lee/*Military Times*)*

Private First Class Ross McGinnis, a member of First Platoon, was known for his silly antics at Apache. Before the end of their tour in Iraq, he would earn the Medal of Honor.

(Photo courtesy of Mike Baka)

Specialist Ernesto Martin *(far right)*, who learned English just so he could join the U.S. Army, takes the mike—and the prize—in another round of basement karaoke. Private First Class Gerry DeNardi holds a lighter in appreciation behind him.

(Photo courtesy of Rick Kozak /
  Military Times)

Sergeant Ian Newland, of First Platoon, stands in front of his family's new home in Colorado. Behind him are his daughter Haley, wife Erin, and son Dryden.

(Photo courtesy of James J. Lee / Military Times*)*

This is the outside of Combat Outpost Apache, a building that sits on the grounds of one of Saddam Hussein's palaces in Adhamiya.
(Photo courtesy of Armando Cardenas)

Second Platoon members Private First Class Armando Cardenas *(left)* and Specialist Ernesto Martin *(right)* make a toast at Christmas in Apache's newly constructed dining area.

(Photo courtesy of Ernesto Martin)

First Sergeant Kenneth Hendrix *(left)* and Captain Mike Baka *(right)* add some cheer to Charlie Company's Christmas celebration at Apache.

(Photo courtesy of Mike Baka)

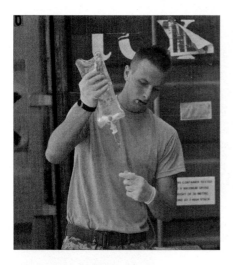

Medic Tyler Holladay readies an IV bag while waiting for injured soldiers to arrive at the aid station June 21, 2007.

(Photo courtesy of Rick Kozak / Military Times)

(From left to right) Battalion Commander Lieutenant Colonel Eric Schacht and battalion Chaplain Ed Choi check in on Charlie Company with Captain Mike Baka and First Sergeant Kenneth Hendrix.

(Photo courtesy of Mike Baka)

Members of Third Platoon pose in front of an up-armored Humvee.

(Photo courtesy of Jeremy Rausch)

In preparation for deployment, Charlie Company's Family Readiness Group held a Christmas party. Third Platoon's Staff Sergeant Juan Campos sits on Santa's lap.

(Photo courtesy of Cathy Baka)

Captain Baka works on improving relations with an Iraqi family in Ad-hamiya.

(Photo courtesy of Mike Baka)

(From left to right) Second Platoon's Specialist Ernesto Martin, Sergeant Billy Fielder, and Private First Class Armando Cardenas pretend they're being chased by a Bradley driven by Private First Class Daniel Agami.

(Photo courtesy of Ernesto Martin)

Second Platoon's Private First Class Daniel Agami *(left)* and Private First Class Gerry DeNardi *(right)*, out on patrol, play with Iraqi children.

(Photo courtesy of Gerry DeNardi)

Second Platoon's Private First Class Anthony Hebert was known for a big grin, as well as for making his friends laugh.

(Photo courtesy of Gerry DeNardi)

Second Platoon's Sergeant Ryan Wood naps in the back of his Bradley.
(Photo courtesy of Gerry DeNardi)

Second Platoon yells, "Hooah!" in formation in front of Platoon Sergeant First Class Tim Ybay at Apache.

(Photo courtesy of Gerry DeNardi)

Medic Timothy Ray checks a chart at the aid station after coming back to Apache following an attack.

(Photo courtesy of Rick Kozak / Military Times)

Soldiers from Charlie
Company patrol Adhamiya.

*(Photo courtesy of James J.
Lee / Military Times)*

Sergeant Jake Richardson *(left)* points out insurgent positions to his
gunner while Sergeant Erik Osterman retrieves an AT-4 rocket launcher
during a battle in Adhamiya.

*(Photo courtesy Sergeant Mike Pryor/2nd Battalion, 82nd Infantry Division, public
affairs)*

A cloud of dust and smoke envelopes Staff Sergeant Michael Mullahy seconds after he fired an AT-4 rocket launcher during a firefight in Adhamiya.

(Photo courtesy Sergeant Mike Pryor / 2nd Battalion, 82nd Infantry Division, public affairs)

(From top to bottom) Sergeant James Lee, Staff Sergeant John Gearhart, Specialist Lindsey Morgan, Specialist Chris Logan, and Specialist Nicole Crottie, all members of the 630th Military Police Company, sit next to a destroyed Humvee at Apache after their company responded to an attack on a Charlie Company Bradley fighting vehicle in Adhamiya.

(Photo courtesy of Rick Kozak / Military Times)

Sergeant Erik Osterman gives a hug to a fellow soldier after an attack that killed five Second Platoon soldiers and an Iraqi interpreter.

(Photo courtesy Rick Kozak / Military Times*)*

Charlie Company soldiers carry their wounded to the aid station at Apache on June 21, 2007.
(Photo courtesy Rick Kozak / Military Times*)*

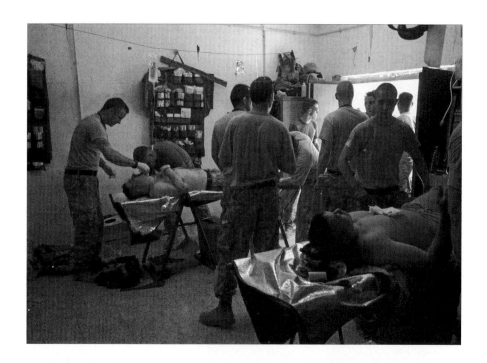

Medics treat the wounded at the Apache aid station on June 21, 2007.
(Photo courtesy Rick Kozak / Military Times*)*

Sergeant Derrick Jorcke *(left)* and Corporal Oscar De Alba *(right)*
mourn the loss of five friends June 21, 2007.
(Photo courtesy of Rick Kozak / Military Times*)*

Private First Class Gerry DeNardi *(left)* and Private First Class Armando Cardenas *(right)* prepare to go out on patrol.

(Photo courtesy of Armando Cardenas)

Staff Sergeant Robin Johnson *(right)* gives Private First Class Gerry DeNardi *(left)* a friendly head rub before DeNardi heads out on patrol.

(Photo courtesy of Gerry DeNardi)

Charlie Company soldiers check e-mail in the Internet hallway at Apache.

(Photo courtesy of Mike Baka)

Private First Class Tyler Norager messes around in the female port-a-potty at Apache. Charlie Company is an infantry unit, so besides one female interpreter and an occasional reporter, there were no females at Apache.

(Photo courtesy of Gerry DeNardi)

A Charlie Company soldier walks across the motor pool at Apache after coming back from patrol.

(Photo courtesy Rick Kozak / Military Times)

Private Omar Avila sits with his niece Haylee back home in Texas. Avila credits Haylee with saving his life.

(Photo courtesy of Omar Avila)

(From left to right) Cathy, Hannah, Mike, and Elizabeth Baka gather for a photo after Mike Baka returned home from Iraq.

(Photo courtesy of Cathy Baka)

Specialist Ruben Chavez *(left)* and Sergeant Ely Chagoya *(right)* dance salsa at a club after returning home from Iraq.

(Photo courtesy James J. Lee / Military Times)

Charlie Company soldiers gather for a toast to the friends who didn't come home from Adhamiya.

(Photo courtesy James J. Lee / Military Times)

On July 7, McKinney went on a night mission and acted the way his men like to remember him, forcing Seashore and Pritchett to sing the song from the Oreo commercial "Ice cold milk and an Oreo Cookie . . ." and playfully yelling at Seashore for not singing his favorite *Sesame Street* song. Everything seemed normal. Everybody laughed. Everyone seemed sure they had their first sergeant back.

But when they returned from patrol, McKinney reverted to the harried, hollow man he'd been since June 21. He stayed up all night preparing for the battalion's change of command the next day, when Lieutenant Colonel John Reynolds would replace Schacht. The man who dusted his Kinder Egg toys convinced himself he would fail, leaving Captain Greaves with a bad mark.

They passed inspection with perfect marks.

But Reynolds had to reassure the first sergeant that he was doing a good job.

Soon after, Seashore found McKinney sitting in a wooden shack that served as a supply room, all by himself. "I don't know how to handle this," he told Seashore.

Seashore adored his new first sergeant, and even as a young soldier, he did his best to console the older man. All day long, he would come up with excuses to check in on McKinney.

"Hey, what's up, First Sergeant?" Seashore would ask. "What's on your mind?"

And every time, McKinney would answer the same way: "This place is a mess. I'm failing this company."

Seashore would remind him of all the good he had done, of all the changes in the living conditions for the guys at Old Mod, of how much better everyone was doing since McKinney had moved people to platoons that better fit their situation, and of how well he'd done on the battalion inspection he'd been so worried about. Other companies hadn't fared so well, and the new battalion commander had no problem making it known who had failed.

But nothing Seashore said seemed to soak in.

McKinney went to see Captain Greaves.

"Sir, I'm failing the company," McKinney said, standing in Greaves's room at Old Mod. Greaves looked dumbfounded. He couldn't think of any areas in which McKinney had been doing poorly. Considering they were both new to the company, Greaves thought things were going pretty well.

"First Sergeant, I don't know where you're getting this," the young captain said. "I think you're doing a great job."

But Greaves knew that McKinney refused to sleep and that he zoned out by himself for several hours at a time.

McKinney would go to Greaves again and again with the same complaint: "I'm not doing enough."

On July 10, Greaves ordered McKinney to take some sleeping medication and to get ten hours of sleep. "You're on the verge of endangering soldiers by not sleeping," Greaves told McKinney. "You can't go on patrol again unless you sleep."

Greaves saw that McKinney looked ill and he knew his first sergeant had not slept for a while.

That night, Seashore got a visit from his platoon sergeant, who asked Seashore to watch McKinney on patrol the next day. "Top's not himself," the platoon sergeant said.

The next morning, McKinney showed up at Greaves's room at 2:00 A.M. to go over the morning's mission, as they had scheduled. Greaves was certain McKinney had been in bed by 5:45 the previous evening, two hours shy of Greaves's mandate, but still a good night's rest.

Except McKinney's men saw McKinney wandering the halls after 5:45.

After the platoon had gathered for the mission, Greaves asked McKinney to give the safety briefing to make sure the men knew the evacuation plan if they were to have casualties.

McKinney gave Greaves a blank look, unable to give a briefing he'd given many times before. Greaves gave the briefing instead.

And then sent McKinney out on patrol.

Greaves feared that if he sent McKinney back to bed, even though he so obviously needed sleep, his soldiers would lose confidence in their first sergeant, and that it would damage McKinney's self-esteem. He decided there were no apparent indications that McKinney wasn't capable of completing the mission.

But as soon as they left Old Mod, McKinney acted confused when he got a call on the radio. His gunner, Private First Class Roberto Lefurgy, watched as McKinney stared at the hand mike and took deep breaths, as if he were hyperventilating. Greaves realized his first sergeant wasn't going to answer and took the call instead.

There was no singing that day. McKinney played with a round from his M-4 and didn't say a word to his soldiers. At one point, Lefurgy, Pritchett, and Seashore couldn't tell if McKinney was asleep or if he had zoned out again.

That day, he didn't drink any water in the 117-degree heat. He obsessed that there would not be enough for his men.

They had a different interpreter that day, but even the Iraqis who had been treated like brothers in previous months felt like outsiders after June 21. The soldiers had a hard time trusting anyone. The platoon finished their mission, McKinney in and out of a fog throughout. The interpreter didn't want to walk all the way back to his own truck because it was too dangerous, but McKinney's men balked because they didn't want to change the seating order. Everyone had an assigned place.

"Let him in!" McKinney yelled, seeming tense and angry.

Seashore again asked his first sergeant what was wrong.

McKinney threw the M-4 round to the floor of the Humvee, opened the door, and got out.

"Fuck this!" he yelled.

The interpreter heard a gunshot and quickly looked around, thinking there was a sniper. He saw First Sergeant McKinney fall toward him. He saw white smoke, and he noticed teeth on the ground.

Lefurgy started yelling, "Hey! Where's the sniper? Where's the sniper?

But Seashore knew there was no sniper. He had heard McKinney yell, "Fuck this!"

Then McKinney turned around and looked at Seashore. McKinney pointed the muzzle of the M-4 beneath his own chin.

Just as McKinney pulled the trigger, Seashore saw his face change—as if McKinney realized what he was doing and did not want to do it. McKinney turned his head to the side even as the round came out of the barrel.

Seashore jumped out and pushed McKinney over so he could treat the wound. But when he saw his friend's eyes close, Seashore began to shake and back away in fear and hurt and horror.

McKinney's men evacuated him to Apache, where he died at the aid station. The autopsy showed that the bullet went in at an angle, as if he'd jerked his head to the side at the last minute, just as Seashore described.

At Old Mod, Staff Sergeant Gregory ran into Hendrix's room. "First Sergeant McKinney got shot!" he said.

Hendrix ran down to the TOC, where they told him McKinney was dead. It was an accident.

"Accident?" Hendrix exclaimed. "C'mon, he's a first sergeant. Who accidentally shot him?"

But then Chaplain Choi pulled him aside and told him McKinney's death had been no accident, that he had killed himself.

"What?" Hendrix asked, needing to be convinced. "McKinney seemed fine. I mean, we're all stressed out. He seemed like he was tired, but you know what? Fuck. We're all worn out."

But suicide somehow made more sense to Hendrix than an accident or even a sniper.

"It's been confirmed," Choi said. "His men saw it."

Sergeant First Class Floyd was working at the TOC at Taji, his last shift before a planned flight to Old Mod to see his friend. Over the radio, he heard a report come in that sounded almost like there had been an accidental discharge. Then someone called him directly to tell him it had been a suicide. Floyd couldn't fathom such a thing. McKinney had no history of mental illness, and he loved his soldiers too much to desert them.

Within days, Floyd moved into the room next door to Hendrix at Old Mod, taking over as first sergeant for his best friend's men. Immediately, he brought in Lefurgy, Seashore, and Pritchett to make sure they understood that they hadn't done anything wrong, that McKinney would never have deserted them if he had been himself, and that Floyd had loved their first sergeant like a brother. Floyd would take care of McKinney's men.

Hendrix and Floyd were devastated, but somehow not surprised. Hendrix thought about how the deployment had affected him, and he thought about the day the two of them stood waist deep in water and blood and their own tears trying to recover Hendrix's men.

Floyd wanted answers.

"Why didn't they send him to mental health?" he asked, as he and Hendrix talked, sitting on the bunk that had been McKinney's. "All the signs were there."

"I don't know," Hendrix said, shaking his head, rethinking all the answers that had played through his mind. "We've all been running around. It's hard enough to take care of yourself."

Floyd felt his own guilt. Why hadn't he kept in better touch? Why hadn't he pushed the issue when McKinney told him at the memorial that he needed to talk?

"You couldn't have known, man," Hendrix reassured him.

Floyd couldn't believe Captain Greaves sent McKinney out after blowing the safety briefing, but he told Hendrix the CO had been devastated by the death.

"I don't know why he let him go," Floyd said. "I know he saw changes. But it's not easy for a commander to say, 'First Sergeant, you can't do that.' I've never had a commander say that to me." And McKinney cared about his reputation. He wanted to appear strong for his soldiers.

Beyond missing a man both Hendrix and Floyd had known and admired for a long time, McKinney's death hit on a personal level. The idea that someone so strong could, in a second of hopelessness, take his own life scared the hell out of both first sergeants. Hendrix went to see Captain Strickland.

"Sir?" Hendrix said. "Do I seem OK?"

"First Sergeant, you're the most squared-away man I have," Strickland said, instantly understanding the fear. "We're all tired, but you still seem pretty alert, pretty together. You seem OK."

"But if I start acting funny . . . ," Hendrix started.

"We'll look out for each other," Strickland said. He told his first sergeant to take some time out for himself with Chaplain Choi or the mental health team at Taji.

And Hendrix did. He went in for a long conversation with Chaplain Choi. But from then on, the chain of command watched the first sergeants. McKinney's death, with all its warning signs, felt like a leadership failure. Captain Greaves could barely talk about McKinney's loss.

Floyd began the process of comforting his men. He sent a few members of Alpha Company to the mental health team, and was stunned and appreciative when their doctors called him. The doctors wanted Floyd to understand just how McKinney's death had affected his men and just what they would need. At the clinic, Lefurgy and Seashore and Pritchett took classes about stress management. They learned what they needed to do to be able to sleep. They talked to people outside their unit about how they felt, free of judgment. And they felt that Floyd cared about them because he paid attention to their anguish.

Each soldier had to work through each death in his own way. One of McKinney's crew had lost his brother to suicide, so he went back to that space in his life to find a way to heal again. Another bottled up his emotions. A third had been pretty aggressive, but wasn't after McKinney died. Floyd noticed, and shifted people around to help them cope.

All of the first sergeants paid a little more attention to their troops after that. But as Floyd watched after his men, he couldn't stop thinking about what he should have done for his best friend, even as he thought about Adhamiya's affect on all of them.

At Old Mod, Floyd and his soldiers prepared for McKinney's memorial service as they would any other soldier's—as if he had died in battle. Floyd comforted his men, but cried himself for the loss of a father, a husband, and a fishing buddy whose silly antics had cheered him so many times in the past.

At the end of the service, Hendrix put his hand on Floyd's shoulder.

"McKinney might have shot himself," Hendrix said. "But he didn't kill himself. Iraq killed him."

CHAPTER 22
Charlie Company Responds to Alpha's Catastrophic Loss

The insurgents seemed to be stepping things up, but still aiming for the government and the Americans. On July 15, when Iraqi police and soldiers ambushed a house in Adhamiya, they found that the building—and a corpse inside—had been rigged with explosives. The explosives detonated when the Iraqi forces entered the house, but no one was injured.

On July 18, Charlie Company was tasked for a clearance operation for zone 19 as part of a handover operation for troops who would be replacing them in Adhamiya. But the guys argued against it: The road was black—forbidden for travel. They had been warned there was another deep-buried IED and told to avoid it. Even without the warning, second platoon knew to stay away: No one lived in the houses lining the street.

"Is there going to be route clearance?" Sergeant Jorcke asked Ybay as the platoon sergeant briefed his men at Taji. "There's no way we're going out there without route clearance."

Ybay said he would check into it, and then laid out the plan: Second platoon only had two Bradleys left, so they would put ten men in each vehicle. The same thought ran through all of their minds: If there were another deep-buried IED, they could lose ten men. Stepping into the Bradleys had never felt so much like stepping into a trap.

Ten men.

But at the last minute, the brigade scrubbed the 3:00 A.M. mission.

A dust storm meant that medevac crews couldn't fly. And there were some problems with logistics: The Iraqi army wouldn't be able to go with them.

At about 9:30 A.M., second platoon learned that Alpha Company would perform the mission at 10:00 A.M. The storm had died down and the Iraqi soldiers were ready. "Holy crap," DeNardi said, when they heard the news. "Does Alpha know it's black?"

There was no way to contact them to find out. And Alpha Company was new to the area and wasn't as familiar with the routes.

That morning, Alpha Company had its first catastrophic loss when one of their Bradleys rolled over a deep-buried IED, killing all five men inside.

Second platoon remained at Taji that day. But third platoon and the scout platoon were already out in sector. When Sergeant Johnson rolled up on the burning Bradley one month after seeing Agami die, he felt as if he'd never left the scene of the first deep-buried IED. It looked the same: flames too high and hot for anyone to react, the carnage of his friends strewn across several blocks, soldiers trying to destroy the insurgents still shooting at them. First Sergeant Floyd was there that day, and First Sergeant Hendrix. As they tried to protect their men once again from the sight of a massacre, and to gather the dead soldiers they would never leave behind, they wondered how they could rally their guys to ever patrol Adhamiya again.

They added four names to the battalion memorial wall:

Specialist Daniel Gomez, twenty-one, the platoon's medic, wasn't available to help that day. Gomez had been inside the Bradley. In high school, Gomez played football and served as commander of his Junior Reserve Officer Training Corps. He wrote a paper for an English class about what medics do, and then he became one.

Sergeant First Class Luis Gutierrez-Rosales, thirty-eight, served as platoon sergeant for Alpha Company's first platoon and was well known throughout the battalion. He had been in the army for eighteen years, had served in the California Conservation Corps before joining the military, and had an eight-year-old daughter named Amber, whom he adored.

Specialist Zachary Clouser had also played football and earned himself the nickname "Babyface" because he looked younger even than his nineteen years. He loved to hunt and fish, but loved even more to spend time with his six brothers and sisters.

Specialist Richard Gilmore III, twenty-two, had loved to ride his dirt bike, go fishing, and play the saxophone with his brother, and they'd hoped to open a restaurant together when Gilmore got out of the military. He had joined to take care of his family: his wife, Jimmiesue, and his toddler son, Malakiah, and daughter, Alexis.

Alpha Company also lost an Iraqi interpreter that day.

CHAPTER 23
Charlie Company Mutinies and Is Torn Apart

Second platoon reacted as if they'd been out with Alpha Company. As if they had recovered the bodies. As if they had lost four more friends.

In essence, they had. When they heard about the explosion, each man replayed in his mind the day they'd lost Agami, Leemhuis, Wood, Montenegro, and Hebert. They'd known the Alpha Company men well. They always saw each other on battalion missions, and Sergeant "Goot," as the guys called Gutierrez-Rosales, had traveled throughout the battalion before arriving as a platoon sergeant in Alpha.

They were furious. At Taji, they gathered in between their hooches, not even trying to hold back their tears. "We knew there was a five-hundred pound bomb on Route SoCo," Jorcke raged, referring to Route Southern Comfort. "We've known it for months. It's black. Didn't they know it was black?"

"I just want to blow it all up," DeNardi said. "Blow up the whole city."

"What if we'd gone out?" Cardenas said. "Ten men. Gone."

"We'll take care of you, bud," Sergeant Billy Fielder said. "We're done."

"We're all done," Jorcke said.

Ybay could see that June 21 affected his men like a scab that wouldn't heal up. They said they weren't ready to go out, and he wouldn't force them. Ybay said he would stand by them. He said he would not

267

send second platoon back in sector. Every member of second platoon was taking sleeping medications that Ybay didn't take, so he didn't understand the confusion and sleepiness that came with the pills, especially since the guys took handfuls of them, desperate for sleep. Dreamless sleep.

He listened to them talk. He could hear that they weren't ready, and he told them that. They talked about what might happen if they went out: Would they perform the mission properly?

Ybay went to battalion to check in on the situation and see what was needed of second platoon. Second platoon marched themselves as a group over to the mental health clinic as much to demand an explanation as to seek help. How could they be expected to continue fighting? They hadn't talked as a platoon, and they needed to. Their former platoon leader, Maravilla, who had moved to battalion to serve as the executive officer, advised them to talk to mental health about why they could not patrol.

In the clinic, they talked about the ethical repercussions of taking out their anger on the civilians of Adhamiya, as well as how it could affect their own lives. Most of them were in their early twenties. None of them wanted to end their careers with jail time.

"If we go out, I'm going to murder someone," one of the guys said, teeth bared. Others agreed, nodding their heads almost shamefully, as if they couldn't quite control the urge. The need.

"If we go back in sector, we're going to do some stupid shit," an NCO said.

"There comes a time when you need to stand up," the counselor said.

"For the sake of not going to jail, we need to be unplugged," Jorcke said. To a man, the platoon agreed, including the remaining squad leaders: Gregory, Morris, and Villa; and team leaders: Fielder, Brown, Jorcke, Specialist Ruben Chavez, Specialist Stephen Breen, and Sergeant Michael French.

But their commander had a different idea: He had been expecting second platoon in Adhamiya for their scheduled patrol that evening. In fact, he didn't realize they weren't coming until someone told him they were not out on patrol. Strickland called Ybay.

"They're not coming," Ybay said. But for whatever reason, Ybay did not tell Strickland that his men had been taking sleeping pills and had taken a trip to the mental health clinic. He didn't know how bad the situation was at Taji.

Strickland thought second platoon refused to go out because they were scared, so he asked Ybay to remind them of the things they'd talked about in the past: If you refuse to go out, these are some of the things that could happen.

"A scheduled patrol is a direct order from me," Strickland told Ybay. It wasn't that he necessarily had to have the platoon out there that night—which he later acknowledged—but he couldn't have a platoon refusing to follow an order.

But nothing was connecting. It was a normal patrol. It wasn't like second platoon to refuse an order because if they didn't go out, someone else would have to. And into the thirteenth month of their deployment, they'd never backed down because of fear.

Ybay had been filling in as platoon leader because Maravilla had moved to battalion, which meant Ybay played both the role of father figure and disciplinarian, putting him in an odd spot with his guys. Rather than being able to stand up for his men to the platoon leader, who would then report to Strickland, Ybay felt he had to make his men execute the orders. They had a new platoon leader, but he'd only been in the slot for ten days. At that point, he didn't even fit into the equation.

Strickland was baffled. He'd asked Ybay to give the men a direct order, and they had refused. He felt as if they were thumbing their noses at him. Normally, it would take a lot to piss the commander off, but that day took him to his breaking point.

"If you're given an order, you've got to execute," he told Ybay.

But he still didn't know everything that was happening at Taji.

Strickland let the new battalion commander know his men refused to patrol. He had to. Reynolds demanded that they meet up at Old Mod.

Ybay asked for volunteers to roll with him to Old Mod. As far as the men knew, it was only to get their platoon sergeant to the base, not to go out on patrol. But Hendrix and Strickland believed the men were coming out to begin their patrol schedule.

When Ybay asked the men willing to head out to raise their hands, nobody did.

Martin struggled, thinking about first platoon, which was still in second platoon's sector by themselves. He wasn't afraid of punishment, but on that day, third platoon had seen the same carnage Martin had seen June 21 when his entire squad died.

Martin raised his hand.

Specialist Randale Charley saw Martin's hand go up.

"God damn it, Martin," Charley said, then raised his own hand.

Then Cardenas realized his buddies had signed up.

"God damn it, Martin," Cardenas said, and grabbed his gear. "You're not going out without me."

Ybay called Strickland.

"I've got seven men who are ready to go," he said. They drove from Taji to Old Mod. When they got there, Hendrix could hear in Ybay's voice how much it hurt to say his men were not ready to patrol—would not patrol. As Ybay finally explained what was going on back at Taji, Hendrix and Strickland realized that everyone needed to go to bed. Second platoon would not go out on patrol that night.

Hendrix understood where second platoon was coming from, but he was worried about first and third platoons, too. They were also missing their friends. Second platoon had been hit hardest, but the company was just too tight. The men who died June 21 had soldiers who called them "best friends" throughout all of the platoons. Everybody was hurting.

As second platoon closed in on itself, third platoon was supposed to return to Taji. Instead, they remained at Old Mod for eighteen days without a break after responding to Alpha's Bradley.

Third platoon was angry.

"What the hell?" Halbasch complained to Johnson after yet another patrol. "I get it, but we're still going out. We're still risking our lives."

Third platoon called it a leadership issue. They were never upset with the squad leaders in second platoon: The battalion executive officer—Maravilla—should not have told second platoon they were correct in their decision not to roll out and that they should go to mental health to make it stick. Someone should have explained what the mission was. Ybay should have told Strickland about the sleeping medications before the situation was blown out of proportion. And no one should have ever promised second platoon they wouldn't have to go out again. The men felt betrayed by Ybay's promise, but Hendrix believed Ybay was right to expect his men to follow orders when the circumstances changed.

But Halbasch felt sad, too. DeNardi was his best friend, and he considered him—as well as several other members of the platoon—a hero.

"They could have said, 'We don't approve of how this mission was handled,'" Halbasch told Johnson. "'You shouldn't have sent Alpha on a black road.' Instead, it was like little kids who didn't get their way. It casts a really bad light on Charlie Company."

Johnson, who loved Ybay and loved second platoon, felt his emotions fighting with each other.

"I think it could have been handled differently," he told Halbasch. "There were a thousand other things second platoon could do. Call them pogues. Call them fobbits. They'd done their time." Fobbits are troops who never leave the forward operating bases.

But Johnson ran back and forth between listening to Ybay and listening to second platoon: "Don't be mad at Sergeant Ybay. Don't be mad at the guys."

He wanted everyone to remember where they had come from—what they had been through together.

At Taji, Jorcke and the other noncommissioned officers fought for their men and insisted they had made the right decision. "As a soldier, we're supposed to do our jobs," Jorcke tried to explain to Ybay. "But we don't feel like we're doing our jobs. Right now, it's more important for us to bring everybody back alive."

Colonel Reynolds asked for a list of everyone who hadn't volunteered to go to Old Mod with Ybay. Ybay offered it up.

On the nineteenth, Reynolds relieved the squad leaders of duty for cause. They were read their rights. "I'm so disappointed in you," said Reynolds, who had been in command for ten days and knew none of them—and didn't know Adhamiya. He had never set foot there.

Though the soldiers of second platoon were never formally charged, the mutiny was recorded in their files as counseling statements. Everyone in the platoon had administrative flags placed on those files, stopping all of their promotions and awards and prospective schools for when they returned home. That decision came from Reynolds.

Hendrix, knowing his men, decided to consult them, to make them part of the decision about what needed to happen next. He pulled all the NCOs from the company immediately after the platoon refused to go out. He asked Chaplain Choi and Captain Strickland to leave. The soldiers needed to talk to their first sergeant.

"What do you guys all want to do?" Hendrix said, when he had his men to himself. "Stay at Apache? Or do you want to leave?"

Half said they wanted to stay, but it became clear quickly that their idea of the mission differed greatly from battalion's: They wanted revenge. "We got to be able to lay the wood to them," one said. "If I do stay, you got to let me break down some doors."

"I can't let you do that," Hendrix said. "The overall mission has to be more important than what happens to one platoon."

More of the men said they couldn't take it anymore. They were done. They were tired of watching their friends die.

"Hey, look," Hendrix said, trying to look each man in the eye in turn, and trying not to think about the sergeants who weren't there. "I can't take it anymore either."

The sense of loss hit them in another wave, and Hendrix broke down. His men were crying and miserable, yet they should have been proud of all they had accomplished. Suddenly, the mission seemed clear to him.

"We need to take everyone home," he told them. He had decided to get Charlie Company out of Apache and out of Adhamiya. "I'm not going to lose any more soldiers in three months in the same shithole." He wasn't worried only about his men. Hendrix had bitten his fingernails down to the bone, and there had been talk of removing him from command after McKinney died. Hendrix had seen casualty after casualty after casualty. So many men had been injured. He had soldiers who might not walk again, who might never go to college because their brains had been rattled, and who might never have the opportunity for a wife and children because they'd been so horribly disfigured. If he, a first sergeant with three prior combat tours, was having a hard time holding up, he couldn't expect more of men barely out of high school experiencing death for the first time.

And he was afraid second platoon's anger and grief would spread to the rest of the company.

Hendrix and Strickland talked about what needed to happen next.

"Sir, second platoon has hit the point of no return," Hendrix said, his heart heavy. He was so proud of his men, but he knew they could no longer operate as a platoon. "They need some new NCOs."

Immediately, the NCOs were flown out of Apache. Staff Sergeant Nicholas Peltier and Sergeant Jorcke were assigned to an engineer brigade and would not return to Germany until a month after Charlie Company, a sixteen-month tour. They would perform escort duties for engineers clearing roadside bombs. The recently promoted Corporal Ron Brown was assigned to Alpha Company of the 1st Battalion, 25th Regiment. Specialist Oscar De Alba was sent to Headquarters Company. Staff Sergeant John

Gregory became the NCO in charge of the tactical operations center. He'd lost half of his squad June 21.

Second platoon ended up with new sergeants and new privates, but felt abandoned.

"They just pushed Jorcke out of the battalion," Cardenas said, not saying anything DeNardi didn't agree with as they sat on their bunks at Old Mod. "Our leaders just don't care. They knew they shouldn't send Alpha, and then they broke us apart."

The idea that awards and promotions were delayed infuriated them.

"You're talking about heroes," DeNardi said, including Cardenas as he listed them off. "These are guys who save lives, and they can't get awards."

Army Commendation Medals and Bronze Stars were put on hold. Privates first class due for promotion missed specialist for two months. A sergeant had to go through the board process again.

Osterman also watched what happened to second platoon as a former insider. He felt that Hendrix and Strickland removed the wrong men, and he told Jorcke so as he prepared to leave for the engineer battalion. "I would have moved a different platoon sergeant in," he said about Ybay, angry over an issue he saw as black and white. "If you lose control of an entire platoon, how do you function? How do you not know your entire group of guys was on meds? How do you have an entire group of guys saying, 'I won't go'? That whole situation fucked up so many people, including those outside the platoon."

Jorcke told Osterman there had been a misunderstanding, but that no one seemed willing to listen.

"What really confused all of us is that we were read our rights for dereliction of duty and failure to obey a lawful order from the commander, and all of us were flagged and sent to the four winds," Jorcke told Osterman. "But we were never given a lawful order. We were given a choice to go to Old Mod, and after all the deaths of our comrades from our platoon, our company, and our sister company, why the hell would we volunteer to go out unless it was to wreak havoc upon the insurgents who did this to our fellow soldiers and the citizens of Adhamiya? We would never refuse to go out in sector to close with and destroy the enemy: It's our job—we're infantry. But cordon and knocks, especially after your best friends have just died and the populace won't give you any info because they are more afraid of the insurgents than of you is a hard pill to swallow. The chain of command was told that we refused to go out in sector, and not that we were given a choice by our platoon sergeant."

But everyone agreed they had, in fact, decided to refuse if they hadn't been given that choice.

Osterman hated to see NCOs flagged, especially when they were never formally charged with anything.

And Jorcke felt like a scapegoat. He blamed the fallout, in part, on Reynolds.

"He doesn't know any of us," Jorcke said. "I honestly believe, if he had been with us the whole time, he would have said, 'There's something deeper going on here.' We just lost five men. If we had actually gone down that road, we would have lost an additional ten because that's how many people we had riding in the Brads."

As far as Strickland was concerned, the investigation ended as soon as he talked to his men. He lifted the flags a couple of months later and tried to let the men know that even though he didn't agree with their decision, he respected that they wanted to look out for their soldiers. The goal had not been to punish them. He understood they had acted out of frustration after twelve months of hell. He understood the army does not have in place a way for troops to stand down if they feel incapable of containing their rage. Charlie Company's leaders needed to reorganize the platoon so it could continue to function, but every man had performed too well to punish them for a day that could have been much worse had they actually gone out in sector.

In their minds, they had followed the same principles Sergeant Wood had when he turned in his platoon sergeant for unlawfully killing an Iraqi. And in Strickland's mind, they had already faced enough punishment.

Months later, when Jorcke saw First Sergeant Hendrix again, he didn't feel anything but admiration. He told Hendrix he understood why second platoon had been disbanded, though Jorcke felt nothing but pain after being pulled away from his men.

"We definitely have unfinished business," Jorcke told the man he would always call "Top." "We can't ever say, 'I left Iraq and my buddies didn't die in vain.' But in a way, the disbanding was good. We got to come back home alive—what was left of our platoon."

And that was the plan.

CHAPTER 24
The Battalion Faces Its Last Casualty

After trying to comfort Chaplain Choi, after working hard not to "replace" Doc Gomez after the Alpha Company medic died in July in the second catastrophic IED explosion, and after studying his medical books even harder after losing his friends, Specialist Tyler Holladay had also earned the title "doc."

But somehow he knew he would be next.

The medics fell under the command of Headquarters Company. In Adhamiya, they were assigned to the line companies as they were needed. For Holladay and the other medics, this meant that they didn't fall in anyone's chain of command. Of course, if an NCO told Holladay to do something, he did it. But if someone was injured out on his patrol, Holladay ran the show. Even officers would obey his orders—to help hold bandages, to provide cover, to evacuate.

Holladay's affinity to Headquarters also meant the men of Charlie Company, from the highest sergeant to the lowest private, felt safe talking to Holladay about everything from bad dreams to headaches to jock itch.

But even as Charlie Company headed out of the worst areas of Adhamiya, Holladay remained behind. Alpha Company needed him.

Holladay had met his first casualty on the streets of the city. The twenty-one-year-old former high school athlete joined the army when he realized he'd spent too much time on high school sports, and he wasn't going pro. But his stepfather was a medic in the National Guard, and his grandfather a medic during World War II, so Holladay visited a recruiter.

At first, he was a little unsure of his skills. He'd had plenty of training, and seen plenty of gory movies to try to get used to what he might see, but actually sticking his hands down in the pulsing blood of a human being—of a friend—had surpassed what his imagination could encompass.

But Holladay, tall and blond and lanky, with dark smudges under his blue eyes, earned the trust of his men quickly. Like most fresh medics, Holladay hesitated on that first casualty. An Iraqi civilian had been shot twice, and Holladay couldn't save him. No one could have.

His second casualty was an Iraqi army colonel. The officer had been shot in the back and the bullet came out his chest. This time, Holladay caught himself thinking about what to do for about two seconds, and then went to work, the knowledge he'd gained in training and watching the other medics poured out through his hands. Holladay had to seal off both the exit and entrance wounds. No problem. The medics stabilized the man at the aid station and sent him to the hospital.

The American casualties reminded him that his men were not invincible. For all the body armor and helmets and guns and armored vehicles, they could still die, and die horribly. In March, when the military police company had hit that daisy chain of roadside bombs, Holladay had been working the aid station. He helped fill body bags with the liquefied remains of fellow soldiers. That day, the possibilities solidified into one thought: "You're not only going to die here, you're going to be disfigured. It's going to hurt. It's going to be quick. And it's going to be messy."

Over the course of a year, he treated more than one hundred people.

But like his friends, he always went out. The Blue Spaders needed him, and no amount of gore could convince him that he should put his own safety ahead of anyone else's.

On the morning of July 31, a perfectly normal day after a fairly calm week, Holladay went out on patrol to search abandoned cars. They littered the streets of Adhamiya, often placed there to secure roads or because the owners simply couldn't get gas or supplies to keep them running. Everyone was in a lighthearted mood, joking around. "Hey, Ty," one of the men said. "I bet you could pimp this ride." Holladay was known for washing and waxing his car every day back in Germany—and souping it up with ground effects and hubcaps and mufflers and tinted windows.

They both laughed. Most of the cars in Adhamiya had been blasted by bombs or bullets, and often lay on their roofs with the tires all missing. "I could totally pick up chicks in that," Holladay said, taking a knee on the crumbling sidewalk between the car and the wall. He pulled security, weapon and eyes up, while someone else checked the car and marked its coordinates.

He listened to one of his favorite songs, "Hey There Delilah," by Plain White T's over his IPod, singing along as he watched the street: *And I'll be making history like I do . . .*

"OK, bud, let's get out of here," Holladay's gunner said.

Holladay took two steps back.

"You know, if this car had a nice coat of paint and maybe a windshield, I'd be wanting to take it home," Holladay said. "Do you think it'd pass the German safety standards?"

Then he heard a loud bang. The bullet went in through his back and out through his stomach, just above his hip and just below his body armor. A stomach wound.

"Shit," Holladay muttered. Nobody wants to mess with a stomach wound.

But Holladay quickly realized he couldn't depend on the medic.

He was the medic.

He couldn't retreat inside himself or he wouldn't be able to tell the gunner what to do. Holladay had to stay calm.

Immediately, his gunner went for the wound with a dry Curlex bandage.

"No, man," Holladay said, trying to sound as normal as possible even as he panicked inside. "I need a wet dressing."

The other soldiers also get first aid training, and several of the medics helped their soldiers through combat lifesaver courses, but just like Holladay on his first case, the gunner froze up a bit.

"You work on the back," Holladay said. "I'll take care of the front."

In back, all the gunner would have to do was stop the bleeding. And the back wasn't nearly as ugly as the exit wound in front, so he'd have less reason to panic.

Holladay realized his large and small intestines must have been hit. He could feel his stomach filling up, so he knew there was internal bleeding. He knew what the chances of survival were. He started thinking about the people who were important to him: the other medics back at the aid station. Holladay turned to his gunner.

"Let Kupau know I love them and I'll miss them," he said. And then he passed out.

His men loaded Holladay into a Humvee and raced back to the aid station at Apache, and from there transported him by helicopter to the Green Zone.

For the next three hours, Alpha Company kicked in doors and tried to find the person who had shot Holladay. They didn't know if their medic was dead or alive.

The bullet had entered right where the appendix sits.

But Holladay's appendix had been removed when he was a child. If he'd had an appendix, he would have died.

Instead, doctors at a military hospital in Baghdad stitched his intestines back together. He couldn't eat for several days, but would require no further surgery. He flew to Walter Reed Army Medical Center to recover.

Holladay was the last member of the 1-26 wounded in Adhamiya. In fifteen months, thirty-one men of the 1-26 were killed and one hundred twenty-two wounded, making it the hardest-hit battalion since the Vietnam War. Charlie Company suffered the most, with fourteen men killed. Second platoon lost nine men.

CHAPTER 25

Charlie Company Works Toward Healing

After June 21, the battalion decided that Charlie was finished. Their so-called mutiny only confirmed that decision. In the background, Baka fumed. "I tried to tell the command," he told Hendrix when the first sergeant came out for a visit to Taji. "It kills me that June 21 had to happen before anyone would listen."

Baka knew his history: Units in Vietnam and World War II had been wiped out but were constantly replenished with new men who would come to the same fate. But this was a different war. There would be no multitude of patriots joining to fight against a threat by the Germans and the Japanese to take over American soil, no draft to prevent the perceived domino effect of communism spreading from Vietnam outward.

This was a volunteer force, not backed by any public outpouring of support as the years went on in Iraq with no measurable progress. A volunteer force doesn't have to stick around. They could finish their tours and head out, as many midlevel officers—Baka's cohorts at West Point included—and enlisted were in fact doing. If the generals bragged about how quiet it was in Baghdad, why not switch some companies out? And if it were so quiet in most of the city, why not add to Adhamiya's ranks? Why leave them with two hundred men?

"I don't get it, sir," Hendrix said, running his hand over the buzz of his hair. "They've proven themselves again and again, but I don't know how any of us continue to function."

They had theories: Charlie Company knew the area better than any-one else and consistently accomplished the mission. If officials put more troops in Adhamiya, it might look as if they had a problem there. And maybe fourteen dead men don't equate to fourteen dead brothers to the logisticians who still saw them only as part of the army machine: The soldiers knew what they signed up for.

Nobody signed up for Adhamiya.

They signed up because they had read *Band of Brothers* and wanted a taste of that camaraderie. They loved the old John Wayne movies and pictured war as a blaze of glory, rather than helplessness against hidden bombs. They believed in the soldier creed and leaving no soldier behind and battle buddies.

But in Adhamiya, they began to believe they were cogs in the ma-chine, which only made them look out for each more fiercely.

And they had to. Even the officers called the new battalion com-mander "Lord Farquaad" for his striking resemblance to the Shrek char-acter, but not to his face, a sign that his personality lined up too closely with the cartoon. Reynolds had come to the battalion in July to replace Schacht, who had flown back to Germany because of his son's death. But that meant Reynolds came in at the tail of the tour without having to ex-perience any of the misery. His first encounter with his new soldiers had been First Sergeant McKinney's suicide, and then second platoon's "mu-tiny." From that point forward, his main goal appeared to be punishment.

Baka told Hendrix what was going on, furious that anyone would see anything but courage in Charlie Company, which Reynolds referred to as a "problem child."

"He wants to downgrade Monte's Silver Star to an Arcom because he was in second platoon," Baka told Hendrix, jaw tight and fists closed.

"What?" Hendrix said. "But he died before that even happened. That doesn't make sense."

"He doesn't want the platoon to have any recognition," Baka said.

Because Baka was in charge of awards and promotions, he had argued with his boss—respectfully, of course—saying Montenegro deserved every bit of recognition possible.

"Sir, with all due respect, he died before that happened," Baka had said, just as Hendrix later repeated. In January, when Hill died and Grose was injured, Montenegro had jumped up on the vehicle, recovered his weapon, and continued to fire to cover his men.

But Reynolds believed that the platoon had behaved so badly that none of its members deserved anything. Reynolds sent the recommendation up with comments that it should be downgraded to an Army Commendation Medal—or Arcom—an award often offered at the end of a soldier's tour of duty just for keeping his nose clean.

Montenegro's medal did eventually get downgraded to a Bronze Star with Valor, but so did every other recommendation sent up to brigade that didn't involve an officer.

It wasn't just Charlie Company. In the cartoon, Lord Farquaad was such a perfectionist about rules that common sense got lost. At Old Mod, Reynolds would get frustrated with his company commanders because the soldiers weren't wearing their long-sleeved uniform tops inside the building with no air-conditioning, or because soldiers didn't salute Reynolds when they saw him. They had been used to living on a base where officers didn't necessarily want their troops to point out who was in charge to the enemy. They had also grown accustomed to leaders who commanded respect, rather than demanding it.

None of this was good for morale, but the officers tried to shield their men from the wrath of a commander who had showed up too late to play ball, but who loved to take credit for every bit of progress that had been made.

But with the help of the brigade commander, Colonel J.B. Burton, Captain Strickland made plans to move his company out of Adhamiya. From Old Mod, the company—with exception of first platoon, which remained behind to train the company's replacement—patrolled Kadhamiya and Rusafa, Shiite neighborhoods just one road and one river away from Adhamiya. But in their new neighborhoods, the streets were paved and clean, and no bullets flew.

"Wow," DeNardi said, upon first encountering the new neighborhood. "Civilization on one side and chaos on the other."

"Dude, don't let your guard down," Cardenas said, unable to believe they were still in Iraq and they didn't need to fear for their lives at every turn of a dusty road. "I don't trust any of them."

But as it turned out, they wouldn't have any serious encounters in the three months they would spend in neighborhoods south of Adhamiya. In fact, the hardest part of patrolling the neighborhood—full of children and shops and friendliness—was trying to come down, to not shove guns in the faces of civilians not used to battle-weary soldiers.

Alpha Company picked up part of Charlie's old sector in Adhamiya, even after the loss of their Bradley. First Sergeant Floyd and Captain Greaves went out in sector with their soldiers as often as possible. A couple of times, soldiers told their NCOs they were too frightened to go out, but rather than encountering bravado that beat them down, Floyd would send that soldier off to mental health. Or he'd offer to ride along. He understood how the losses and fear had affected his best friend, First Sergeant McKinney.

And Floyd was proud of his men. They'd fought hard. They never backed down. And they understood and filled in when Charlie finally got a break.

Strickland cut Charlie Company's rotation schedules way back. They didn't have to do the left-seat/right-seat training with the troops coming in to take their place at Apache because that had already been done. Rather than twenty-four hours at Taji, Strickland had the guys spend several days so they could go to the movie theater, hit the pool, or hang out at the PX looking for new music, video games, and movies. The tank platoon now attached to Charlie Company helped fill in some of the patrols, but they just didn't go out as often. They didn't need to. Outside Adhamiya, life remained fairly peaceful.

DeNardi took full advantage of that time, developing bronzed cheeks and blonder hair at the pool, trying to find new music at the exchange, and chancing the Iraqi-sold black-market movies, which might include people standing to buy popcorn in the foreground while somebody videotaped a show at a movie theater.

But DeNardi was a lightning rod.

On a trip to Taji at the end of August, he walked over to Burger King. In Iraq, there's never a McDonald's right across the street. It's Burger King or nothing. At Taji, the food court consisted of several food stands: Cinnabon, Pizza Hut, a Green Beans coffee shop. At Burger King, troops ordered at one window and picked up their food at another. So DeNardi ordered his burger. Then he heard a fairly common sound: "Wah! Wah! Wah! Incoming! Incoming! Incoming!"

He did what one does on a base in Iraq when warned of mortar rounds: He looked around to see what everyone else was doing. Usually, when the alarm rings out, the mortar has already hit somewhere. DeNardi turned toward the picnic tables in front of the stand, saw that everyone was still eating, and turned back to the business of picking up the burger he'd already paid for.

But as he turned back to the stand, the mortar hit, sending the Burger King stand and DeNardi flying from the blast. After DeNardi landed, he thought, "I'm not going to get killed at Burger King."

So he ran for a concrete bunker.

But after a while, he saw a Cinnabon worker hobbling around. All the workers at the concession stands were what the military calls "foreign nationals"—mostly from third-world nations where making a living was so difficult that the Iraq war seemed like a dream come true—Iraq, with its designated bathrooms on American bases for "foreign nationals" and "men" and "women."

DeNardi waited a moment, and then dashed out to pick shrapnel out of the Cinnabon worker and bandage him up. But then the manager of the Pizza Hut started crying and said there were two people behind his stand who needed help. DeNardi figured lightning doesn't strike twice—obviously forgetting that he attracts it—and ran back behind the Pizza Hut.

Misery. There were body parts everywhere, and the sight of burnt tissue and bone and the smell of roasted flesh sent him right back to June 21. Still, he forced his way through it. The blast had blown the leg off the first man he encountered, and the man's second leg was barely attached. He had a chest wound. He was going to die.

DeNardi ran to a Conex where another wounded man lay, but he was almost dead, too. A third man had shrapnel in his neck. When DeNardi checked the medical kits always available in big white boxes throughout the bases in case of a mortar attack, he found a whole lot of nothing. So DeNardi tore off his shirt and used it to make a tourniquet. Someone else ran over with aid bags. DeNardi was covered with blood, none of it his own. The guy with the shrapnel in his neck was quickly losing blood. DeNardi couldn't get the IV bag from the medical kit to open, and then he couldn't get the needle in. He took off the gloves he'd donned to protect himself from blood-borne diseases, such as AIDS or hepatitis, so he could better grasp the needle.

Just then, medics came running over and said they would take care of it.

And base officials came over the loudspeakers with another announcement: "All clear."

"All clear, my ass," DeNardi muttered just as his platoon sergeant, Ybay, and Staff Sergeant Robert Morris came running over.

"Dude, I look like Carrie," DeNardi said, giggling a bit after his calm disappeared.

"Oh my god!" Ybay said. "Are you hurt?"

"No, no," DeNardi said. "It's not my blood."

They took him back to the hooches to get cleaned up, Ybay almost in tears from relief and DeNardi trying to act as if none of it were a big deal, but grinning a bit at his new nickname: the Hero of Burger King.

And he still had his hamburger receipt.

The next day, he went back to the Burger King stand, which had already been rebuilt.

They wouldn't give him his Whopper.

Trying for another burger was just DeNardi being DeNardi. It's easier to deal with anything if a joke's involved. But after again seeing burnt tissue and torn limbs, DeNardi slept in a bunker. He didn't want to go like that.

Halbasch, his best friend, talked DeNardi into moving back into the hooches. Each trailer had three rooms, each room had two beds, and everything was near bathrooms and showers. This was their only opportunity to live like humans, and Halbasch worried about DeNardi sleeping in a cement cave with the scorpions and snakes and camel spiders.

But about two weeks after DeNardi's experience at Burger King, Halbasch had a day off. He and several other guys—Specialist Eduardo Rodriguez, Specialist Ruben Chavez, Sergeant Oscar Gonzalez-Barerra, Sergeant First Class Widmark Quashie, and First Lieutenant Matt Martinez—were watching *Prison Break* in Halbasch's room when a rocket hit and destroyed Martinez and Quashie's rooms.

Immediately afterward, they heard, "Wah! Wah! Wah! Incoming! Incoming!"

Second platoon came running over.

"Holy crap, man, are you OK?" DeNardi said, color up, eyes wide. He'd been terrified he would find his friends in pieces.

The guys who had been watching the movie couldn't see for the dust in their eyes, but nothing hurt.

"I'm golden," Halbasch said, rubbing grit from his eyelashes.

No one was hurt because they had all been in Halbasch's room watching the movie, rather than in their own rooms.

Within minutes, ambulances and the bomb squad arrived, and contractors repaired the damage to the rooms within an hour.

Even with the mortars, Strickland hoped the trips to Taji after the second IED would help the men regain a sense of safety, to decompress and mourn their friends, to sleep and to relax at the pool, to eat well at the football-field-sized dining facilities complete with ice cream and all the energy drinks even DeNardi could stomach. This method went back to World War I: Get the men out of battle, let them rest, let them think about something beyond killing and being killed.

The trips were a treat even for officers higher in the chain of command because it was the only time they could be alone. Hendrix had his own containerized housing unit, or CHU, which he only saw once a month, but he outfitted it with rugs so he could walk around barefoot. He brought in a TV and bought sheets for the bed. Normally, they had about twenty-four hours to shower, wash clothes, and resupply. Hendrix would visit the battalion to report in with the command sergeant major, and then he'd go sit in his room. He'd sleep, call his wife, or watch movies.

After they'd lost the two Bradleys, Strickland made sure they had a couple of days, rather than just twenty-four hours.

But it didn't take much to remind them of what they'd lost. The guys would ask DeNardi to play songs for them, and then someone would ask for "Adhamiya Blues." He couldn't sing it. The lyrics had been in Wood's pocket the day he died.

The entire battalion suffered. Sergeants began getting rough with the Iraqi interpreters, convinced they had more information than they were giving up. Soldiers began fighting with each other. Not only was everyone on edge, almost three hundred people had been crammed into one building at Old Mod—with the interpreters.

Chaplain Choi realized the men would need more than sleep and time at the pool to get through the rest of their tour. He asked each platoon to come see him once a month, and he brought in a mental health team. Not everyone seemed as eager to talk with the counselors because the men didn't know them. They did know Choi had witnessed even more horror than they had. He always tried to be on the scene for last rites. He also realized that lower-enlisted soldiers might not be eager to speak about everything that was bothering them if their platoon sergeant was in the room with them, so he had meetings by rank, too.

Some of his mental health efforts were a little less obvious: Choi set up Thursday-night movies, complete with popcorn, and organized battalion sports competitions.

In the meantime, Hendrix, Floyd, and Sergeant Major McClaflin continued to try to improve the living conditions. McClaflin set up a dining area so they wouldn't have to eat in their rooms every night.

As they continued to patrol, Charlie caught news updates about Adhamiya: A roadside bomb exploded near a college, killing one and injuring another. A bomb exploded at a prominent cleric's home, killing the cleric's brother and injuring two children.

And on August 20, Rear Admiral Mark Fox, deputy spokesman for Multinational Forces–Iraq, and Brigadier General Qassim Atta, an Iraqi spokesman, announced that the situation in Adhamiya had improved.

"There is good cooperation and coordination between the people in Adhamiya and the security forces," Atta said at a joint press conference. "This cooperation resulted in detaining so many terrorist groups and al Qaeda (in Iraq) leaders, and also finding a large amount of weapons and explosives that terrorists intended to use for operations against civilians."

"Well no shit," DeNardi said, as he and Cardenas watched the announcement on the Armed Forces Network television station. "You send in one thousand men where we patrolled, and things are gonna improve."

"Aww, don't be bitter man," Cardenas said, joking because they both bled bitterness. "Be happy for the people of Adhamiya!"

"Also," Atta continued, "this improvement resulted in providing services to this area, and the commanding operation there makes visits every day. And the good cooperation resulted in good results in many places, like in Adhamiya neighborhood and Sadr City and also in Baya neighborhood."

"Also, kiss my ass," DeNardi said, rising up to point his backside toward the television. "I don't care if I ever see Adhamiya again."

"I wonder how they got the Iraqi army out of bed?" Hendrix joked, as Atta continued with his speech about Iraqi forces working well with the Americans.

"Maybe they found it was more effective if they let them sleep while they were out on patrol," Cardenas said.

In September, after the cleric's brother was killed, the Iraqi army raided the Abu Hanifa Mosque and found weapons and evidence that training had taken place there. But no one was inside the mosque: Someone had alerted them to the raid.

Outside Adhamiya, the men finally learned what it meant to use the counterinsurgency manual. Halbasch drank chai with the locals for the first time since he arrived in Iraq. Instead of patrols looking for bomb-making equipment, they met a lot of the neighbors and officials. All of Charlie Company still functioned on high alert, which made it hard not to enter a house with weapons up and doors thrust open with no warning to the residents. It made it hard to sit in one place long enough to drink a cup of tea, because in the past, that meant drawing snipers like camels to water.

But in zone 17, the new area, the children played in soccer fields. There was no sewage. And people who smiled at them meant it.

The guys even started to joke again. One day, Hendrix woke from a deep snooze on the balcony at Old Mod. When he went inside, he wondered if he should dare sleep ever again around Charlie Company. All through the building, the guys had pasted posters of Hendrix to nearly every wall, apparently passed out from too much drink. While he slept, they had placed empty near-beer cans all around the first sergeant's cot, and then photographed him.

"What the hell?" McClaflin said, laughing so hard he could barely stand after walking through Old Mod. "Who in the hell?"

"I don't know," Hendrix said, laughing, too. But when DeNardi walked by with Sergeant Robert Lambeth, Hendrix couldn't help but notice the extra bit of sparkle in their eyes.

"That kid . . . ," he muttered.

And laughed again.

CHAPTER 26
Charlie Company Goes Home

The men of Charlie Company walked into the small gymnasium tucked behind a shoppette back home in Schweinfurt. They arrived home in waves, platoon by platoon, with the Headquarters Company crew arriving last. The first troops in the door walked through a paper banner as if they were quarterbacks heading into a football game. There was music—the usual "Red, White and Blue" and "Proud to Be an American." Women and children stood with WELCOME HOME signs.

Each man looked—and hoped—for something different.

Ybay saw his wife and children and broke down with relief, so emotional he couldn't even tell his family hello.

Richardson looked for his wife and tiny daughter. And looked again, hope and pain filling his face at the same time. He circled the gym several times before facing the truth.

They weren't coming.

Cardenas looked for no one, and instead sat on a bench on the side of the room with all the other single guys wishing they could go get a beer, trying not to look as their married friends kissed their wives.

In the days following, more groups of soldiers returned.

Captain Baka's wife was at his side instantly, daughters dressed prettily and smiling for daddy.

Osterman watched only for his men, clapping them on the backs as if they hadn't just gotten off the same plane. "Welcome home, man." His wife was still in Iraq.

Charlie Company had returned to Germany, but they would never leave Adhamiya.

They spent the next few days in briefings and debriefings, taking tests to determine whether they had any combat stress or traumatic brain injury issues and trying to readjust to driving on streets with traffic lights and no roadside bombs.

It should have been easy.

Home.

Safe.

But they had all gotten so used to being alert to the enemy or planning for all the things that could go horribly wrong, that home did not feel safe. Baka tried to adjust himself in his Chevy Trailblazer so that, if an EFP came through, it might take off only one limb instead of both legs or both arms. DeNardi fought with friends who he believed couldn't possibly understand what he'd been through. Hendrix declined to tell his wife even the most basic tales of Adhamiya. And Osterman struggled to reconnect with his wife after both of them had been diagnosed with post-traumatic stress disorder.

All of this, army officials say, is normal, the expected result of war, which leaves soldiers "hyperalert." They call the symptoms the normal things a person needs to survive in combat: hyperawareness, an inability to sleep or even a feeling of being emotionally numb. In Adhamiya, soldiers could get by with those symptoms, but surviving at home would require building and maintaining relationships with family and friends, being able to get a good night's sleep, and not being afraid every time they went out in traffic.

The symptoms stop being normal when they tear relationships apart, lead soldiers to drink or use drugs to try to numb their feelings, or cause guilt so deep that every other emotion can only be anger. Charlie

Company made it through the war zone, but not all of them would live through their welcome home. Many would leave the military. And many would be back in Iraq within a year, starting the whole cycle again.

They would try to battle the memories by embracing all that they had missed while they were in Adhamiya.

Sitting on the back patio, looking out over storybook German homes, Ely Chagoya pulled out his guitar for the first time since his return to Germany. Tentative at first, he soon started singing sweet Spanish songs about lost love. He sang a song he wrote himself about a homeless man who returned to the same park bench every day because that's where his lover said she'd meet him.

"The song is about him being the only guy I ever knew who had really fallen in love," Chagoya said. "I quit playing in Iraq because I feel what I play. In Iraq, it was like eating but not being able to taste the food. But when you stop yourself from feeling, it goes all the way around. You don't feel good. You don't feel bad."

He tried playing again immediately after returning to Germany, but fiddled with it for about five minutes before placing the guitar back in its case. "I just wasn't ready for it," he said. But now the numbness was beginning to lift. "You think about what you did over there. How it was. When you remember the details, you think about friends you have no more and places you don't want to be any more. It's not so much that you forget but that you're just so numb. For all the crap we went through, I feel like I'm OK right now. But if I feel like I'm starting to fall apart, I'll go talk to someone."

He said he'd watch out for his men, too. "They're like little kids," he said, laughing about the boys' nights out at the local clubs. "I don't want nothing to happen to them. You're trained to think and react a certain way for fifteen months, and then it's like 'OK, you're off. Go relax in your apartment. Go have fun.' But you feel weird being normal."

For Chagoya, relaxing meant a lot of time alone. He talked to his friends back home. But it was hard to spend time with men who reminded him of his dead friends. "You're going from that to normal," he said. "You're scared of feeling. The moment you start feeling is the moment you'll start remembering."

And he couldn't justify the deaths of his friends.

"If you had asked me a few years ago, I would have said, 'Hell yeah!'" he said. "But now it seems like we never know what the Iraqis are doing. How do you think we feel being led by someone who's blind? You will listen to their problems, but you will not trust them. I don't see how we did anything over there. If we did, it's not worth what we lost."

He went back to his guitar, playing for himself, and the feelings began to return, flowing through his fingers and out through his songs. As he talked about his men, he cried.

"I'm proud of my soldiers," he said. "That's it. Some days, even though they thought they might die, they went out with me. I'm proud of them because they didn't back down. I don't expect people to understand it. You weren't there when your closest friend died. You weren't there to help carry wounded soldiers back in. You have to go out regardless if you believe in the war or not."

He gathered his friends in close, bringing the "brown squad" in for a barbecue and a night out at the clubs, Chagoya running the floor with the moves he'd taught Mock. Smooth and decked out for dancing, Chagoya took control.

Cardenas danced for a bit, and then sat on a couch at the edge of the club, his eyes deep pools of sadness behind his glasses. "There's always someone missing," he said, determined not to cry. "Mock. Montenegro. Nobody really says it, but it's on everybody's mind. They're not here."

Cardenas struggled to get used to not carrying a weapon. He refused to leave the barracks without a friend, a battle buddy. He couldn't bond with the new guys, and had to work to keep his voice level when he talked about what had happened to his NCOs in second platoon.

"Even in garrison, they moved all our NCOs to a different barracks so we still aren't together," he said. "They said it's because they're all getting out of the military, but it doesn't feel right." As he talked, he twisted the bracelets that ran up his arm. Each carried the name of a dead friend. He would eventually collect—and wear—fourteen of the Killed in Action reminders.

"Not a single guy in our company who died was worth it, because we didn't see any progress," he said. When his family and friends ask him about his experience, he goes back to the sentiments expressed in generation after generation of service members who hoped only to protect others from what they had lived through themselves: "Don't ask what I did in Iraq,' " he told them. "Just pray for me."

One year later, he would ask his family to pray for him again as he returned to the war zone.

Carlos Perez grinned his big happy grin, surrounded by friends, safe with a beer, dancing as if he had never stopped. If he kept grinning, maybe the other emotions wouldn't surface. Shots all around. Cheers to Monte and Mock and Hartge and Sizemore and Marsh and everyone else we lost who we loved. Dance. Drink. Grin. They're watching over us. Another round.

A year later, Perez would be out of the military, working at a meat-packing plant near Fort Riley.

"I'm fine," he said. "I don't have anything that affected me, other than when there's a loud noise, my heart starts racing."

He's had a couple of bad dreams, but he's had a lot of happiness, too. He married his wife, Eva, who is also a soldier, on November 22, 2008, and they have already started a family: His first child is due in the fall of 2009.

Perez still talks to Hartge's mom, telling her stories of her son as he remembers them. "He was my best friend, and she loves me," he said.

Avila flew to Germany—wheelchair, bandages, and all—to see his crew. He would remain at Brooke Army Medical Center for more than a year, facing a constant barrage of surgeries and decisions almost too hard to bear: His foot wasn't healing correctly. Would it be easier for him to have it cut off and use a prosthetic limb?

Doctors had waited until he was stable to show him a mirror. The fire had darkened his skin, but his model-handsome face retained the high cheekbones and strength; and his beautiful eyes often seemed to look only toward his niece.

When he first arrived at the hospital, he hovered between life and death, for burns covered 75 percent of his body. Campos died in the same hospital, his burns even deeper. That scared Avila's family, and they were determined to help him decide to live. His family had immediately dropped everything, eventually moving to San Antonio to be with Avila as he healed.

"Haylee's waiting to meet you," his mother whispered in his ear, referring to his brand-new niece. "But you'll have to come out to see her."

Ever since then, Avila has referred to his niece as his guardian angel.

"I spend my time appreciating life," he said. "You go over there thinking you're either going to come back or you're not. You never think you're going to come back like this."

At the burn unit, he has met combat vets who were burned as badly or worse than he was. Jay Fain, McKinney's soldier who lost his leg, arrived soon after Avila. The two spent all of their time together.

Avila joined knowing there was a war, but while he was in college, he said it bothered him that people were dying and he wasn't contributing. Immediately upon arriving in Charlie Company, he knew he would be a lifer because he loved the men he served with so much.

"I'd do it again," he said. "But I would have lived every minute to the fullest had I known."

Avila and Perez had been roommates before heading to Adhamiya. They had switched out with other soldiers so they could be together. Perez was thrilled to see his friend when he returned to Germany, and the guys took Avila out to the bars, helping with his wheelchair, making sure he was comfortable, buying him drinks.

"I kept it to myself," Perez said. "But I lost it. It hurt. He needed help for everything he did. I stayed in the restroom and cried. I just couldn't believe it was Avila. He was the biggest dude we had in the platoon."

But as always, his friends were there for him. Chalfant comforted Perez in the bathroom.

"Man, if he can cope with it, we can cope with it," Chalfant said. "He doesn't let it bring him down."

"It made me realize I can't let it hurt me," Perez said. He calls his friend often, laughing that it's still the same old Avila, telling jokes and laughing about rattraps and Tasers.

Driving home from the hospital a year after Perez's breakdown at the bar, Avila tells a friend he'll call her back. He doesn't want to talk on the phone and drive at the same time.

Avila's getting out of the military, medically retired at 100 percent disability. He can't open a Coke bottle or put on a sock, though he can now shower by himself and dress, except for the buttons. He has learned to adapt: He opens bottles with his teeth.

"Little by little, I'm getting there," he said. "But I don't know what I'm going to do. I'd like to go back to school."

In the meantime, he explains to burn doctors what his experience was like and, in the process, tells them the story of Charlie Company. "I really don't mind," he said. "I want to speak for them."

But he gets defensive if anyone calls him a hero, even as he recounts the day when he fired his weapon to protect his friends as his hands and feet burned down to the bone.

"I was just doing what any of us would do for a friend," he said.

After coming home from Iraq, Ernesto Martin also left the military, even after he had spent so much time learning English just so he could join. But he missed the camaraderie, and he joined the reserves to try to regain it.

Oddly, the hardest part of the deployment had been when his crew was moved to Headquarters Company after Second Platoon's mutiny.

"I went out in sector like three times," Martin said.

But he understands why.

"When Montenegro died, that was my whole squad," he said. "I was the only one left. I was supposed to be dismount for the Bradley, but we were short of drivers, so they changed the board the night before so I would drive another Brad."

Instead, he rode behind them, and from the driver's seat, he saw everything.

"It happened right in front of my eyes," he said. "I was supposed to be with them. I guess it wasn't my time."

Now, he doesn't even tell people he was in the army. If someone asks, he tells them to get a job in an office or in finance. If his family asks and really wants to know, he tries to explain. He tells them about his friends and why they were brave enough to keep going out even with all the horror they had seen. He tries to explain why it was so hard for him not to go back out in sector while his friends still did.

"I doubt it was about the mission," he said. "It was about ourselves. We knew we had to go out there, but it was just about each other, making sure everyone could come back safe home."

Erik Osterman drove his freshly worked on Jeep up the autobahn toward home, puffs of smoke trailing behind him. But he arrived at an empty house. A home that had been empty for almost a year, making it seem all the lonelier. His wife would not return from Iraq for another month, and things still seemed up in the air. He couldn't reach her on the phone, and she didn't always reply to his e-mails. For the first six months, she—Tonya—had been in Ramadi, but she didn't have a cell phone. The Internet made things worse because Osterman expected to always be in touch with his wife, and the Internet in Iraq isn't reliable.

They didn't talk to each other when Osterman cleaned the blood out of trucks or when his wife's unit was hit by mortars, and he could feel them growing apart.

They second-guessed each other: Was there really no way to get to a phone? You really couldn't send one e-mail in two weeks? Are you with somebody else? Osterman was in Iraq for five months before he talked to his wife on the phone. The couple had come home on leave together, and when they returned to Iraq, they learned she was pregnant. The army sent her home. She miscarried. The army sent her back to Iraq.

"I can't believe anyone would be so callous to think she was ready to come back to a war zone after experiencing that," Osterman said. Especially since both of them had been diagnosed with PTSD after their first trip to Iraq in 2004. They had met in Samarra.

When he got home from that deployment, Osterman told a counselor he was having some problems at home. "I was really angry when I came back last time," he said. "We came back to garrison, and the stupid stuff just made me so angry."

His doctor prescribed antidepressants, but Osterman said that made him feel somehow worse. "It made me zone out so I would do things and not care," he said. "It allowed me to not care about inhibitions." He stopped worrying about the repercussions of his actions, which didn't help his situation.

And even with the diagnosis—mild PTSD and anger-management issues—his chain of command acted as if he were trying to get out of work or, eventually, out of deploying, which infuriated Osterman. "You can tell who those guys are," he said. "They're the ones who develop symptoms right before we're supposed to leave."

After the deployment to Adhamiya, he expected that at least one-third of the company "would be screwy."

"When you're home, you have to deal with it," he said.

In Adhamiya, he had tried to dwell in another world. He filled his computer with photos he took of flowers in places seemingly able to bloom only violence, or of little girls grinning as they played where friends had died, or of a bit of curlicue latticework in a building pocked with gunfire. "I spent a lot of time just thinking and reflecting," he said. "I tried to find things that were beautiful. My real coping mechanism would be to see how the other guys are doing. Because of the first deployment, I'm used to it. But I will never be the same."

When he arrived home, he didn't stop worrying about his men.

"This time, I don't know," he said. "We've lost a lot of guys."

They were pulled out of Adhamiya, which would seem to be exactly what they wanted, but Charlie Company felt insulted. "I felt that when we left, it was unfinished," Osterman said. "Every goal, we went above and beyond what was expected. Yes, Adhamiya was a safer place, looking at the statistics, but the bombs just got bigger. It might not be the locals setting them up, but they were allowing it."

When they returned to Schweinfurt, Charlie Company hadn't won a war or a battle. But their pride in each other remained untouched.

"Just know that each soldier fought for something," Osterman said. "They fought for each other."

Robin Johnson played on the floor with his ten-month-old daughter Mia. She'd been born while he was home on leave, and they'd had six days to bond before he returned to Adhamiya. "When I left, she was this tiny six-pound thing," he said, grinning as the baby bustled across the carpet. The window behind him served as a background for a giant WELCOME HOME poster, his wife's proud proclamation that her soldier was home. She had gotten out after their tour together in Samarra, when she had been a medic and he had learned to respect female soldiers.

But Johnson's grin quickly disappeared when he started talking about Adhamiya, and about June 21.

"It's the worst possible feeling in the world," he said of his arrival at the scene. "Your friends are torn apart. You can't even tell who your friends are. Rylance had to watch Agami trying to get out of that hatch for ten minutes." But Rylance had tried to comfort Johnson by putting those last moments in a different light.

"I didn't get to hear that last joke over the radio, and he did," Johnson said. "He got those last moments."

At first, no one would tell Johnson what had happened to his friend just before Johnson got there with the quick reaction force. "Don't worry," they told him. "It was fast."

"Guys will try to protect you from the details, but then they had to get it off their chest," he said. "There was nothing they could do for him. You can't lift the front of a Bradley. The only way for him to get out was for them to pick up the front of that Bradley."

Johnson had been raised Boston–Irish Catholic, but even after years of seeing poverty in South Boston, nothing prepared him for how June 21 would test his faith. How could he love a God that allowed his friends to die so horrifically?

"When something like that happens, the last thing you want to do is talk about God," he said. "You want to hurt. You want to feel that pain. God? I hated him right then."

But he had a hard time finding comfort elsewhere.

Johnson didn't believe they had accomplished anything, though they found, detonated, and destroyed more IEDs in their battalion than anyone else. They caught high-value targets with an almost foxhound-like efficiency. "We are proud of these things, and we are proud of each other," he said. "We only had 110 guys patrolling; the unit that relieved us brought in a battalion. The new unit had 1,100. No one else could have done what we did. It sounds cocky and arrogant, but we know we're the best. But are we proud of what we accomplished there? No.

"We know we made a difference, but we just don't feel like it. We got sucker punched, and we were forced to back down."

Johnson continued to try to reassure the guys that Ybay did what he felt he had to do, as well as reassure Ybay that the guys did the same.

"I wanted to step in and tell second platoon, 'Absolutely not. Don't go,'" he said about the day they refused to go out. "But I didn't face the same repercussions as second platoon because I was with the scouts. I said, 'If you don't think it's right, don't do it.' God, there was fallout for that for a long time. But I remember Ybay telling the first sergeant, 'My platoon isn't going out again.' They thought he had their backs. But he's a professional noncommissioned officer. He's able to put the blinders on and say, 'Roger.' The younger guys? They act with their hearts.'"

From a distance, Johnson struggled to figure out if the company and battalion leadership had come up with a good solution after the "mutiny."

"In a way, they were put someplace where they wouldn't have to go out again," Johnson said. "But as an NCO, they took these guys' leaders away and put them with people they didn't know and didn't trust. Before, they knew, 'If I go down, Sergeant Fielder is going to come and take care of things. Sergeant Fielder? He's fearless. They know he'd die for them. That's what made Charlie Company and second platoon so great. You know they'd die for you without a second's hesitation. That's why it hurt so much when the guys were left on their own."

None of it changed the way he felt about Charlie Company and second platoon.

"I could not have worked with a finer platoon," he said. "The things I saw these guys do were straight out of a movie—running through grenades, blast sites, enemy fire, strictly to get to their guys. It was amazing to be a part of. Not one person in our platoon ever ran."

Chrissi McKinney waited to meet her husband's men. More than anything, she wanted them to know McKinney had loved them, that he never would have hurt them.

"I wanted to tell them I was sorry for what they witnessed," she said. "They were different after that. It affected them." She gathered Seashore and Lefurgy—the last men to see her husband alive—to her. They told her what they knew. That they thought First Sergeant McKinney was asleep, and that they were worried because he used to sing a special song from *Sesame Street* as they went out. He always liked to sing.

But he wasn't singing.

She also wanted some answers. She tried to talk to Greaves, but he refused to come near her, not even responding to her requests. Others in the chain of command said they felt guilty about McKinney's death, but no one apologized for not looking out for him. He should have gone to mental health, and she didn't understand why his lack of sleep wasn't apparent, why he would be sent out on a mission to save face, rather than allowing the troops to see that everyone needs some help sometimes.

"He did not commit suicide," she said. "He did shoot himself, yes."

The difference, she said, is that there was no decision involved in Jeff McKinney's action, no way he would have left his men behind like that.

"The most important thing to know is Jeff was not himself," she said. "They know Jeff would never do that."

In the warm living room of McKinney's father's Texas home, photos of the first sergeant sit on every surface. As Charles and Rhonda, Jeff's stepmother, talked about their son, neither of them could stop smiling. "It feels good to talk about him," Charles said.

"He could be so patient," he said. "Like Job." Patience stood as another trait that set the first sergeant aside, even as a child. Once, he and his dad went fishing. They fished all day long.

And fished.

And nothing bit.

"Why don't we call it a day?" Charles said.

"No, Dad," his son answered. "Let's just stay until the fish are biting."

"He always persevered," his dad said. "And we know he wanted to come home. That's all he talked about—his family."

When he saw the soldiers in the dress uniforms coming up his front drive, Charles screamed and ran to a back bedroom. As a Vietnam vet, he said he finally understood something his mother said while he was overseas: "My mom said she cried until her heart hurt."

But his pain went deeper when he found out the details behind his son's death.

"An IED, you about halfway expect that," he said. "But for them to watch it happening. It was almost a betrayal. They let him down. They let him die."

At a McDonald's in Washington, D.C., a much thinner version of Doc Tyler Holladay talked excitedly about flying home to Germany to see his guys. As their medic, he was used to being able to check in on them. And they were used to knowing exactly where to find Holladay.

And he was tired of the hospital. No twenty-two-year-old wants to be stuck in a hospital by himself in an area where he doesn't know anyone. His visits to the McDonald's nearby became so routine that the clerks knew what time to expect him, and that he could eat an amazing amount of food.

"I could never get away from zone 19," he said, reflecting on his time in Adhamiya. "And sure as hell, I got shot in zone 19."

But he didn't spend much time thinking about the day he was shot. He thought about the days before that.

"You have to identify the bodies," he said of the medics. "You have to bag the bodies. It's hard to get their expressions or that burnt charcoal appearance out of my mind. These are my friends. That's something you'll always remember."

He needed to get home to make sure the rest of his friends were OK.

DeNardi immediately got to work setting up his room in the barracks—movie projector first so he could watch "300" as he worked. He broke out his favorite artsy-college-kid clothes—loafers and all—and set up his futon and put away videos. As he worked, his door opened and his friends checked in.

"Hey, Irish Bar tonight, man?" Halbasch said.

"All over it," DeNardi said.

He'd already had a friend in the barracks tattoo "Strength" and "Honor" down his forearms in memory of Mock. Over the course of a year, he would add a tattoo that would memorialize something special about each friend who died.

But he didn't know what to do to help his friends who had lived through the anguish that would follow after they reached the safety of home. At first, he and Halbasch spent every spare minute together, but eventually, that was to the exclusion of everybody else. They disagreed with the way the company was being handled: Baka had left for West Point and Hendrix for Fort Jackson, South Carolina, and Ybay now served as first sergeant.

"We had a lot of anger when we got back," Halbasch said. "That transition coming home was really hard. And with Ybay getting first sergeant, it was worse, because he treated us like a basic training unit, like a bunch of kids."

A lot of the guys were using drugs, and he and DeNardi were both drinking too much. "One night, somebody went out and got really pissant drunk," Halbasch said. "He knocked on Ybay's door in the middle of the night and demanded that he come out. He had a beer bottle. He just snapped."

His buddies dragged the soldier away before he could get in trouble.

A couple of guys went AWOL, including Cieslak, the soldier who was moved to second platoon after becoming violent when an Iraqi threw a grenade under Baka's Humvee. Cieslak moved to Poland, where he had family.

Nobody seemed surprised by any of it.

"We just sheltered ourselves," Halbasch said. "We just stayed in DeNardi's room and watched TV. I hated it. There were a lot of things I hadn't dealt with. Not having Wood or Agami around just killed me."

But then, even the two best friends had a falling out. Halbasch had talked to DeNardi one night about burning through money and fighting with his friends. "He got drunk and just started calling me out," Halbasch said, laughing. "Then we patched things up. Things got a lot better after that."

DeNardi went home for his grandfather's funeral and ended up eloping with an old friend. Halbasch went to Fort Benning, Georgia, to serve as a drill sergeant and also found himself engaged.

The 1-26th Infantry was disbanded soon after they returned home, and Charlie Company became part of the 2nd Battalion, 28th Infantry Regiment, the Black Lions. Their company motto is "Strength and Honor."

DeNardi and Cardenas returned with them to Iraq in November 2008.

First Sergeant Tim Ybay sat behind his new desk talking to his wife, Maybelline, on the phone. She didn't much care that he had a unit full of guys moving back into the barracks and playing a little too hard to suit army regulations. Ybay had family responsibilities, and he needed to pick up the kids and be home in time for dinner.

"Got that, babe?" she asked.

"Got that," he said, grinning. He wanted nothing more than family time.

Even with news of the "mutiny" spreading throughout the military, each of Charlie Company's platoon sergeants was chosen to serve as a first sergeant within the battalion: Quashie, Thomas, and Ybay would all begin immediately.

"They're the best," Ybay said about Charlie Company. "This is an overall. They're a bunch of great guys. I'm proud of them. The accomplishment of the unit itself—I'm really proud of them. I'm happy for the unit's accomplishment."

But he had a hard time determining whether that accomplishment actually meant progress in Adhamiya. "Do I think it got better?" Ybay said. "Me personally? No. It was the same."

As he started to talk about the men who died, tears built up in his eyes, then fell on his desk.

"Sizemore would always say, 'Enough of the war stories,'" Ybay said. "I didn't understand that until this deployment. You have to talk about the good times." But the pain of the losses, he believed, fed into the way his men had behaved in Adhamiya, and that, as an NCO, is hard to prepare for as a unit trains for battle. No one trains for anything but success, and if there's success, why would there be mental health issues, a need for vengeance, and, frankly, fear?

"The battalion and company commander's outlook on the platoon was we had to change the environment," Ybay said. "That's what it boils down to. We still got to continue to drive on. We got some new soldiers."

But some were sent away.

"Sergeant Brown—we'd still give him a big hug even though he was gone," Ybay said. "It was hard for me. Staff Sergeant Gregory was one of my leaders. Corporal Brown was my gunner. But I had a mission. The company had a mission. We still had to execute. But no matter where you guys go, you're still part of second platoon. I would like to come back in formation with all my guys. They did outstanding."

Captain Strickland, also sitting at a new desk because he had taken Baka's place while the company was in Iraq, said Adhamiya gradually got better, but the men weren't around to see it.

"This company set the conditions for the good things that are happening now," he said. "There's a safe-market initiative, and the gas station is up and running. People aren't afraid to leave their homes. The soldiers may not see it, but I think if you do look at the big picture, they'll see we did make a difference. It may have sucked at the time, but sacrifices have to be made for progress.

"But the big question is, are those people who will be affected, will they appreciate the sacrifices? It hinges on whether they go down the road we want them to go down."

Adhamiya did seem to improve after Charlie Company left. The United States worked more with the Sunni Awakening, providing paid positions for former insurgents. When Charlie Company was there, the same group had been called a militia, and the policy from the top was not to provide weapons or money to former insurgents. Charlie would have to wait to see what would happen in the town in the long term.

Strickland said the loss of the second Bradley marked a turning point for the whole theater. He had three platoons working one of the most violent areas in Iraq. The Blue Spaders didn't see the surge until it was too late.

"If there had been an increase of combat power in Adhamiya, I think the dynamics of what happened would have been different," he said. "It was so traumatic to just everybody in general. People started paying attention: 'Oh my god. There are only three platoons in Adhamiya.'"

He did wish he could have better seen the mental toll Adhamiya took on his men. He didn't find out they were taking sleeping medications until after he ordered them to report to Old Mod. But even afterward, he had to do something to make sure his company could continue to function. The army recently began teaching ethics classes to its soldiers to avoid the My Lai situations the military had seen in Vietnam, and the Abu Ghraib situation it saw in this war. But beyond telling the men how to behave, there is no standard operating procedure for what to do if a platoon is past the point. One guy? Sure. Baka had encountered that when he moved Cieslak to headquarters platoon to cool out after roughing up civilians. But a whole platoon? During Vietnam, platoons had refused to go out because the draftees didn't support the war, and there had been cases since the beginning of warfare of platoons running scared in the face of overwhelming strength. This was something different. This hadn't been brought up in ROTC.

"I didn't want to punish them," Strickland said. "I understood what was going on. But they had to understand you couldn't do something like that and have nothing happen." And it wasn't purely Strickland's decision. Reynolds wanted to make sure the men were punished. "We had a new commander who wanted to make an example and put his foot down," Strickland said. "The investigation's closed. In my mind, it was done after I talked to all of my guys. But the battalion commander wanted a piece of paper with a signature. He got it." The men were flagged.

Even without the punishment, Strickland and Hendrix agreed that they needed to move the men around. Second platoon could no longer function as a group, and they had seen enough. It was time to get them out of Adhamiya.

"Within the company, we made some adjustments," Strickland said. "Some for a fresh start. A couple went to a different battalion, and a couple went to Alpha Company. After looking into it, I didn't feel the need to punish anybody. It was hard. The infantryman in me wanted to say, 'Why are you having these issues?' But the person I am understands.

"I understood why they did what they did," he continued. "Some of the NCOS, I was disappointed in them because they failed to lead their men through difficult times. They let soldiers influence their decisions. But on a personal level, I applauded their decision because they stood behind their soldiers. I was disappointed, but I thought they had great courage. It was a Jekyll-Hyde moment for me."

Lieutenant Colonel John Reynolds tends to heap praise on all of his companies—except for Charlie.

"Charlie Company had a number of issues," he said, sitting in his office in Schweinfurt. "One of them is leadership. Tied to that is morale. They were a challenge. You have to heal with your mind. You still have to go out in the morning, even when you're hurting. Charlie Company was the problem child."

But it's hard to keep Reynolds on track. Through several questions about Adhamiya, he gave answers about all the mayors he had talked to and the schools he had fixed. "I personally talked to local leaders," he said. "I told them, 'No more IEDs.' We were the centerpiece trying to make these connections. It was building momentum."

In Adhamiya?

No, no, not in Adhamiya.

While Charlie Company had been getting hammered in Adhamiya, Reynolds had been based at FOB Liberty. From there, he worked with some of the officers from the battalion.

"I didn't experience a lot of things they were doing, but I knew the people," he said. When talking about the change of command after Colonel Schacht's son had died, he said, "Oh, it was easy. You trust the people. The incident rate was quick. It was a high-op tempo. But it was nothing I did not expect. The transition was the best you could probably get."

By any definition, his first days weren't easy, and it is hard to understand his nonchalance. "A couple of days later, you lose a first sergeant to suicide," Reynolds said about his transition. "Then a couple of days later, you lose more to a deep-buried IED."

He felt prepared for the deployment because he had served as the executive officer of the 2nd Battalion, 2nd Infantry Regiment, on a previous tour to Iraq.

And, Reynolds said, everyone experienced pain.

"My driver, Sergeant Mock—I brought him to this battalion," Reynolds said. "It just shook me to the foundation when he died. He was the guy sitting next to me fighting through Fallujah. But like I said, there's pain and we grow everyday."

He said he and the chaplain called the parents and spouses of wounded soldiers every night. "The soldiers still talk to the families, so they find out the command cares: 'Hey, sir, I heard you talked to Zach's mom the other night, and she's very appreciative.'"

He talked about Chaplain Choi's mental health program, and came up with "Operation Healing Hearts," a title Reynolds had thought of in Iraq that he said was a "pretty good quote." He said he told the chaplains and other leaders "to heal minds" and deal with spiritual and anger issues. "I know it worked," he said. "It gave us an opportunity to reflect and gave us an opportunity to heal. It did not affect the mission after that.

"I think I only had one casualty in the last ninety days," Reynolds said, referring to Holladay.

As they waited for Mike Baka to return, Elizabeth helped Cathy remove links in a paper chain to count down the days. "She's asked me a couple of times if we take away all the links in the chain, will he come back sooner," Cathy said. "How do you explain time to a three-year-old?"

But even after Elizabeth greeted him at the gym with hugs and kisses for the man in the pictures Mommy had showed her every night, life seemed as fragile as that paper chain.

Elizabeth cried for the first two days after he came home, not because he seemed unfamiliar, but because every time he left the house, she was certain he would never come home.

"He was gone for thirty minutes," Cathy Baka said. "My daughter said, 'I want him home. Where is he? Is he in Iraq again?' She was dealing with some hard issues."

"At the age of three I never talked about death and dying," Mike said. "She prays about it. A three-year-old praying that none of my friends would die."

"She knew," Cathy said. "She was worried about him."

The homecoming, though eager, wasn't easy. Mike said he wasn't used to listening to a baby cry. Cathy said she felt she had to walk on "pins and needles" until he got used to being home. "I'm used to doing everything myself," she said. "I'm a little apprehensive about parenting. I don't necessarily want to be criticized. But then, going through something like this, you get to know somebody like no other."

Cathy said the two deployments—the first coming twelve days after Elizabeth was born and the second three weeks before Hannah was born—taught her not to take anything for granted. But she worries about the future. "I know when he's going to have bad days," she said. "I know October 17—when Sizemore died—is a bad day. I always ask him point-blank how he's doing. I know he's suffering from PTSD."

Mike told her he wanted to visit the families of the soldiers he lost.

"I just love these guys," Baka said. "It was really personal to me. All the parents I had to call. I'm sorry this is the first time I talked to them. I wish I could have gone back and called and said, 'Hey, your son did a good job for me today.'"

But Cathy knows her husband doesn't understand his effect on the men, and she smiles when he says he doesn't think he did enough.

"I know Mike probably came home because the soldiers loved him so much," Cathy said. "They protected him. He's a pretty loved guy."

"I think that makes it harder, though. He always tries to remember the last conversations he had with the soldiers who died."

When second platoon refused to roll, Baka intentionally pulled away, but it angered him that they had been left in sector for so long. "I knew I would have done things differently, but I wasn't in charge," he said. "I wouldn't say it was the soldiers' fault. But I think there were a lot of failures at a lot of levels that day."

For him, it came down to one thing.

"If you have a company like mine, you don't take out the team captain and expect the rest of the team to operate," he said.

As soon as Reynolds took over as battalion commander, the pair went head to head. It continued when they got to Schweinfurt. Baka headed up the S-1 shop, so he was in charge of promotions and awards. He had received a Meritorious Service Medal for his four-and-a-half years of service in Germany, and he was due to be promoted to major.

But Reynolds didn't invite Baka to the battalion awards and promotion ceremony held just before Baka left Germany for his new position at West Point. And then Reynolds called him the day of the ceremony to apologize for forgetting to invite him.

"I don't really know what that was about," Baka said. "But it didn't matter, ultimately."

Instead, on the anniversary of Ross McGinnis's death, Lieutenant Colonel Schacht would promote Baka to major at Arlington National Cemetery, with the men McGinnis had saved standing around McGinnis's grave.

A year later, in his office at West Point, Baka points to the desk where he has cadets sit as they wait to see the Special Assistant to the Commandant for Honor Matters, Baka's new title. Underneath glass lay several stories about Charlie Company and Ross McGinnis.

"It gives them a chance to think about what's really important before we talk about it," he said. "All I do is talk about honor and courage and integrity."

Now, when he talks about McGinnis and his Medal of Honor, he also likes to tell the story of Private First Class Brandon Waugh. Waugh was the soldier who, when he saw a grenade land in his Humvee, yelled, "Grenade!" and jumped out. The grenade turned out to be a dud, but it got everyone thinking about what they would do in a similar situation, and later got Waugh to thinking about why he didn't do what McGinnis had done.

"He felt a lot of guilt for jumping out when he saw that grenade, even though it didn't go off," Baka said. "But this young man, in his eyes, was given an opportunity to redeem himself."

Waugh, now a sergeant, returned to Iraq a year after Adhamiya with Bravo Company, 1st Battalion, 2nd Infantry Regiment. On January 20, 2009, two years after his friend Hill died in Adhamiya, Waugh noticed that the Iraqi police had abandoned their posts. In Adhamiya, that had always signaled danger. Soon, he heard gunshots, and then realized his platoon sergeant had been hit. Waugh headed on foot toward the sound of the gunshots, even as the gunman tried to hit other soldiers. The gunman had hit Waugh's platoon sergeant in the leg, but had tried to keep shooting to kill when his weapon jammed, Baka said. The platoon sergeant then shot the man and killed him.

Waugh evacuated his platoon sergeant, talking to him through his pain while simultaneously arranging for a medevac to land.

"Waugh took charge of the platoon and kept everyone under control, kept the platoon sergeant under control," Baka said. "All these young soldiers in his platoon got to see that. That's impressive."

There's another story he doesn't like to tell. When Baka recommended that Hartge go to West Point, he also recommended another soldier, Private First Class Raymond "Ross" Powell. "He had a 1500 on his SAT and his dad was an Air Force Academy grad," Baka said. "It just made sense that he might want to go." Powell had served with second platoon, but in June 2007, he left for the U.S. Military Academy's Preparatory School in Fort Monmouth, New Jersey, so that he could get ready to attend West Point.

But even though the students there crave the combat experience Powell could bring them, he had a hard time bowing down to cadets younger and less experienced than he, but who outranked him, Baka said. He had been diagnosed with post-traumatic stress disorder, and Baka said he'd had some alcohol violations at the school. One time, while sitting with his dad at a bar near the school, someone made a joke about the fourteen names Powell had tattooed on his arm. That ended in a fight.

Eventually, Powell was sent to Fort Benning, Georgia, when school officials decided he might not be ready for West Point. While at Fort Benning, Powell hurt his hand and found himself at the Warrior Transition Unit at Fort Gordon, Georgia, awaiting a medical discharge.

On November 30, 2008, Powell ran off the road with his Ford Explorer and hit a tree. When the police found him the next morning, he was dead.

"I buried him at Arlington in December," Baka said.

At West Point, Baka tries to prepare his cadets for those kinds of stories, for how war might affect his cadets—and their men—psychologically.

"I don't feel I have PTSD," Baka said. "It's a label."

Yet he knows his deployment affected him. A year after returning from Adhamiya, he still can't go to bed before one or two in the morning. For a while, he would have a beer or two every night—nothing to set off warning bells, but enough of a change that he noticed it.

"Why?" he said, rhetorically. "Maybe to calm my nerves? Maybe because I couldn't for fifteen months?"

But after about six months, he, without really thinking about it, stopped reaching for a beer every night.

When he got home, he felt a little paranoid, like maybe he needed a concealed weapons permit. "I need to protect my family," he thought. "There are people in Iraq who know my name."

But like the drinking, that soon went away. He began running again. He trusted that he and his family were safe. He still obsesses over the men he lost, but he doesn't have nightmares or flashbacks. He wonders if it's because he talked so much with Cathy, or because he kept in touch with the families, or because he was willing to cry in Iraq.

"I'm back to normalcy," he said, and with that, he left his office in a castle, climbed into his minivan—necessary after baby Matthew was born nine months and four days after Baka returned from Iraq—and drove off to pick up Cathy and their children.

First Sergeant Kenneth Hendrix rode his Harley-Davidson in the early morning sunshine at Fort Jackson, South Carolina.

In January.

He bought the new ride as soon as he arrived, which was immediately after returning from Adhamiya. At Fort Jackson he took on a new mission with the only soldiers in the army who could possibly need more than his boys in Charlie Company: basic trainees. Of those brand-new soldiers, 80 percent would head to a combat zone within a year, and he had some things to teach them.

In his home—bright and cheerful and filled with three daughters and his wife—Hendrix has a room all to himself. There he keeps his football memorabilia, his Lazy Boy, and framed copies of stories about his men. He lights up when he talks about that last beer with Jorcke and Montenegro, and laughs every time he hears DeNardi's name. He won't ever have a company like that again, and he said he wishes he could stay with them until he retires.

But as it turned out, he didn't talk much about what he had seen in Adhamiya, even as he taught the newbies what they would need to survive.

Sitting at a local restaurant, Hendrix's hands lay palm up on the table. When he started talking about the men he'd lost, his fingers lightly but quickly rubbed against his thumbs as if he were snapping without any noise.

"As a first sergeant, every single one of 'em was mine," he said. "I'm the one who stayed there in the aid station. All the soldiers. I had to watch those soldiers die."

His nightmares come with the one he couldn't be with: He had been on leave when Campos died, and his NCO appeared often in his dreams.

As did Agami.

"If anything messed McKinney up, because I know it did me, it was Agami," Hendrix said. "You know he didn't die right away. You could tell he put up a struggle."

But he worries just as much about the ones who lived. "I think all the medics in Charlie have serious, serious problems," he said. "They all have PTSD. If they say they don't, they're lying. They just saw too much."

But he knows no one came out unscathed. In Iraq, he talked to Chaplain Choi. At Fort Jackson, he kept all the stories inside, refusing to go to a mental health counselor. "We feel like we're the only ones we can talk to," he said. "Who else would understand?"

In Adhamiya, he and Baka had worked to maintain the professional distance necessary between officer and enlisted leaders. But a year and a half after their tour in Adhamiya ended, Hendrix traveled to West Point where he, Baka, and some other Charlie Company leaders gathered for a leadership conference for Baka's cadets. Baka wanted his students to learn from Charlie Company's combat experience, and they did. Better, Baka and Hendrix drank a couple of beers together, talked about their men together, and shed some tears together. Hendrix had not talked about his experiences in Iraq to anyone until the spring of 2009.

Hendrix understood that if he did anything right, it was getting second platoon out of Adhamiya. He couldn't remember having even one contact while on patrol on the other side of the river. "It gave our guys the time they needed to decompress before we came home," he said. "If we'd redeployed straight from Adhamiya to Schweinfurt, we would have been in trouble."

Even for what the company went through with second platoon—even with his drilled-in belief that when a soldier is told do something, he follows that order—Hendrix is proud that they controlled themselves on the most important level.

"The thing I'm most proud of is that for as much as we went through, it didn't come back that we killed detainees," he said. "We didn't want to taint it. I was very proud of my guys for that."

But he won't go back.

He loves his men too much.

"Maybe things would have turned out differently if I hadn't been there," he said. "But I don't know if I could let myself get that close to another company again and then lose somebody.

"There's definitely a limit to what a person can take."